COMMERCIAL PROVIDENCE

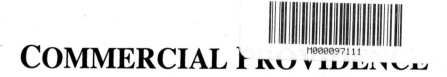

The Secret Destiny of the American Empire

Patrick Mendis

Foreword by Stephen Joel Trachtenberg

University Press of America,® Inc.
A member of the Rowman & Littlefield Publishing Group
Lanham · Boulder · New York · Toronto · Plymouth, UK

Copyright © 2010 by
University Press of America,® Inc.
4501 Forbes Boulevard
Suite 200
Lanham, Maryland 20706
UPA Acquisitions Department (301) 459-3366

Estover Road
Plymouth PL6 7PY
United Kingdom

Library of Congress Control Number: 2010929880
ISBN: 978-0-7618-5243-8 (clothbound : alk. paper)
ISBN: 978-0-7618-5244-5 (paperback : alk. paper)

™The paper used in this publication meets the minimum
requirements of American National Standard for Information
Sciences—Permanence of Paper for Printed Library Materials,
ANSI Z39.48-1992

PRAISE FOR *COMMERCIAL PROVIDENCE*

"Inspired by the Founding Fathers and their vision, Patrick Mendis, an adopted Minnesotan, narrates America's ancient hope, promise, and performance as manifested in our increasingly pluralistic democracy. His is a unique and insightful analysis of the power of freedom and the globalizing spirit of our republic, which is ingrained in the Constitution's commerce clause and in symbols in the nation's capital. Mendis' own history resonates globally: similar to the Kenyan father of President Barack Obama, this former exchange student from Sri Lanka married a white Minnesotan at the University of Minnesota over two decades ago. Having learned from Patrick's interdisciplinary investigation, I recommend it to you very enthusiastically."

~ Senator THOMAS DASCHLE
former U.S. Senate Majority Leader, Distinguished Senior
Fellow at the Center for American Progress, and author of
Like No Other Time: The Two Years That Changed America

"Our forefathers, who came from all sorts of backgrounds, gave us a philosophical republic to self-govern our diverse states. When Chancellor Robert Livingston of New York, a Founding Father, administered the oath of office for President George Washington, he may not have imagined how far we could progress as a union. Yet today, I now see a more diverse nation than ever; one in which the enduring founding vision continues through leaders like Louisiana Governor Bobby Jindal of Asian heritage, Austrian-born Governor Arnold Schwarzenegger of California, and most importantly, President Barack Obama, who has both

African and American roots. In this carefully researched and perceptive book, Patrick Mendis, who was born in Sri Lanka and educated in Minnesota, reveals the secret of America's success story. In doing so, he identifies the reason for its magnetic appeal and its inspirational role as the beacon of hope for the world. Every American should read this book to appreciate the wisdom of our Founding Fathers and their prophetic vision."

~ Congressman ROBERT LIVINGSTON, Jr.
former Speaker-elect, U.S. House of Representatives and
the founder of The Livingston Group, Inc.

"By carefully examining the influence of Freemasonry on the Founding Fathers, *Commercial Providence* provides valuable insights for the student of history and the modern political leader alike. . . . Unlike Dan Brown in the *Lost Symbol*, Patrick Mendis has a serious scholarly purpose when he explores the ancient symbols impressed in the architecture of the American capital city. . . . Mendis presents an optimistic view of the American experiment and a useful framework for leaders in contemporary crisis situations. . . . Aspiring leaders, students of history, and visitors to the nation's capital alike will find *Commercial Providence* an intriguing look at the origins of our American identity, seen through the eyes of the Founding Fathers and the Masonic Architect of the Universe" [From the foreword].

~ Professor STEPHEN JOEL TRACHTENBERG
President *Emeritus* and University Professor of Public Policy
The George Washington University

"In this well-balanced book on America's founding vision and its freedom march, Patrick Mendis explores the pivotal role played by Freemasons like brethren George Washington, Benjamin Franklin, and Paul Revere. Like Alexis de Tocqueville, Mendis perceptively observes

our cherished democratic ideals and dynamics of freedom, and judicious-
ly integrates the original documents and Freemasonry rarely mentioned
in history textbooks. As an award-winning military professor, he supports the task of defense forces as champions of freedom and advocates
the primacy of the commercial mission inculcated in the American story.
This is an optimistic book about America's destiny and a needed antidote
to the current pessimism and historical conspiracy we often read in the
media. I commend it highly."

~ Rear Admiral WILLIAM SIZEMORE (Ret.)
U.S. Navy, the Grand Executive Director of the Supreme
Council 33° of the Scottish Rite Freemasonry, and author
of *Dynamic Freedoms: Our Freedom Documents*

"Patrick Mendis has produced an original and fascinating interpretation
of the political, cultural, and even religious roots and corollaries of
America's historic policy toward trade. His account puts current policy
discussions in a new light. I enjoyed reading this book and think it will
prove valuable to anyone interested in this topic."

~ Journalist JAMES FALLOWS
The Atlantic Monthly and National Public Radio, founding
chairman of the New America Foundation and former chief
speechwriter for President Jimmy Carter

"I got to know Patrick Mendis (long-time protégé of the late Harlan
Cleveland, a former Marshall Plan administrator and NATO ambassador)
at the State Department and was astounded by how much I could learn
from this outsider as well as insider: his infectious optimism about the
future of this country, and, more important, the rigorous analysis and
close reasoning that underlies that optimism. Particularly eye-opening is
his essential thesis that the founding fathers believed that trade and

commerce, rather than religion, would be the glue that held this nation together. Amidst all the other exciting bits of history and analysis, this one has enormous relevance for today."

~ Ambassador FRANK LOY
former Undersecretary of State for Global Affairs under President Bill Clinton and President of the German Marshall Fund of the United States

"With his unyielding patriotic sentiments, Harvard alumnus Patrick Mendis proffers compelling perspectives on Jeffersonian inspiration for democracy promotion and human rights in a hard-edged Hamiltonian world of commerce and finance. His thoughtful analysis of America's founding vision is incisive, optimistic, and innovative. In support of the founding vision, Mendis convincingly illustrates that a Madisonian empire is not only desirable, but also needed to realize an empire of liberty. This naturalized U.S. citizen has a clear and cogent message to our foes as well as our friends: America will succeed; it is embedded in our destiny."

~ Ambassador PAULA DOBRIANSKY
former Undersecretary of State for Democracy and Global Affairs under President George W. Bush and Senior Fellow at Harvard University's John F. Kennedy School of Government

"Dr. Patrick Mendis, a consulting professor of international relations at our Center, is a perceptive scholar of Sino-U.S. relations. As alumni of Harvard University, we both share a great interest in global affairs. He has lectured at prestigious universities in Beijing, Chengdu, Nanjing, Shanghai, and Xian. His previous book is widely praised by Chinese scholars, leaders, and media as it brilliantly connects American founding vision and China's 'Peaceful Rising' in the world's stage. I strongly rec-

ommend this book to you as a valuable contribution to mutual understanding of 'Chimerican' relations."

~ Professor TANG XIAOSONG
President, Center for International Security and Strategic Studies
Guangdong University of Foreign Studies, Guangzhou, China

"Dr Patrick Mendis deepens our understanding of the American spirit by
bringing back Washington, Jefferson and Hamilton, then showing us
how these forefathers laid down the philosophical foundation for the future superpower through a confluence of human values including
morality, justice, achievement and freedom. His analysis on the providential destiny of the United States and the birth of a commercial
civilization is both powerful and enlightening. Mendis forcefully demonstrates how the instruments of soft power are crucial to U.S. national
interests, and provides insight into the close association of American
power with the principles of Freemasonry. His detailed depiction of how
Masonic ideas influenced the planning of Washington, D.C., is revealing."

~ Professor TING WAI
Department of Government and International
Studies, Hong Kong Baptist University and President
of the Hong Kong Association for European Studies

"Patrick has unfolded a panoramic dimension by interpreting America's
growth through commerce. His unique insight remains meaningful for
contemporary America and the world."

~ Professor SHEN DINGLI
Dean of the Institute of International Studies
Fudan University, Shanghai, China

"Professor Patrick Mendis goes beyond Dan Brown's *Lost Symbol* to disclose the true story of the fictional narrative, and the meaning of symbolism in Freemasonry and the American Experiment. The professor is a mind-reader of the Founding Fathers, a judge of ancient symbols, a lover of his adopted country, and a seer of America's secret destiny. Every visitor to Washington, D.C., must read this book to clearly understand and deeply appreciate the wondrous nature of our freedom and the promise extended by American innovation for the rest of the world to enjoy."

~ **Masonic Grand Master AKRAM ELIAS**
President and Co-founder of Capital Communications Group,
and Co-producer—with Academy Award Winner Richard
Dreyfuss—of *Mr. Dreyfuss Goes to Washington*

PRAISE FOR THE WORKS OF PATRICK MENDIS

Trade for Peace, 2009
Foreword by Professor and Dean J. Brian Atwood

"For those who are interested in American foreign and trade policies, this work connects the dots from the Founding Fathers' global vision to the global marketplace within which America competes today" [From the foreword]

~ Professor J. BRIAN ATWOOD
Dean, Humphrey Institute of Public Affairs, University of Minnesota
and former administrator of USAID under President Bill Clinton

"Patrick Mendis, in this carefully researched book, seeks to explain how trade is encoded in the DNA of the United States and expressed in its Constitution. He provides an interesting approach for analyzing the nation's commercial roots."

~ President WALTER ISAACSON
The Aspen Institute and author of *Benjamin Franklin* and *Albert Einstein*

"Get to know this patriotic citizen and award-winning American educator through his unique analysis of the founding ideas of freedom, capitalism, and our Founders' enduring gifts to the world."

~ Senator GEORGE ALLEN
Ronald Reagan ranch presidential scholar and former
U.S. senator and Virginia governor

"Readers will find this book both impressive and useful to help further understand the picture of the American experiment and its future."

~ **Ambassador MAX KAMPELMAN**
former chief negotiator and counselor to the U.S. State Department
under Presidents Jimmy Carter and Ronald Reagan

"In this insightful work, Patrick Mendis approaches the American narrative with a sharp scholarly edge, drawing richly on America's classical roots. All in all, a tour de force."

~ **Professor LINCOLN BLOOMFIELD**
Professor of political science *emeritus*, Massachusetts
Institute of Technology and former White House Official

"Like de Tocqueville, Mendis sees cultural connections that those born in the U.S. often overlook. This fascinating book places international trade at the heart of the American vision for a harmonious world. Economic nationalists . . . will be forced to think again."

~ **Professor ROBERT KUDRLE**
Orville Freeman professor of international trade policy
University of Minnesota

"I found his insights into contemporary foreign policy and international affairs immensely valuable, precisely because his education and experience presented a different, often richer, synthesis of diverse fields than those usually encountered. In this book, he narrates a unique perspective of our nation and its future."

~ **Ambassador RONALD LEHMAN**
Director of the Center for Global Security Research, the U.S.
Department of Energy's Lawrence Livermore National Laboratory

"Patrick Mendis . . . writes with clarity and a lightness of touch rarely found in books of such serious academic purpose. I thoroughly enjoyed reading his work even as I learned from it, and I recommend it heartily."

~ **Professor STEPHEN TRACHTENBERG**
President *emeritus*, The George Washington University

"Dr. Patrick Mendis, one of our most original thinkers on global economic issues, has produced another timely and very interesting volume. Patrick's unique perspectives build on his immigrant experience in the U.S., his Sri Lankan roots, and his impressive experiences as a scholar, a U.S. diplomat, and world-traveling professor to give us new understanding of the interrelationships among history, economics, culture and international relations."

~ Ambassador SHAUN DONNELLY
former American trade negotiator at the World Trade Organization
and U.S. ambassador to Sri Lanka

"This is a timely antidote to ahistorical pessimism."

~ Dean DAVID LAMPTON
George Hyman professor of China studies, Johns Hopkins
University's Paul Nitze School of Advanced International Studies

"As America prepares to reinvent itself yet again, it is important to reexamine the links between the future and the past. Patrick Mendis—master teacher, world citizen, and great American—provides a vehicle for that examination. Seeing clearly through a trilateral prism of Jeffersonian, Hamiltonian and Washingtonian perspectives, this Sri Lankan from Minnesota will help you see too."

~ Professor SHELTON WILLIAMS
President of the Osgood Center for International Studies

"In a time of economic crisis, when corporate and public sector responsibility are absolutely essential, Patrick Mendis offers us the 'back to basics' historical context that we need. Through the lenses of our Founding Fathers and philosophers, Americans are offered new insight on the problems that challenge them—and the world—today."

~ Professor KENNETH E GOODPASTER
David and Barbara Koch endowed chair in business ethics
University of St. Thomas, Minneapolis

"In addition to Chimerica, Dr. Mendis coined words like Chindia, Chirussia, Chifrica, and Chipan to describe China's peaceful rise in the global community."

~ *China Daily*, Beijing

"Replete with information, this book presents a broad conception of American constitutional providence. Mendis has constructed a unique and thought-provoking portrait of history that offers an intriguing lens through which to examine the topics of democracy, trade, and the American spirit."

~ **Ambassador JOHN MCDONALD**
Chairman of the Institute for Multi-track Diplomacy

"This book reads easily and quickly; it's a glorious ride."

Journal of the Scottish Rite of Freemasonry

"With his combined experience in the legislative and executive branches of the U.S. government and the academy, Patrick Mendis synthesizes his unique perspectives of Washington, D.C., and the historical connectedness of trade, peace, and the Constitution. This excellent analysis is prologue and a glimpse into a possible future direction for history."

~ **Dr. MICHAEL GRAHAM**
Vice president of the U.S. Institute of Peace

"In his sweeping and provocative discussion, Mendis traces themes from the writings of Washington, Jefferson, and Hamilton up through the creation of the World Trade Organization and the economic policy dilemmas of a post-9/11 world."

~ **Dr. TIMOTHY TAYLOR**
Managing editor of the *Journal of Economic Perspectives*
The American Economic Association

"Patrick Mendis is a witty, engaging writer with a knack for telling a good story. In weaving together fascinating anecdotes about America's Founding Fathers with reflections on lasting friendships made in Minnesota, my home state, Mendis makes a convincing case that trade is the tie that binds all of us together. In this book, American history comes alive."

~ **Professor JOHN BESSLER**
The George Washington University Law School

"This book examines the importance of trade and commerce by focusing on their origins. Pressure to avoid competition is huge and readers should become vigilant in fighting against protectionist tendencies."

~ **Dr. JOHN HARRINGTON, Jr.**
Associate dean of Johns Hopkins University's Paul
Nitze School of Advanced International Studies

"Like Alex de Tocqueville, Dr. Mendis writes about the promise of America and the wisdom of our Founding Fathers. In this book, he observes that America's inspiring history is still in the future."

~ **Ambassador MICHAEL RETZER**
CEO of Retzer Resources Inc.

"This interdisciplinary book is compelling, entertaining, and enlightening."

~ *Asian Pages*, Minnesota

"At a time when the United States and other democracies are revisiting their founding principles to respond to major global challenges, along comes Patrick Mendis with his unique perspective on how to achieve balance among seemingly conflicting ideals."

~ **Editor WARREN MASTER**
Editor-in-chief of *The Public Manager*

"The book is seen as a new perspective of historical events alongside the visions of the nation's Founders."

~ **Honorable ALVIN LIEBLING**
Senior U.S. administrative law judge, Chicago

"Dr. Patrick Mendis, a Kiva lender who donated his book royalties, now writes that our Founding Fathers' vision, as we at Kiva.org are realizing in collaborating with one entrepreneur at a time in forty-seven different countries, is genuinely global. Read this book to learn more about America's mission in the world."

~ **Co-founder JESSICA FLANNERY**
www.Kiva.org: first worldwide person-to-person micro-loan program

"Dr. Mendis sees cultural connections those born in the U.S. often ignore."

~ *Ceylon Daily News*, Sri Lanka

"He humanizes our nation's Founding Fathers through his interesting analysis of their foundation and construction of our nation's capital city, the Constitution, and commercial principles."

~ **Director STEPHEN JORDAN**
Executive director, the Business Civic Leadership Center
and vice president of the U.S. Chamber of Commerce

Human Side of Globalization (3rd Edition, 2009)
Foreword by Sir Arthur C. Clarke

"This book is ample evidence that the author is at home in the United States, Sri Lanka and in many other lands. His multi-faceted career—working with governmental bodies, universities, volunteer organizations and international institutions—is reflected here as he integrates his Sri Lankan and American values into these essays" [From the foreword].

~ **Sir ARTHUR C. CLARKE**
Fellow of King's College and author of *2001: A Space Odyssey*

"Patrick Mendis—born in Sri Lanka, educated in America, now truly a citizen of the world—has an infectious enthusiasm for the diversity he has experienced. His informal glimpses of people, policies, life and work in a dozen countries show just how various and vibrant 'globalization' really is."

~ Ambassador HARLAN CLEVELAND
President *Emeritus*, World Academy of Art and Science and
former U.S. ambassador to NATO and Assistant Secretary of State

"As individuals, communities, nations, and interdependent beings, we awaken each other. Dr. Mendis describes the process by which observers and travelers can learn such lessons. These are stories that must be told" [From the afterword].

~ Dr. A. T. ARIYARATNE
Founder and president, Sarvodaya Shramadana
Movement of Sri Lanka

"There is no better equipped scholar and researcher of this topic than Patrick Mendis, who was born and raised in a developing country and now lives in the heart of the developed world. [His] book is a multi-disciplinary analysis that is both stimulating and eminently readable."

~ Ambassador JAYANTHA DHANAPALA
Chairman of the UN University and former undersecretary-general
of the United Nations

"This book certainly helps us to reach the shore of a new creation in which globalization will be a blessing for all."

~ Professor M. S. SWAMINATHAN
Member of the Indian Parliament and the chairman of
The M. S. Swaminathan Research Foundation, Chennai

"The book will stimulate intellectual curiosity to further explore a host of challenging issues in globalization, which he calls 'glocalization.'"

~ Professor MIYUKI INABA
Kyushu University, Fukuoka, Japan

"Both the author's descriptions of various cultures and his theoretical observations provide valuable reading for our time."

~ **Professor GEORGE BOND**
Northwestern University, Chicago

"Dr. Patrick Mendis takes the reader through a compelling and compassionate voyage of discovery as he sets sail in the winds of globalization. The vast scale and scope of this work is a feast for the mind and the eyes!"

~ **Professor DEBASHIS CHATTERJEE**
Chairman, Center for Leadership and Human Values
The Indian Institute of Management

"If you are curious about the world and how globalization is affecting the people of the world, read this book."

~ **Professor DEAN CALDWELL**
UMUC Graduate School of Management, University of Maryland

"This book presents a collection of difficult and paradoxical issues in a simple manner while raising another set of challenging questions to reflect on globalization."

~ **Dr. WILLIAM RECANT**
Executive vice president, American Jewish Joint Distribution
Committee, New York

"Mendis' work helps to take the fear out of 'globalization' and thus promotes its eventual acceptance."

~ **Professor HAROLD KEARSLEY**
Graduate School of Diplomacy, Norwich University

"Every American should read these stories to learn more about *ourselves* rather than other countries. After traveling to and working in more than 70 countries, this perceptive author tells you why."

~ **Dr. JERRY ICE**
CEO and President, Graduate School, U.S. Department of Agriculture

"The diversity of experiences written about in this book and the richness of Dr. Mendis' life shine through these pages of shared human aspiration."

~ President ALEX PLINIO
AFS Intercultural Programs Inc., New York

"From one country to another, he observes how hope and freedom interact with poverty, and how ideology can interfere with deliberate steps to a better world. Travel with him and see what you think."

~ Professor RICHARD BROOKS
University of Wisconsin-Madison

"America's fundamental illiteracy about globalization represents a grave threat to its continued positive unfolding, for no nation does more to encourage its spread and no nation can do more to torpedo its future through bad political choices. Patrick Mendis' book helps much to combat that ignorance by providing a traveler's-eye-view of how this unprecedented wave of change is reformatting the planet. We can't get enough of this sort of education."

~ Professor THOMAS BARNETT
Author of *The Pentagon's New Map* and the Baker Center
distinguished scholar, University of Tennessee

Human Environment and Spatial Relationships
in Agricultural Production, 1992
Foreword by Professor Harlan Cleveland

"This study goes beyond the call for a sustainable development strategy by urging policies that help integrate Sri Lanka's ethnically diverse population. At the same time, this study also addresses important meso-economic issues such as land segmentation, crop diversification, and issues of privatization [thus] deserving of scholarly attention" [From the Foreword].

~ **Professor HARLAN CLEVELAND**
President of the World Academy of Art and Science

"An innovative analysis of the interaction between resource endowments and economic forces on the development and prospect for the Sri Lanka tea sector."

~ **Regents Professor VERNON RUTTAN**
University of Minnesota

"For the first time, this study provides a fascinating multidisciplinary approach in order to find answers to many questions, especially returns to scale, raised by tea researchers and policy-makers in Sri Lanka and elsewhere. This book is a very useful addition to the development literature and deserves to be in all research institutions."

~ **Professor and Dean JAGATH BANDARANAYAKE**
University of Sri Lanka

"A skillful blending of economics and geography resulting in a multidisciplinary analysis of the Sri Lanka tea economy."

~ **Professor WILLIS PETERSON**
University of Minnesota

"This is a technically sophisticated and well-written study of an industry which is of considerable importance for Sri Lanka, providing a model for similar studies elsewhere, and taking full account of both geographical and economic considerations."

~ **Professor MICHAEL CHISHOLM**
University of Cambridge

CONTENTS

PART III
ANNUIT COEPTIS, PROVIDENCE (GOD) FAVORS OUR UNDERTAKINGS

PART IV
JAMES MADISON'S UNIVERSAL EMPIRE

EPILOGUE

ILLUSTRATIONS

DEDICATION

To my family—Cheryl, Gamini, Samantha, and Ed
Burdick—who believe in an incorrigible dreamer

FOREWORD

"Study the past if you would divine the future."
~ Confucius, Chinese Philosopher, 551-479 B.C.

A wise European-looking sage sculpture of the
Pennsylvania Avenue side of the National Archives

FOREWORD

The Invisible High Priest of America

> Being persuaded that a just application of
> the principles, on which the Masonic Fraternity
> is founded, must be promotive of private virtue
> and public prosperity, I shall always be happy to
> advance the interests of the Society, and to be
> considered by them as a deserving brother.
>
> **President George Washington**
> Letter to the King David's Lodge of Freemasons
> in Newport, RI on August 22, 1790

A visitor to the National Archives may stop to notice a wise figure in seated contemplation at the Pennsylvania Avenue entrance, inscribed with the message: "Study the Past." By carefully examining the influence of Freemasonry on the Founding Fathers, *Commercial Providence* provides valuable insights for the student of history and the modern political leader alike. It takes the reader on an intellectual and reflective journey to understand the mindsets of the Founding Fathers through little-known linkages between the Pilgrims, Enlightenment philosophers, Thomas Jefferson, Adam Smith, and the Federalists.

Out of many points of historical curiosity, *Commercial Providence* creates one vision of America's founding history. Author Patrick Mendis argues that the American experiment has, since the founding, been grounded in a universal concept of global unity through trade and commerce. Mendis connects American's esoteric history to this founding conviction through a careful study of the Constitution, the Masonic ideas represented in American symbols, and the structural design of the nation's capital. Freemasonry is cast as the invisible high priest in American history, guiding the Founding Fathers at every turn.

History reveals that real world problems are not bound by academic disciplines or formal occupations. Author Patrick Mendis brings an unbounded career and a unique background to his investigation. He was born in Sri Lanka, came to the United States as an AFS exchange student, was adopted by Minnesotans when the civil war erupted in Sri Lanka in 1983, and is now a naturalized American citizen. Through a career spanning academe, government, and the private sector, Mendis has been exposed to an eclectic group of world leaders and scholars. His distinctly American experience adds insight to his perceptive analysis; this book is a testament to what he represents as an American.

Mendis presents an optimistic view of the American experiment and a useful framework for leaders in contemporary crisis situations. His treatise reveals themes of freedom, universal order, and unity in diversity. Unlike Dan Brown in the *Lost Symbol*, Patrick Mendis has a serious scholarly purpose as he explores the ancient symbols impressed in the architecture of the American capital city: through extensive research, he illuminates the shared belief among many Founding Fathers that the birth of a new nation was a providential act.

By examining the meanings of Masonic symbols and beliefs, *Commercial Providence* explores the roots of the Founders' belief in universal and democratic values. The heart of his theory is that the Founding Fathers believed trade and commerce, rather than religion, to be the most effective tools of statecraft and fonts of national unity. Mendis argues that Constitutional architects established a "wall of separation," as Jefferson described the concept, between church and state to protect the fledgling nation from Old World religious strife, tyranny, and persecution. He extends these beliefs and applies them to modern domestic and foreign policy, maintaining that departure from this founding vision will create domestic religious factions and worsen international tensions.

Reflecting American abolitionist Wendell Phillips's assertion that "Eternal vigilance is the price of liberty," Mendis counsels vigilance to the founding wisdom that prescribes trade with all nations and entanglements with none. He concludes that our governing principles were born with conviction, and that without such convictions American policy may spawn dictators and religious zealots to oppose those policies around the world. As a champion of freedom in the world, America stands for none of these fundamentalist endgames.

Thomas Paine could have been describing the first decade of the 21st century when he discussed "the times that try men's souls." In truth, American history is replete with trying times. Through depression, war, and civil upheaval, America has been resilient, undergirded by vigilance to her strong constitutional institutions and founding principles. Our enduring American identity rests upon the foundation of shared convictions and shared history. Aspiring leaders, students of history, and visitors to the nation's capital alike will find *Commercial Providence* an intriguing look at the origins of our American identity, seen through the eyes of the Founding Fathers and the Masonic Architect of the Universe.

Professor Stephen Joel Trachtenberg
President *Emeritus* and University Professor of Public Service
The Trachtenberg School of Public Policy and Public Administration
The George Washington University
Washington, D.C.

American Mercury—born with commercial providence—is the source of American exceptionalism, Manifest Destiny, indispensible nation, and God's crucible nation.

PREFACE

"I believe in American exceptionalism. I believe we were meant to transform history. I believe that the progress of all humanity will depend, as it has for many years now, on the global progress of American interests and values. I believe we are still the last, best hope of earth."

~ U.S. Senator JOHN MCCAIN
July 30, 2000

PREFACE

Providence and Empire

> Providence has given us a torch which our forefathers
> did not possess, and has allowed us to discern fundamental
> causes in the history of the world which the obscurity of the
> past concealed from them.[1]

Alexis de Tocqueville
Democracy in America, 1835

Providence really exists. It was the conviction upheld by the learned Founding Fathers of America, who were preachers, teachers, and nation-builders. For them, Providence was a mechanism through which God— i.e., Nature's God—might influence both natural and human events, as well as the course of history. Like today's debate between the intelligent design movement headed by Christian creationists and Charles Darwin's evolutionary theory of natural selection, the eighteenth century founding generation also contemplated the wondrous nature of the cosmic framework. Their aim was to understand universal order and its relationship to fellow human beings and earthly affairs.

Their perennial argument in favor of Providence was based on a creed that held the existence of a watch pointed to the existence of a watchmaker. Their belief system was thus illustrated by action that required an accompanying actor; without an actor, there is no action. For them, the paradoxically exclusive—yet mutually inclusive—actor and action was shrouded in the mystery of Providence. Dr. Benjamin Franklin, America's first scientist and a versatile sage, confirmed this doctrine at the 1787 Constitutional Convention when he asked: "If a sparrow cannot fall to the ground without his [Providence] notice, is it probable that an [American] empire can rise without his aid?"[2] The embryonic beginning of a philosophic empire in America similarly corresponded to the arcane mysteries of the ages.

Enlightenment writers like Sir Isaac Newton, Immanuel Kant, and others preferred an explanation that God's relevance was more applicable to a life of faith and personal devotion than to a world of physical and natural spheres. For these natural philosophers and the Founding Fathers, the universe existed long before the humans appeared. In effect, God (the Creator embodied in the universe) governs the natural laws that in turn affect human affairs. The Psalmist confirms in the Bible that "the whole Nature [is] the vehicle of his revelation."[3] Deuteronomy separately describes human actions as having corresponding consequences.[4] These two independent observations seem to imply two different realms of machination for the governance of human behavior and natural environment.

Over the course of history, human actions might indeed have been guided by the hand of Providence. The metaphysics of this plausible explanation were at the heart of the mindsets of the Founding Fathers. Certain miracles and special acts (similar to George Washington's reportedly religious experience at Valley Forge in Pennsylvania and the episodes like "the professor" leading up to the Constitutional Convention in Philadelphia) show that Providence appeared to favor the establishment of a new American nation; thus, no natural process was explicitly involved. But apart from this religious and occult (unseen) conviction, scientific debate continued to forge gaps between a providential explanation and natural occurrences in the world, in which the latter caused immeasurable human suffering through earthquakes, volcanoes, tsunamis, hurricanes, and floods. Were these random incidents? Or were they a part of the grand mechanism of Providence, the benevolent equalizer, who saw fit to unleash a natural and Karmic reaction to reward or punish humans for their deeds? These cultured men of faith generally believed that a confluence of both natural and human events mysteriously manifested in what they viewed as America's unfair advantage: a "Special" Providence (as opposed to a general sort of Providence).[5]

In his luminous book *Special Providence*, Walter Russell Mead at the Council on Foreign Relations also explained America's "good luck" as having been bestowed by divine Providence.[6] Though he did not analyze the origin and anatomy of Providence within the framework of the founding vision, his generic discussion essentially advocates quantum mechanics for such a possibility.[7] The process of quantum mechanics introduces new ways of rethinking the founding, and has continued debate on whether America's special Providence has been complicated by natural causes (such as Hurricane Katrina) and other human interventions (like the Civil War, the global conflicts of WWI and WWII, and recent wars in Iraq and Afghanistan). For rational scientists and evolutionary biologists, human suffering caused by events like the Asian Tsunami and Haitian earthquake is simply due to natural occurrences, which may be easily explained in a physically, biologically, and chemically deterministic manner.

Unlike the Founding Fathers, a different caliber of agenda-driven Christian theologians has misconstrued the very nature of the Providence associated with Davidic and Mosaic insights gleaned from Psalms and Deuteronomy. In the aftermath of the tragic events of 9/11 and Hurricane Katrina, two prominent televangelists—Reverends Jerry Falwell and Pat Robertson—informed the American public that God had punished them because "the United States had become a nation of abortion, homosexuality, and secular values."[8] For these myopic and solipsistic members of the faith community, the gaps between science and religion became ideological and political weapons. As if in anticipation of such un-American commentary, the Founding Fathers deliberately and brilliantly pronounced the meaning of Providence in a prism of secular language and human values to neutralize such weaponry.

Religion, Science, and Commerce

The purpose of this book is neither to advance an argument for quantum mechanics nor a debate about religion and science. Still, the interesting and compelling doctrine of Providence is intrinsically interwoven throughout the American experience. It has also opened an inconclusive debate that continues within our "American Experiment" in a quest to restore a sense of balance between Nature's God and man (and woman). While authentic theologians and scientists have engaged in civil discourse on this matter, the events themselves that have been confounded by natural and human actions (like climate change, for example) are more important for this exploration of the restoration of balance between humans and the environment, the market and the government, and individual greed and public goods. This book hopefully provides insight into the psyche of our Founding Fathers, describing how they acted on the basis of their understanding of the world of religious faith, scientific reasoning, and human progress through the American cause for freedom. Their actions reveal a collective intellect in which both science and religion flourished for greater understanding of the mind of the Creator, or Providence.

Their belief in special Providence has been ridiculed by some, while others have found it a source of inspiration. Prussian chancellor Otto Von Bismarck once sarcastically muttered, "God has special providence for fools, drunks, and the United States of America."[9] Yet French author Alexis de Tocqueville used a religious salutation to celebrate the democratic development and freedom he discovered in America. In his perceptive book *Democracy in America* (1835), the Christian aristocrat characterized the American cause for a democratic republic in three dimensions: Providence, the rule of law, and the mannerism and customs of the American people.[10]

De Tocqueville, Nostradamus of American democracy, predicted that Providence would guide the nation into achieving greater equality of living conditions for all its citizens. He emphasized the inescapable influence of Providence, in which "all have been blind instruments in the hands of God."[11] The Frenchman even ventured to say that Providence had positively instructed the birth of democracy in America. In aristocratic nations like France, he argued, ignorant masters appeared to believe that "amazing inequality" resulted from the "hidden law of Providence;" democracies, however, created "no permanent inequality between the servant and the master."[12] De Tocqueville projected in a prophetic manner that America's political freedom and unhindered commerce would continue to reinforce each other. He concluded that "in democracies nothing is more great or more brilliant than commerce: it attracts the attention of the public, and fills the imagination of the multitude; all energetic passions are directed toward it."[13]

These vivid observations further confirm the validity of the founding conviction that the United States was more pragmatic than dogmatic, and the original commercial vision for the country underscored the purpose-driven nature of our democratic republic. Ideological emoters and scientific determinists should reflect on the intentions of providential architecture; the argument has not been about whether unknowable territories in science and religion compete or complement each other. It has instead been about whether scientific enthusiasts, religious doctrinaires, "nominal" patriots, and skeptics can accommodate healthy debate over domestic policy formulation and foreign policy agenda. As the pendulum for those all-encompassing philosophical doctrines of religious idealism and economic realism swings from one end to another, the politics of policy and government action in the United States has always, in these public arenas, been promiscuously calibrated in a Reaganesque-type center.

As de Tocqueville observed, democracy in America is best governed from the center—precisely what Providence dictated. In his book *Human Understanding* (1748), Scottish philosopher David Hume, who greatly influenced the founding generation, also argued that a religious system offering divine reward or punishment was not necessarily the best mechanism to sustain moral, ethical, and political order.[14] Since the Founding Fathers understood the nature of Providence, they neither denied nor endorsed any particular religious belief. Instead, they employed a wide range of Egyptian and Greco-Roman symbols to depict their vision of divinity when they devised the architectural blueprint for the nation's capital; Providence is a celestial voice at the heart of this grand plan for Washington, D.C. Affirming Hume's prescience, the constitutional architects designed a governance system for a commercial republic—both literally and figuratively—to find "more peace of mind . . . . and more favorable reception from the world."[15] Within that architectural and constitutional system, scientific discovery and religious faith are counterpoised to generate creative tension for greater innovation and the pursuit of happiness.

Overview of the Book

The readers of this book are welcome to find cross-fertilization of all these persuasions through the prism of American history in the proceeding chapters. As in these opening paragraphs, I do not intend to subscribe to any singular perspective over another. Rather, the primary focus of this volume is to dissect the anatomy of Providence, which has never been academically and practically espoused in order to understand the command of America's Mercurial power (related to the Roman god of

commerce, innovation, and communication as opposed to the hawkish
and controlling forces of Mars) and the embryonic source from which
our trade, commerce, and finance sprouts. The formulated doctrine,
which I call the "theory of commercial providence," is intended to advance our understanding of the underlying foundation that has been
obscurely displayed in the nation's capital through mystical and symbolic language from ancient occult and esoteric traditions. Mainstream
history textbooks have hardly integrated the metaphysical aspects of our
country's commercial and political evolution, though the pervasive role
of Providence has been widely noted by perceptive observers. In 1840,
for example, Alexis de Tocqueville wrote:

> That Providence has given to every human being the degree of
> reason necessary to direct himself in the affairs which interest
> him exclusively; such is the grand maxim upon which civil and
> political society rests in the United States. The father of a family
> applies it to his children; the master to his servants; the township
> to its officers; the province to its townships; the state to the prov-
> inces; the Union to the states; and when extended to the nation, it
> becomes the doctrine of the sovereignty of the people.[16]

The dominion of Providence has been an entirely magical and logical
notion, and it has persistently served as an exhilarating and powerful
force for Americans; consequently, the United States was never established to be a pusillanimous nation. The French visitor observed that "all
the gifts which are bestowed by Providence with an equal hand [have]
turned to the advantage of the democracy."[17] In American democracy,
the invisible hand of commercial providence is the cause of social and
economic equality—and the source of global human progress. De Tocqueville concurred when he wrote, "If we carefully examine the social
and political state of America after having studied its history, we shall
remain perfectly convinced that not an opinion, not a custom, not a law, I
may even say not an event," explained "the origin of that people" but the
effect of Providence.[18] In fact this creed, which resonated from the Puritan Fathers, has been the nucleic source of America's exceptionalism.

In this book, I present a clinical analysis of "special" Providence to
better understand the genesis of exceptionalism, which is often venerated
by "God bless America." The employed method of examination is inspired by William Shakespeare's statement: "What is past is prologue."[19]
As a student of American history and international affairs, I was natural-

ly inclined to use a Shakespearean framework to interpret the future history of the United States and the continuation of America's exceptionalism, which benefits the world.

Roadmap of Commercial Providence

Following the celebrated notation of Providence by de Tocqueville, I fast-forwarded the book one hundred years to capture a similar observation made by President Franklin Delano Roosevelt in chapter **one**. Echoing de Tocqueville, the president said that the new generation of Americans has "a rendezvous with destiny."[20] In this chapter, I further explore the doctrine of Providence and the role of religion in America to provide a conceptual framework. With this introduction, the book is divided into four segments according to the abstract outline of the U.S. Constitution's commerce clause, the Great Seal of the United States, the Egyptian and Greco-Roman origin of commercial providence, and the codification of American Mercury.

The birth of a new nation in Part I of the book contains three chapters. The original national motto, *E Pluribus Unum*, "Out of many, one," describes the founding instruments and concepts in chapter **two**. The chapter includes a survey of the role of the Constitution's commerce clause not just as a powerful unifier of the thirteen original states, but in reconciling inhabitants with the world of international trade relations. In chapter **three**, Freemasonry is discussed as the subtle (and secular) "high priest" of the American foundation. The American experience of the Pilgrims and colonists is explained in chapter **four** to demonstrate how democratic and republican ideas emerged from the two cradles of civilization at Plymouth, Massachusetts and Jamestown, Virginia.

Part II outlines the development of a philosophy for the commercial republic. Chapter **five** analyzes Adam Smith's primary thesis in *Wealth of Nations* (1776), which is associated with the colonists in Jamestown. His *Theory of Moral Sentiments* (1759) can be linked to the Pilgrims, and presents the power of ethical calculus in individual and public decision-making. Smith's two frameworks then influenced Alexander Hamilton and Thomas Jefferson, and this ingenious tradition of rivalry is analyzed in chapter **six**. Chapter **seven** reveals the philosophical and practical aspects of the Constitution's commerce clause as the vector of national unity and the unrelenting force of globalization.

In Part III, the concept of *Annuit Coeptis* or "Providence (God) favors our undertakings," is employed to examine the physical manifestation of the meta-physical concept of Providence. Chapter **eight** explores George Washington's decision to locate a parcel of sanctified land in the Potomac delta for his namesake capital, and how this act connected with the ancient ideas of Pythagoras. The anatomy of commercial providence is described in chapter **nine**. The idea of a commercial empire denoting a Mercurial ruler and the sacred attributes of Constitution Avenue (which runs from the Dirksen Senate Office Building to the new edifice of the U.S. Institute of Peace by the State Department) is displayed in chapter **ten**. The Virgoan Federal Triangle as the altar of commercial empire is discussed in chapter **eleven** to illustrate the power of American Mercury through the Federal Trade Commission, the Commerce Department and the Ronald Regan International Trade Center, among others.

In Part IV, the segment on James Madison's universal empire is the most provocative. I explore the original meaning of *Novus Ordo Seclorum*, which is generally described as the New World Order. In chapter **twelve**, the medieval motives of religious fundamentalists are studied to investigate the way in which a certain religious "faction," which Madison characterized as a danger, exploited government power to change the original American motto. They also attempted to modify the establishment clause of the Constitution to falsely reclaim their so-called Christian nation. In the concluding chapter **thirteen**, Madison's universal empire is explained by Jefferson's idealistic vision of an empire of liberty, which is achieved through Hamilton's commercial and financial instruments and institutions like the Federal Reserve Bank (the Fed).

In the closing analysis, I revisit the ideas of philosophic empire, Providence, and most importantly, the influential role played by Benjamin Franklin and other Freemasons as the precursor to the founding of the commercial republic. The book concludes with a re-examination of the mystical power cloaked in Providence and isolates its perplexing gravitas as the dominant force behind American Mercury's invisible attraction. It was this magnetism that prompted my own American journey, in which I learned about the adopted country of my providential choice and its hidden laws of nature. This inspiring education was communicated through the universal language of symbolism on display in the architecture of our nation's capital, from which freedom reigns over much of the world by way of America's philosophic empire of commerce—the empire prophesied by Sir Francis Bacon and other philosophers.

ONE

A Rendezvous with Destiny

I also know that Islam has always been a part of America's story. The first nation to recognize my country was Morocco. In signing the Treaty of Tripoli in 1796, our second President, John Adams, wrote, "The United States has in itself no character of enmity against the laws, religion or tranquility of Muslims." . . . We are shaped by every culture, drawn from every end of the Earth, and dedicated to a simple concept: *E Pluribus Unum*—"Out of many, one."[1]

President Barack Hussein Obama

The new generation of Americans has "a rendezvous with destiny."[2] When President Franklin Delano Roosevelt echoed those prophetic words in 1936, he described "a mysterious cycle in human events"[3]—like the Boston Tea Party and the Revolutionary War—that led to expelling political and religious tyranny on July 4, 1776. Yet the most auspicious day of this era was actually April 30, 1789; the exalted city was New York; and the celebrated man was a great military leader. His dreams, visions, and ideals (and more importantly, the acts of Providence) brought thirteen colonies together in Philadelphia to form a new country. Thomas Paine, a Revolutionary philosopher and writer, characterized this

historic incident as the "Birth of a New Nation," and movingly celebrated the purposeful creation in these memorable words: "We have it in our
power to begin the world over again."[4]

The world leader was none other than George Washington, who took
the oath of office as the first president of the United States of America
and initiated the first administration. Chancellor Robert Livingston, Masonic grand master of New York, administered the oath. After his pledge,
Washington closed his eyes devotedly, kissed his Masonic Bible solemn-
ly, and said reverently: "So help me God."[5] Ever since, most American
presidents have seemingly followed the practice of faithfully placing
their hand on a Bible and wishfully declaring the four-word codicil. The
action has repeatedly demonstrated that the new nation detested the religious oppression that was a hallmark of world history, and
simultaneously embraced all religions.

The tradition of taking an oath that alluded to Christian deity ignited
a debate on whether the first president actually recited, "So help me
God," and every president henceforth pursued Washington's example.[6]
Even if he voiced those questionable four words, Washington—the most
famous Freemason in the world—used the term God in a generic sense to
represent no particular religion, but to encompass the very essence of all
religious faiths. In his first Inaugural Address, President Washington
clearly articulated:

> In this official act my fervent supplications to that Almighty Be-
> ing who rules over the universe, who presides in the councils of
> nations, and whose providential aids can supply every human
> defect, that His benediction may consecrate to the liberties and
> happiness of the people of the United States.[7]

Given his prior patriotic and heavenly observations, the president
subtly distinguished the connection between religious authority and political freedom, which has played an ambiguous but positive role in
America as it worked mysteriously toward realizing the nation's new
destiny. Washington attributed such a non-visible power to "the Great
Author" in his address. In other instances he referred to the Almighty
Being as Providence, or Heaven, although he sometimes made personal
appeals by calling on the Director of Human Events, the Great Ruler of
Events, the Supreme Ruler, the Governor of the Universe, the Author of
the Universe, the Supreme Architect of the Universe, the Grand Architect, or the Great Creator.[8] Dr. Benjamin Franklin, another famous

Freemason, used similar phrases to identify the Almighty Being. The common recognition of this powerful personality as an obscure and unseen force of divinity points to the occult (hidden) promise and inherent destiny that lies at the heart of America's democratic enterprise.

The Great Architect of the Universe

President Washington's imparted sentiments resonate more with Freemasonry and esoteric linguistics than the language of the Bible, and there was no mention of God in the Inaugural Address. In reflection of his faith, the first president not only took his oath on a Masonic Bible, but also never gave a paramount position to either Jesus Christ or the Christian Bible elsewhere. In his well-balanced book *Founding Faith,* Steven Waldman, former national editor of *U.S. News & World Report*, concludes that Washington "rarely referred to Jesus Christ or Christianity in his writings" and "often spoke of God, Providence, the Great Architect, and other formulations for the deity,"[9] deriving all from the earliest civilizations. As various religious forces within the church and state coexisted in restless equipoise in the ensuing years, the president and other Founding Fathers communicated America's concealed mission in a murky language of Masonic and ancient symbolism. In his *Secret Destiny of America*, prolific Freemasonry author Manly Hall reveals:

> The rise of the Christian Church broke up the intellectual pattern
> of the classical pagan world. By persecution . . . [the Church]
> drove the secret societies into greater secrecy; the pagan intellec-
> tuals then reclothed their original ideas in a garment of Christian
> phraseology, but bestowed the keys of the symbolism only upon
> those duly initiated and bound to secrecy.[10]

This is why a plethora of symbols in the nation's capital drawn from Greco-Roman and Egyptian civilizations exists. Together, they convey a multitude of meanings to various levels of human understanding. In this clever strategy, symbols speak universally and differently to each person's individual taste, intellectual grasp, and religious faith.

Freemasonry, which has ancient and European origins, is a beautiful system of esoteric and exoteric morality veiled in allegory and illustrated by olden rituals and arcane symbols. In his book *Fire in the Minds of Men*, James Billington, director of the Woodrow Wilson International

Center for Scholars in Washington, D.C., writes that Freemasonry is "a moral meritocracy" among "men of intelligence and ambition," who "often experienced with Masonic lodges a kind of brotherhood among equals not to be found in the aristocratic society outside."[11] These men believed that Masons were "creating in their fraternal societies the 'natural' condition of cooperation that prevailed among those earlier, artisan masons who shaped stones for a common building."[12] Fervently convicted of a "Divine Architect,"[13] these Freemasons pursue a vision of a secular order backed by a moral force to establish a better society for all.

To this end, these Freemasons believe in a Supreme Being or a Great Architect—an omnipresent and omnipotent, divine source of power that created the world and everything in it. In his book *Faiths of the Founding Fathers*, Professor David Holmes at the College of William and Mary in Virginia writes, "When the Founding Fathers use such terms as 'the Grand Architect' to speak of God, they are using language that comes directly from Freemasonry and not from the Bible."[14] Thus, the bedrock of American ideas derived not from a particular religious faith but from a reservoir of European Enlightenment ideas and wisdom traditions.

In 1781, the Articles of Confederation did acknowledge "the Great Governor of the World;"[15] however, six years later the U.S. Constitution neither referred to God nor Jesus. When Alexander Hamilton was asked why the framers omitted the word God from the Constitution, he cheerfully replied, "We forgot."[16] On the other hand, two days after President Thomas Jefferson wrote a letter to the Danbury Baptist Association on January 1, 1802 (endorsing a doctrine of a "wall of separation between church and State"[17]), he attended a religious service in the U.S. House of Representatives. These statesman-like words and deeds signify the accommodation of a personal relationship between a faithful and their God, and the rightful role of religion in the public arena. As such, the Constitution states that Congress should "make no law respecting an establishment of religion, prohibiting the free exercise thereof."[18] This carefully drafted principle was a solid foundation for the endurance of the republic.

Given all these deliberations, it was quite certain that Christian ideals were implicitly and minimally infused into these documents. But the guiding spirit and language of the U.S. Declaration of Independence and the Constitution manifestly derived from the ideas and ideals of Freemasonry and Reverend Dr. James Anderson's *Constitutions of the Free-Masons*, which was originally published by the Grand Lodge of England in 1723.[19] The edited version was reprinted in 1734 by Dr. Benjamin

Franklin, provincial grand master of Pennsylvania,[20] and distributed among over one-hundred lodges in all thirteen colonies by 1765.[21] The basic principles of the constitutions were contained in a federal system of a grand lodge with self-governing local lodges, a process of electing officers by ballot, a method of limiting the governing power by constitution, a form of judicial review process, a scheme of majority rule by protecting the rights of minority, and most importantly, a moral code for religious tolerance. By the time of the American Revolution and the founding of the nation, a learned, enlightened, and morally vigilant citizenry was well-prepared to self-govern the new republic. Despite sectarian rivalries and political persuasions, a continued esteem for Masonic philosophy in eighteenth century America galvanized the spirit of unity, religious optimism, and the "universal needs of humanity."[22]

In her book *Moral Minority*, Dr. Brooke Allen also points out that the United States was not founded on Christian principles at all, but on the humanist ideals of European luminaries.[23] In fact, the Preamble to the U.S. Constitution is written in the form of a social contract with people, not of a covenant between the American nation and God. Allen also confirms that the Christian God or Jesus Christ was conspicuously absent in the grand scheme of things and that the character of the founding documents originated from John Locke and other Enlightenment thinkers.[24]

A Religious Nation

As literary enthusiasts in the Age of Enlightenment, the Founding Fathers were a pantheon of true believers and spiritual seekers; many of them—including John Adams, Franklin, Hamilton, Jefferson, James Madison, Paul Revere, and Washington—were Deists and Freemasons. They certainly did not want the United States to be a Christian nation, but a religious nation based on humanism and rationality. As members of the elitist American Philosophical Society in Philadelphia (a counterpart to the Royal Society or the "Invisible College" in London), Adams, Hamilton, Franklin, Jefferson, the Marquis de Lafayette, Madison, the Reverend Peter Miller, Paine, Charles Thompson, and Washington all applied scientific thought and esoteric knowledge to their personal affairs and political strategies.[25] Franklin was the founding president of the Society and later Jefferson became president while also serving as the third president of the United States. Their collective conscience in religious and spiritual matters permeated through scientific and divine notions of a Creator, the Author, or Nature's God.

Some religious writers and others have claimed that America has a Christian origin; however, Reverend Billy Graham—the legendary "America's Pastor" who has offered prayers at Presidential Inaugurations from Dwight Eisenhower in 1953 to George W. Bush in 2001[26]— affirmatively declared that the United States is not a Christian nation. In an interview televised on May 30, 1997, Sir David Frost of the British Broadcasting Corporation (BBC) asked whether the United States was still a Christian country and the pastor indisputably asserted: "No! We're not a Christian country. We've never been a Christian country. We're a secular country by our Constitution in which Christians live and in which many Christians have a voice. But we're not a Christian Country."[27] Exactly two hundred years prior to Reverend Graham's affirmation, a legal document in 1797 explicitly revealed to the Islamic country of Tripoli that the United States was indeed a secular nation. The Barbary peace and friendship treaty with Tripoli (now Libya)—negotiated by President Washington, ratified by the Senate, and signed by President Adams— clearly stated:

> [T]he Government of the United States of America is not, in any sense, founded on the Christian religion; as it has in itself no character of enmity against the laws, religion, or tranquillity, of Mussulmans [Muslims]; and, as the said States never entered into any war, or act of hostility against any Mehomitan nation.[28]

Indeed, such reflective comments and documentary evidence are needed to complement the founding vision implanted in American symbols. As Karen Armstrong elaborates in *The Case for God*, "Ideas about God come and go . . . the struggle to find meaning even in the darkest circumstances must continue" because "the idea of God is merely a symbol of indescribable transcendence and has been interpreted in many different ways over the centuries."[29] Likewise, the Founding Fathers' shared notion of God was depicted symbolically on the reverse side of the Great Seal of the United States, in which the Latin words *Annuit Coeptis* lie above an unfinished pyramid and Freemasonry's watchful Eye of Providence, or the All-Seeing Eye: "Providence [God] has favored our undertakings." In her previous book, *A History of God*, former Catholic nun Armstrong explains that words such as God were "seen as symbols of a single transcendent Reality;"[30] however, the language falls short of describing the real meaning behind the symbols.

For the Founding Fathers, Masonic symbolism had the ability not only to address this disadvantageous situation in describing Providential
Agency, but also to portray the religious nature of the country in a secular manner. Disapproving of the founding secularism, Professor Charles
Eliot Norton, translator of *Dante* and a respected scholar of art history at
Harvard University, confirmed in 1884 that the "elaborate and allegorical
character" adopted by Congress for the Great Seal of the United States
was "a dull emblem of a Masonic fraternity."[31] Despite such disagree-
ment, the Masonic device was intended to illustrate a force of unity
through a "public religion,"[32] as Benjamin Franklin advocated. In his
book *American Gospel: God, the Founding Fathers, and the Making of a
Nation*, Jon Meacham, editor of *Newsweek*, champions the founding secular cause and crystallizes the concept of Franklin's "public religion,"
calling it the "American Gospel."[33] Embedding the Enlightenment philosophies and ancient ideas of Masonic and esoteric symbols in the
architecture of the nation's capital made the meaning of God common to
all, applicable to changing circumstances, and open to life-altering prayers during national calamities like the great San Francisco earthquake in
1906 and Hurricane Katrina in 2005.

Purpose of the Book

There is no city in the world that projects the power of symbolism
more than President George Washington's Federal City. The original city
is a perfect square measuring ten miles on each side, with cardinal points
at which it rotates 45 degrees to resemble the Masonic square and compass symbol. The city is purposefully located on the Y-shaped Potomac
delta. Washington employed the wisdom traditions he learned as a Master Mason and as a member of the American Philosophical Society to
identify the ideal location for the new capital. He also relied on methods
that celebrated the ancient Greek mathematician and Masonic philosopher, Pythagoras, and his mystery school of divine teachings. That
mathematical and philosophical knowledge convinced President Washington of the celestial meaning contained in the premier real estate site,
which notably resembles the Pythagorean-Y. This belief system further
persuaded the president to circumvent the sufficiently established cities
of Boston, New York, and Philadelphia for the linearly-connected southern spot, and to favor placing the Federal City on the banks of the
malaria-ridden marshlands of the Potomac delta near Georgetown, Maryland (Figure 1.1). Professor Francis Fukuyama at the Johns Hopkins

University School of Advanced International Studies writes, "The Masonic influence in the city's design is unmistakable, and indeed is still often denounced by conservative Christians as a satanic conspiracy. George Washington was of course a Freemason."[34] Available historical information suggests that it is indeed a Masonic-inspired city and does not contain even the slightest evidence of Christian inspiration.

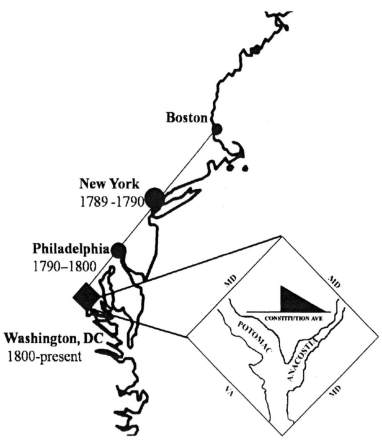

FIGURE 1.1: The linear connection of Boston, New York, Philadelphia, and Washington, D.C. The years indicate the periods in which each city hosted the nation's capital until it moved to Washington, D.C., in 1800.

British writer Ian Axford describes the world's foremost "Masonic City"[35] as constructed according to Pierre L'Enfant's original master plan: the city plan included a consequential collection of triangles, circles, and rectangles upon which a number of important monuments for war heroes, political leaders, and Freemasons were erected—without any religious endorsement, but with Masonic meaning and symbolism. The heavenly-directed American pyramid—i.e., the Washington Monument—is similarly purpose-driven, much like the Egyptian structure without the capstone on the reverse side of the Great Seal of the United States. A triangle (Delta, in the Greek alphabet) containing the All-Seeing Eye floats on top of the unfinished pyramid surrounded by rays of divine light. Like the streets radiating from the Capitol to the White House, through Pennsylvania Avenue over the hypotenuse of the Federal Triangle, underscored by the Constitution Avenue denominator, the geometric city also signifies the Greek letter D: the first letter of the name of God (The name of God was represented by Greek *Theos*, Latin *Deus* in Bible translation). In his *Morals and Dogma*, Masonic philosopher Albert Pike writes:

> It is to be noted that the name of God in Latin and French (Deus, Dieu), has for its initial the Delta or Greek Triangle. Such is the reason, among ancients and moderns, for the consecration of the Triangle, whose three sides are emblems of the three Kingdoms, or Nature, or God.[36]

The pyramid—both the American one in the Washington Mall and the Egyptian symbol on the Great Seal of the United States—is the universal house; the delta-like apex is the eye of the Great Architect of the Universe. For Egyptians, the pyramid is the shrine tomb for the god Thoth; for Greeks, it is the god Hermes; and for Romans, it is the god Mercury. For George Washington and other Masonic brethren, the concept of an American pyramid personified Universal Wisdom, or the God of antiquity. It was this God that they described as Providential Agency or Nature's God—a generic word to explain the ultimate reality of God, Brahman, Allah, Dao, or Nature itself as the Universal Builder.

What does this founding Doctrine of Providence mean to America, and to the universal appeal it holds for the world?

In this book, I present the theory that the Founding Fathers' understanding of Providence was essentially commerce-centric for the republic to achieve the Jeffersonian vision of an Empire of Liberty through Hamiltonian instruments of trade, commerce, and finance. Since its founding, the Hamiltonian mission has either contributed to, or been associated with, every American life; however, Jefferson's ideals of human freedom and civil rights were achieved much later during the Women's Suffrage movement in 1920 with the passage of the Nineteenth Amendment to the U.S. Constitution, and the Voting Rights Act of 1965 for African Americans, for example. Along with the symbols of Mercury (the ruler of Virgo and Gemini in astrology) displayed in the nation's capital, over fifty mysterious zodiacs and eminently-featured Virgoan images[37] reveal the esoteric orders of the Freemasons and other ancients, to whom the Roman god of Mercury signified commerce, communication, and innovation. The hidden symbolism of "commercial providence" is pronounced in the U.S. Constitution's "commerce clause" as a grand strategy to not only preserve, protect and defend the nation, but also to realize James Madison's "Universal Empire"[38] created abroad in America's image—first, as an extension of the Hamiltonian realism of the commercial republic, then as a way of gradually promoting Jeffersonian idealism and democracy. The latter involves human struggles, as witnessed in the Suffrage and the Civil Rights Movements (and as in Tibet, Myanmar, Sudan, Iran, and elsewhere in the world). Hamiltonian instincts, on the other hand, are as natural as commercial desires for greater wealth and greed—as illustrated in emerging countries like China, India, Russia, and elsewhere.

How then is the manifest commercial providence of the nation's capital a source of national power for the formation and governance of a global empire, or a Madisonian Universal Empire?

To that end, the old notion of Manifest Destiny is no longer capable of acquiring more land and expanding American influence around the world. The founding vision entrenched in symbolism dictates that the original mission is to integrate the global community through trade and commerce. This is America's secret destiny, born of commercial providence. With the North American Free Trade Agreement (NAFTA), the United States began to visibly demonstrate the commercial providence with neighbors Canada and Mexico, and then led the establishment of the World Trade Organization (WTO) in order to create an "empire of commerce." Both Hamilton and Jefferson agreed on international trade despite their philosophical rivalry on other issues of national importance.

In this theory, I illustrate how in an evolutionary process, the origin of the city's architectural design has somewhat modified the founding national identity to accommodate the changing circumstances and politics of global realities. Yet the vision of the commercial republic endures with Providence, followed by democracy promotion abroad especially when the latter serves as a convenient (but historically paradoxical) conveyor of the part of America's founding vision that associates with human rights and individual freedom.

"In God We Trust" on Money

In a Darwinian-like competition for survival of the fittest, commercial providence has adapted itself in times of hostility or gravest difficulty to reinforce the founding motto of unity, *E Pluribus Unum*, "Out of many, one." For example, in a direct response to fear of the atheistic Communism of the former Soviet Union and the rise of McCarthyism in the United States, the eighty-fourth Congress passed a joint resolution to replace the original dictum with "In God We Trust." The new slogan officially took the place of *E Pluribus Unum* when President Dwight Eisenhower signed the resolution into law on July 30, 1956, affirming the so-called Judeo-Christian origin of the national identity. Congress ordered the new national motto placed on all U.S. currency, and added the phrase "Under God" to the Pledge of Allegiance.

The idea of placing God on money originated from Reverend Mark Richard Watkinson, a Baptist minister of the Gospel at Ridleyville in Pennsylvania, at a time when religious sentiments ran high during the Civil War. The Reverend was convinced that "the bloody conflict was God's punishment on the nation for failing to recognize Him in the Constitution."[39] In a letter dated November 13, 1861, Watkinson appealed to President Abraham Lincoln's Secretary of the Treasury Salmon Chase, saying that the "Almighty God" must be recognized "in some form on our coins."[40] Secretary Chase agreed, saying, "The trust of our people in God should be declared on our national coins."[41] He then authorized the phrase "In God We Trust," which first appeared on the two-cent coin in 1864.[42] A year later, Congress allowed the director of U.S. Mint to engrave the motto on all gold and silver coins. The phrase may have had its inspiration from the fourth stanza of Francis Scott Key's *Star Spangled Banner*, which he wrote in 1814: "Then conquer we must, when our cause it is just, And this be our motto, 'In God is our trust.'"[43]

In 1907, President Theodore Roosevelt—another preeminent Freemason—believing that religion and money should not be mixed, tried to have the words removed from newly designed coins because he felt the practice was "in effect irreverence" and "dangerously close to sacrilege."[44] The president believed that invoking God as a defender of liberty was noble; however, an association with money would "cheapen" the divinity.[45] In the end, growing public outcry put a stop to Roosevelt's plan. Like the president, Supreme Court Justice William Brennan thought slogans like "In God We Trust" and "One Nation Under God" have "lost any true religious significance."[46] The religious mottos were later challenged in courts and found to be constitutional since they do not endorse any particular religion. (Nevertheless, non-Abrahamic religions—like Buddhism and Hinduism—and agnostics, atheists, and other non-believers in America may be offended by axioms that isolate them and demean their belief systems).

Unlike the original motto, the religious tone of the new slogan has been unleashed at moments of crisis to affirm national identity. For instance, in the midst of the Civil War and the fear of the Cold War, America collectively and affirmatively reacted without much deliberation for unintended consequences. It was an evolutionary process punctuated by human events and emotional exuberance. In hopeless and powerless situations (like the 9/11 tragedies and Hurricane Katrina), the struggle to find meaning is certainly natural and favored by religious groups. Karen Armstrong describes this occurrence as new: "The modern God—conceived as powerful creator, first cause, supernatural personality realistically understood and rationally demonstrable—is a recent phenomenon."[47] History, however, attests that religion has often been viewed as a means of generating social cohesion and national unity.

Yet, America's religious transformation resembles the God of antiquity. The brilliant adaptation in times of threat and terror further signifies the vitality of Franklin's notion of "public religion." As God and money circulate among people on a daily basis, there is no need to find God in places of worship. This is where the rivalry of Jefferson and Hamilton meets to validate the common view of "Providence" as an insurance policy for commercial affairs.

The founding motto *E Pluribus Unum* still appears on U.S. coins even though it is no longer the official national slogan. Since 1956, that tribute has been given to "In God We Trust," and the phrase is inscribed on all "greenbacks," or Federal Reserve Notes. Like a heavenly-sent endorsement, money seems to conquer all things where God fails—an acknowledgment of Hamiltonian instincts. The design of the original motto was actively deliberated by Adams, Franklin, and Jefferson, and is as universal and genuinely American as the enduring commercial republic. Without the power of unity inherent in *E Pluribus Unum*, the self-preservation of American democracy would continue to struggle for a national identity.

In a free and diverse society, Americans are more likely to be bound by the universal human values championed by Jefferson than religious fundamentalism. This is the occult (unseen) promise and the continued existence of ancient hope for America. Jesuit scientist and French philosopher Pierre Teilhard de Chardin seemed to have captured this occult vision: "We are not human beings having a spiritual experience; we are spiritual beings having human experience."[48] He observed that human beings are moving toward "Point Omega"[49] as an organic evolution that transcends all human differences, not just the secular and the sacred. With what appears to be a similar vision of unity, the Founding Fathers encapsulated the new nation's eventual rendezvous with destiny in its original motto, *E Pluribus Unum*—a rendezvous later enshrined with "In God We Trust," as if the American project were a grand design of the Great Architect of the Universe.

President Harry S. Truman, dressed in his Grand Master's Masonic regalia, once wrote: "Freemasonry is a system of morals which makes it easier to live with your fellow man, whether he understands it or not."

PART I

THE BIRTH OF A NEW NATION

"They [the United States of America] are the hope of the world. They may become a model to it. . . . They may exhibit an example of political liberty, of religious liberty, of commercial liberty, and of industry. The Asylum they open to the oppressed of all nations should console the earth."

~ *French statesman ANNE ROBERT JACQUES TURGOT*
March 22, 1778

TWO

E Pluribus Unum: Out of Many, One

No nation on this globe should be more
internationally minded than America
because it was built by all nations.[1]

Harry S. Truman
Thirty-Third U.S. President and 33°
Masonic Grand Master

President Barack Obama is a testament to the audacity of ancient
hope. The Founding Fathers envisioned such inevitable possibilities
when they created our global nation, *E Pluribus Unum,* "Out of many,
one."[2] Distinguished author Walter Isaacson, the president of the Aspen
Institute, writes:

Benjamin Franklin will . . . have been pleased, even tickled, by
the election of Barack Obama as president. He believed that
America's fundamental virtue, the key to creating a pluralistic
democracy, was balance—the humility to allow people of
different faiths, backgrounds, and ethnic origins to be equal
participants in the nation's civic life.[3]

When Obama's African father from Kenya met his white American mother from Kansas at the East-West Center of the University of Hawaii, neither realized the seemingly providential power of freedom and democracy that brought them together. They took different journeys following the birth of their son in the fiftieth state of the Union, Hawaii, leaving Obama to find his own destiny.[4]

Almost all U.S. presidents, from George Washington to our forty-third President George W. Bush, have maintained a providential worldview.[5] In his first Inaugural Address on April 30, 1789, President Washington praised the "invisible hand" of the "Grand Architect of the Universe" for directing the affairs of our nation.[6] He elaborated:

> No people can be bound to acknowledge and adore the invisible hand, which conducts the affairs of men, more than the people of the United States. Every step, by which they have advanced to the character of an independent nation, seems to have been distinguished by some token of providential agency.[7]

John Adams described his view of providential occurrence as "reverence and wonder" at America "as the opening of a grand scene."[8] In his second Inaugural Address on January 20, 2005, President Bush proclaimed, "When our Founders declared a new order of the ages . . . they were acting on an *ancient hope* that is meant to be fulfilled. History has an ebb and flow of justice, but history also has a visible direction, set by liberty and the Author of Liberty"[9] (italics added). Of course, neither Bush nor Adams prophesied the arrival of a half-American and half-African president, which would change the course of history by prompting the birth of a new "visible direction," and the opening of a "grand scene." The presidents seem to have recognized the divine providence that had been bestowed on the American cause and embedded in our national motto: *E Pluribus Unum*.

The Latin dictum may be traced back to Horace's *Epistle*, in which it refers to the creation of one nation in Rome.[10] Interestingly, just as thirteen American colonies joined together to form a single cohesive nation (the United States), so the motto *E Pluribus Unum* contains thirteen letters. More importantly, however, the traditional notion of a global nation reflects a "melting pot" of various religious, ethnic, and racial backgrounds to create an interconnected human community as God's crucible nation. President Barack Obama ostensibly epitomizes this American idea and the founding ideals. In his keynote address at the

Democratic National Convention on July 27, 2004, the then-candidate for the U.S. Senate seat in Illinois eloquently explained the meaning of America and its founding vision:

> For alongside our famous individualism, there's another ingredient in the American saga, a belief that we are all connected as one people. If there's a child on the south side of Chicago who can't read, that matters to me, even if it's not my child. If there's a senior citizen somewhere who can't pay for their prescription and having to choose between medicine and the rent, that makes my life poorer, even if it's not my grandparent. If there's an Arab-American family being rounded up without benefit of an attorney or due process, that threatens my civil liberties. It is that fundamental belief—it is that fundamental belief—I am my brother's keeper, I am my sisters' keeper—that makes this country work. It's what allows us to pursue our individual dreams, yet still come together as a single American family: *E Pluribus Unum*, "Out of many, one." . . . There's not a black America and white America and Latino America and Asian America; there's the United States of America.[11]

Like Alexander Hamilton (born on the British island of Nevis, raised on the Danish island of St. Croix in the Caribbean, and educated at King's College, now Columbia University, in New York), President Obama had an unorthodox journey. His pathway took him from Hawaii to Indonesia, from Harvard and Columbia Universities to the south side of Chicago as a community organizer and state senator, and then from the land of Abraham Lincoln to the United States Senate. His giant leap to the presidency of the United States marked a meteoric ascendance, which was apparently providential. The embodiment of his life, work, and vision is a pleasant endorsement to the Americanization of global citizenry.

As other Founding Fathers described earlier, Benjamin Franklin had his own explanation for such providential episodes. In his later years (more precisely at the Constitutional Convention of 1787), the American sage and astrologer told the delegates:

> I have lived, Sir, a long time; and the longer I live, the more convincing proof I see of this Truth, *that God governs in the*

Affairs of Men. And if a sparrow cannot fall to the Ground
without his Notice, is it probable that an Empire cannot rise
without his Aid? (italics original).[12]

   With the inherited financial crisis of 2008, the ever-increasing
national debt, and two wars in Afghanistan and Iraq, President Obama
appeared as the national leader at a pivotal moment in American history.
His demonstrated (and often controversial) religious faith indicates a
subscription to the notion of power from a providential agent. He has
also implicitly sought blessings from the Author of Liberty to visualize
unseen elements of the audacity of ancient hope. These are reflected in
his life story—"genuinely an American tale"[13] according to *Newsweek*—
and his own writings. They are also referenced in a famous speech on
"Politics of Conscience," in which Obama described his unconventional
spiritual journey to a "common destiny."[14]
   Like President Obama, President Bush looked to his faith in God for
guidance. The president confirmed in his second Inaugural Address
following the 9/11 attacks, saying on January 20, 2005:

We go forward with complete confidence in the eventual
triumph of freedom. Not because history runs on the wheels of
inevitability; it is human choices that move events. Not because
we consider ourselves a chosen nation; God moves and chooses
as He wills. We have confidence because freedom is the
permanent hope of mankind, the hunger in dark places, the
longing of the soul.[15]

   For all Americans, freedom matters most. As a divine and universal
gift, freedom brings people together—just as it did for the thirteen
diverse colonies that formed the Union. In other parts of the world,
however, freedom has manifested itself paradoxically. For example,
countries such as the former Yugoslavia and Soviet Union were
Balkanized by racial, ethnic, and religious divisions. In order to flourish
and unify, freedom must exist in the presence of commerce and the
absence of tyranny. Eventually, these two dynamics will unite people and
nations together—just as the European Common Market initially did
before ultimately becoming a full-pledged European Union. A common
love of freedom and commercial interest also brought the American
Founding Fathers together, despite the fact that they were each
independent thinkers to varying degrees of rationality, empiricism,

reasoning, and of different national backgrounds and religious faiths. For example, Franklin invented his own scientific instruments and astrological charts; Washington proved diplomatic and commanding; Adams grumbled about such domineering characteristics; Jefferson tinkered with them, and then removed the divinity of Christ in *The Jefferson Bible*; and Madison defended all these qualities as natural rights and advocated freedom and liberty to exercise them.[16] They were still a unified flock despite the plurality of their points of view, and were both international and universal in their commercial mindset. The legacy within America and across the globe indicates a spiritual nature of freedom that is common to all.

Union through Commerce, Not Religion

Both secular and religious rulers alike have relied on force to concentrate power since antiquity. History attests that religion may unify empires (like the Roman, Ottoman, or British Empires) by distinguishing one from another. In human evolution, however, neither a single religion nor a divined authority has proved to be a cause for unity amongst all God's children. After learning of the tyranny of Christendom and of the imperial dynasties and sultans in Europe and elsewhere, the Founding Fathers deliberately wanted to move away from so-called divinely-ordained leadership and religious suppression. For those men, the power to govern would derive from the governed.

The new American nation would be a nation of religious tolerance and liberty for all without interference from the state. Many of the Founders were Christians; however, their secular thinking superseded their religious conviction and faith factor to overcome such tribal-like divisions not only the realm of religion, but also in their racial, ethnic, nationality, and ideological differences. Professor Frank Lambert at Purdue University confirms that the free marketplace of religions gained legal status as the Founding Fathers began the daunting task of uniting thirteen disparate colonies together. To avoid discord in an increasingly pluralistic and contentious society, Lambert maintains that the Framers of the Constitution protected religious matters from government intervention to guarantee the freedom of exercising choice for all.[17] Indeed, though Christian values and ideas influenced public matters, the Founding Fathers often addressed them in private. They were certainly aware that human freedom eventually triumphs over the power of religious, terrorist, and fanatical forces.

The best available alternative to all these historical and religious factions is commerce that unites people. With this in mind, Franklin— along with other men of commerce such as Hamilton, Jefferson, Madison, Paul Revere, and Washington, to name a few—helped lay the foundation for the most enduring and successful commercial republic in the history of human civilization. Influenced by European Enlightenment philosophers, these leaders of American thought used the pathways of trade as a tapestry to hold the nation together. For example, the Founding Fathers maintained a neutral religious position to provide a world of market opportunities for American traders. This also allowed them to better manage partnerships with Anglican merchants in England, Catholic agents in France, Muslim traders in Libya, Hindu buyers in India, Buddhist sellers in Sri Lanka, and Confucian suppliers in China. The unifying power of trade also illustrates the endurance of the American republic that emerged through many disagreements amongst the Founding Fathers and the thirteen colonies, and was sustained as a politically and militarily powerful force with the ability to fuse opposing self-interests.

As businessmen and plantation owners, American leaders believed that a commercial republic would not only direct human passions away from the violent conflicts caused by religious, ethnic, and ideological divisions, but inspire each person to pursue one's calling in life through profitable enterprises. In one of his *Federalist Papers,* Hamilton assured the public that "commercial republics, like ours, will never be disposed to waste themselves in ruinous contentions with each other," because they are "governed by mutual interest" that would "cultivate a spirit of mutual amity and concord."[18] The Founders reasoned that a commercially-motivated system would help maintain social order and human equilibrium while promoting individual freedom. In turn, they realized such a system must be made globally appealing and universally practiced to manage the dissimilar religious persuasions and racial divisions throughout the world.

By nature, we are of mixed human stock (even self-proclaimed Aryan Adolf Hitler had Jewish blood).[19] Although we are all God's children, our ethnic, racial, and religious identities have created unnatural boundaries that serve to fracture the whole of humankind in the same way that artificial national borders distinguish one country from another. A system of commerce expedites reversal of these fragmented social constructs, just as it did in moving the habitually flirtatious Franklin, the scandalously womanizing Hamilton, and the pleasantly courting Jefferson beyond their Christian or other religious morality. Other prominent politicians—such as President Bill Clinton, U.S. Senator Larry Craig, and South Carolina Governor Mark Sanford—have also illustrated the frailty of human nature, which often triumphs over religious virtues and traditional family values to bond with other racial, religious, ethnic, and sexual orientations through marriage, friendship, or liaison. This entangling thread is indeed the Americanization of human diversity.

In his book *All Connected Now*, Walter Anderson of the World Academy of Art and Science explains that our life in the "first global civilization"[20]—a new world order—emerged with America's commercialization of modern biological and communication technology. The synergy of American innovations—like organ transplants and pacemakers, the Internet and the World Wide Web (WWW), and the Global Positioning System (GPS) and satellite communications—have not only benefited the entire world but have also united people beyond their unnatural boundaries. Rapidly growing global movements of capital, people, goods, services, and ideas through scientific discoveries and technological advancements add increasing complexity to political governance. This is especially true when domestic and foreign policies are inextricably linked, and the former often extends to the latter. As such, the founding commercial vision was determined to gradually eradicate the differences that divide us by uniting all peoples as a global nation. This is America's providential destiny.

Toward A Theory of Commercial Providence

American textbook authors and scholarly writers have hardly integrated concurrent facts about American history and the influence of Freemasonry in the formation and progress of the commercial republic. Departmentalization of academic disciplines, pride in specialized knowledge, and the so-called secretive and esoteric nature of Masonic tradecraft may have prevented academics from examining the interconnected nature of the American Experience and Freemasonry. The ideas and ideals of Freemasonry, one of the largest and most well-known global fraternities dedicated to the universal "Fatherhood of God and the

Brotherhood of Man,"[21] played an enormously influential role in the
Revolutionary War, America's founding, the drafting of the U.S.
Constitution, and the design of the Federal City.[22]

This book examines the often-neglected area of synchronized history
and proposes a theory that Freemasons—including the most famous,
Washington and Franklin—used the wisdom of antiquity and esoteric
traditions to conceive the commerce-driven republic to achieve the aims
of the three national mottos (in Latin) symbolically depicted in the Great
Seal of the United States[23] (Figure 2.1). Ultimately, the theory postulates
that the powerful imprints of Freemasonry and the esoteric symbols
(such as images of Virgo and Mercury) prolifically inscribed on the
architecture of the nation's capital are openly concealed—yet
simultaneously revealed—to project the commercial providence of the
purpose-driven nation.

FIGURE 2.1: The front and back sides of the Great Seal of the United States
include 13 stars, 13 arrows, 13 olive leaves and 13 berries as well as 13 letters
each in *E Pluribus Unum* and *Annuit Coeptis*. The pyramid contains 13 layers of
72 stones; the significance of the number is not limited to the original 13 states.

The following four facts and interpretations briefly introduce the
primary contours of a theory of commercial providence—the sacred idea
that is embedded, in secular terms, in the foundation of the United States
to realize a global mission:

First, the plethora of arcane symbols and Latin phrases found in
American iconography (drawn from Greco-Roman and Egyptian
civilizations) is itself mysterious to many Americans. Those few who are

knowledgeable in the wisdom traditions and initiates of mystic fraternities (like the Rosicrucian Order) and Freemasonry are privy to the hidden and encrypted meaning of the symbolic language. For example, the banner bearing the Latin phrase *E Pluribus Unum* on the Great Seal (held in the beak of a bald eagle grasping a thirteen-leaf olive branch in its right talon and thirteen arrows in its left talon) is easily recognizable to most Americans—yet its origin and meaning is mystifying. In *Freemasons in America*, Paul Jeffers describes the numerical meaning of the eagle's feathers and its association with Freemasonry:

> On the obverse [of the Seal] is an eagle whose dexter wing has thirty-two feathers, the number of ordinary degrees in Scottish Rite Freemasonry. The sinister wing has thirty-three feathers, the additional feather corresponding to the Thirty-Third Degree of the same Rite conferred for outstanding Masonic service. The tail feathers number nine, the number of degrees in . . . the York Rite of Freemasonry. Scottish Rite Masonry had its origin in France; the York Rite is sometimes called the American Rite; the eagle thus clothed represents the union of French and American Masons in the struggle for Liberty, Equality, and Fraternity.[24]

Benjamin Franklin, who preferred the turkey as the symbol for the United States, eventually conceded that the power of America's symbols must be universal, saying, "Eagles have been found in all countries, but the turkey was peculiar to ours."[25] Thus, the new nation used the power of ancient symbols and Masonic traditions to unite the country, not only native and colonial Americans but with nations around the world as well.

Second, prominently featured on the reverse side of the Seal is a pyramid of thirteen layers of stone (representing unity), which depicts the sanctified idea of building a Union both through a republic of colonies and from a melting pot of Americans. On top of the unfinished pyramid is Freemasonry's watchful Eye of Providence enclosed in a triangle. The upper motto is a 13-letter Latin dictum, *Annuit coeptis*, meaning, "He [God] has favored our undertakings." The lower maxim, *Novus ordo seclorum*, stands for "the new order of the ages." The nation's birth year of 1776 is dated on the base of the pyramid in Roman numerals: MDCCLXXVI.[26] Collectively, the Great Seal signifies earthly affairs and spiritual life. However, the founding vision was purposefully concealed from the public eye; the back side of the Great Seal was not revealed to the American public until 1935. Following the advice of his Vice President Henry Wallace (then the Secretary of Agriculture), President Franklin Delano Roosevelt put the pyramid side on the one-dollar bill to intimate that his "spiritual New Deal" would be the beginning of a new commercial order blessed by the providential "eye of the Architect of the Universe."[27] Roosevelt and Wallace were Masonic brethren and they believed that the revelation would gain benedictory advantage for the New Deal.

Third, the extraordinary birthday of the United States on July 4, 1776—the date of destiny—was calculated according to planetary movements, astrological significance, and commercial importance. On the eve of the Declaration of Independence in Philadelphia, when the ascending constellation Sagittarius (representing the ruler of Jupiter and governor of prosperity) aligned with the fixed star Regulus (representing rulers or regulators in general), John Hancock, the president of Congress, signed the document.[28] This Freemason, along with astrologer Benjamin Franklin[29] and other signers, understood the significance of the auspicious occurrence on that day: success in war (Mars) and commercial enterprise (Mercury), according to mystic schools and Masonic traditions.[30] With such occult knowledge, Dr. Ebenezer Sibly (himself a Master Mason, British physician, and astrologer) published a nativity chart for the new nation in 1787 and illustrated "the situation of the heavenly ordinances at the time the Americans chose to declare their defection from the mother-country."[31] He wrote, "They [Americans] know there is a secret power in the magnet, which they can neither see nor comprehend. They are sensible of all the phenomena and surprising properties of air, though they cannot see it, nor demonstrate its particles . . . and question the ordinations of Providence."[32] Astrologer Sibly then predicted, "the Americans shall not only be permanent and durable, but shall be supported by those three grand pillars of state, wisdom, strength, and *rising commerce*; an advantageous and universal traffic to every quarter of the global, with great fecundity and prosperity amongst the people" (italics added).[33] The propitious American event was also noteworthy because it was unprecedented in world history; no other nation-state on earth has had such a precise birth date or similar creation.[34]

Fourth, the symbolism of embellished zodiac signs—over fifty zodiacs[35]—found on federal buildings and landmarks in Washington,

D.C., illustrates the renewal and universality of America's commercial destiny and friendship with other nations. The founding architects used occult symbols to communicate their choice of a universally-embraced means (commerce) to pursue the will of a universal being (Providence). For example, President Washington integrated both America's commercial origin and his understanding of nature's order (as articulated by Pythagoras) into the architectural design and the location of the nation's capital in the Potomac delta. When President Washington consecrated the Capitol with corn, oil, and wine—each Masonic symbol represented the accompanying ritualistic Greco-Roman commodity—he was, in fact, affirming the commercial foundation of the nation.

The Commerce Clause In the United States Constitution

The Constitution of the United States has pivotally been a unifying and universal force for an orderly and law-abiding society from the very beginning. Its "commerce clause" certainly served as the catalyst for defining our commercial republic and its economic behavior. The trilateral clause in the Constitution fosters such relations with Native Indians through interstate commerce and through trade with foreign nations. Thus, the Constitution embodies the nation's sacred nature of oneness, universality, and Providence. The expanded constitutional framework also departs from religious-based domination to create secular governance (i.e., the separation of church and state) so that all Americans may live in harmony. To signify this founding notion, Christian or other religious icons are conspicuously absent in American symbolism and in the nation's capital and its architecture.

Instead, the founding ideas are contained secularly and symbolically in Greco-Roman-Egyptian architecture like the Washington Monument (i.e., the American pyramid) and the astrological signs found in the commercially-oriented Federal Triangle. The triangle begins with the Andrew Mellon "Zodiac" Water Fountain at Pennsylvania and Constitution Avenues, and then continues to the western end of Constitution Avenue by the Albert Einstein Memorial and the site of the U.S. Institute of Peace. These landmarks, including the U.S. Department of Commerce and the Reagan World Trade Center, denote America's "commercial providence" through the Roman god Mercury (counterpart to Greek messenger god Hermes). This "Mercurial" triangle corresponds to the Virgo constellation in the skies, which encircles the Washington Monument, the Capitol, and the White House. In astrology, Mercury is the ruler of Gemini and Virgo, and is the only sign that is assigned to both the masculine and feminine. This illustrates the gender neutrality of the founding vision.

The American nation is Mercurial in nature and organization, and that is precisely the governing framework the Founders envisioned to guide our commercial republic just as the messenger god Mercury guided commerce and communication in Roman mythology. (This Mercurial vision contrasts sharply with Robert Kagan's famous notion that "Americans are from Mars,"[36] which he used to justify President George W. Bush's war policies). After all, twenty-first century America is all about the same global geo-economics embedded in several hundred ancient and arcane symbols that were impressed into the architectural landscape of Washington, D.C., during its construction.[37]

Metaphorically speaking, the tapestry of commercial providence is not easily discernable or even immediately apparent unless we step away from the dance floor of the nation's capital to the balcony of George Washington's Providential Agency. In the postulated theory, I examine the already "openly-secret" commercial providence lodged in the founding vision and try to unveil the mask behind the monuments, symbols, and architectural designs to delineate the purpose-driven American Mercury.

Freemasonry in America's DNA

At the founding of the United States, Thomas Paine—a British-born French citizen and later, an American émigré—articulated a grand strategy for the new nation: "Our plan is commerce, and that, well attended to, will secure us the peace and friendship of all . . . Her trade will always be a protection."[38] Paine suggested that the "Birth of a New Nation" should mark the initiation of a "Democratic Republic"—a term that combined the essence of democratic Greek and republican Roman civilizations—and that it should become the "United States of America." The Founding Fathers firmly endorsed Paine's vision and enthusiastically adopted his unified theme for the thirteen colonies, which were renamed the United States of America. Just as these men intended, the United States evolved into a commercial civilization and a relatively peaceful, prosperous, and stable nation of which the world has borne witness.

In essence, the Constitution is the heart of the American statecraft, tradecraft, stagecraft, and soulcraft that combines both the secular and sacred spaces in our lives as well as in the Federal Triangle architecture. Freemasonry, often referred to as "the Craft," has not only unified this secular-sacred nexus, but its ancient symbols and Masonic tenets reveal a confluence of many sources drawn from both antiquity and modernity.[39] Our Constitution is a fittingly welcome innovation for a commerce-driven nation that pursues its global destiny to create a harmonious and rule-based international order in the image of our commercial republic. Harry S. Truman, the highest ranked 33° Masonic grand master of Missouri and our thirty-third president (a convenient occurrence associated with Providence), captured the fundamental character of the United States when he said, "It will be just as easy for nations to get along in a republic of the world as it is for us to get along in a republic of the United States."[40] The American republic was inspired by the universal brotherhood of Freemasonry and set in motion by American Revolutionaries. It began with the Boston Tea Party, which was at the center of the commercial self-interests and the hearts of New Englanders, who both engaged in and benefited from international trade and commerce.

In a Mercurial republic such as ours, past becomes prologue. In his Farewell Address, President Washington guided the nation with his doctrine that "our commercial policy should hold an equal and impartial hand: neither seeking nor granting exclusive favors or preferences."[41] Jefferson reiterated this in 1799 when he said, "Commerce with all nations, alliance with none, should be our motto."[42] Obviously, the Founders were united in the belief that commerce binds nations and peoples together. The Nobel Peace Prize laureate president agrees that "our commerce . . . bind[s] us together;"[43] Obama's own personal story, from his Kenyan father and white Kansan mother, narrates this well. The progeny of interracial (and inter-religious) unity may be an example of America's founding promise and ancient hope. This hope was also exemplified by Thomas Jefferson when his human spirit touched the life of Sally Hemings,[44] and their African-American descendants emerged as part of one people at the founding of our commerce-driven, secular nation.

President George Washington, who served as worshipful master of Alexandria Lodge No. 22 in Virginia in 1788-89, said of his membership in the fraternity: "The object of Freemasonry is to promote the happiness of the human race."

THREE

Freemasonry as a Catalyst and High Priest

> In this age when different cultures are killing
> each other over whose definition of God is better, one
> could say the Masonic tradition of tolerance and
> open-mindedness is commendable. . . . Moreover,
> Masonry is open to men of all races, colors, and
> creeds, and provides a spiritual fraternity that does
> not discriminate in any way.[1]
>
> **Dan Brown**
> Author of *The Lost Symbol*

For many Americans, Freemasonry is a mysterious and secretive organization; nobody seems to know with certainty as to how, when, and where the symbolic and ritualistic fraternity was formed. It is widely accepted that it may have begun with stonemasons in the Middle Ages.[2] Some scholars and historians have attributed the origin of the craft to the Knights Templar in Europe, and even to the Pharaohs in Egypt.[3] For the most part, Masonic legends have proliferated from tracing the celebrated origin of the great builders and ancient philosophers to King Solomon and the construction of his Temple in 967 B.C. in Jerusalem.[4]

Similar legendary traditions also evolved following the controversies of the medieval Knights Templar, a powerful military and religious order that was established to protect pilgrims to the Holy Land. The order severed its patronage of the Roman Catholic Church when Pope Clement V, under pressure of King Phillip IV of France, dissolved it in 1312. The Knights Templar then nearly disappeared in France, and some Freemasonry historians claim that modern Masonry acquired secrets, symbols, and terminology such as "degrees," costumes, and rituals from the Templar.[5]

When first introduced to Tuscany in Italy, Freemasonry was not forbidden by the Church of Rome. After Pope Clement XII dispatched an inquisitor to arrest a number of heretics and other offenders, the Grand Duke set them free and declared himself patron of the order. The Duke, Francis of Lorraine, went on to sponsor Masonic lodges within his province. On April 28, 1738, the Pope directed a bull *In Eminenti* against the Grand Duke and condemned the order.[6] According to ancient Church practice, a bull is not promulgated until it has enforcement power. Still, the Vatican's Code of Canon Law prohibited church followers from joining "Masonic sects or any other similar associations" believed to "plot against the church"[7] well into the twentieth century. Following this first public attack on Freemasons, Pope Pius IX renewed the condemnation in 1865. In 1882, Pope Leo XIII issued another encyclical referring to a "pernicious sect"[8] that was at war with Jesus Christ. Two years later, the Pope announced that "Freemasonry's goal was the destruction of the Roman Catholic Church, and that Freemasonry and the Roman Catholic Church were adversaries."[9] The Church incorporated the attitude of previous papal encyclicals into the 1917 Code of Canon Law, which reaffirmed earlier Church practices and enforced the edict with automatic excommunication from the Roman Catholic Church. In 1983, the Congregation for the Doctrine of the Faith stated that "the Church's negative position on Masonic associations"[10] remained unchanged, and Pope John Paul II reiterated that "Catholics enrolled in Masonic associations are involved in serious sin and may not approach Holy Communion."[11]

Despite this, many Catholics have practiced Freemasonry throughout the years including Daniel Carroll, a prominent Founding Father, close friend of Benjamin Franklin, and most importantly, older brother of first Roman Catholic Bishop in the United States. Bishop John Carroll "did not consider the papal ban applicable"[12] to the United States, which had a whole different experience than in Europe, particularly in Italy and

France. In general, the Catholic Church in America views Freemasonry as other social fraternities like the Rotary and Lions clubs, which have charitable inclinations.[13]

Two types of Masons defined early Freemasonry. In medieval times, Freemasons were mostly comprised of Operative Masons (i.e., the stonemasons), who built the great cathedrals, castles, and other marvels of Europe. Speculative Masons sought to improve their inner spiritual life, and were more interested in the esoteric traditions of antiquity than stonemasonry. This Speculative branch, whose practitioners were also known as Esoteric Masons, focused on the ethical development of personhood through practicing the moral and spiritual tenets of Freemasonry. Although various historical interpretations exist, these Speculative or Esoteric Masons were widely referred to as "Accepted" Masons. These great builders and philosophers provided the framework to create something new and beautiful from dispersed material, and the fraternity appropriately developed its motto *Order ab Chaos*, "Order out of chaos," in the same vein to signify continuous human development of the external material life and the interior temple of divinity for enlightenment.

Since the establishment of the Grand Lodge of England in 1717, the history of Freemasonry has been meticulously documented.[14] Within three decades following that time, the Masonic fraternity had spread throughout Europe and the American colonies by promoting Enlightenment ideals and emphasizing personal development and philanthropy. Membership within the ancient and secretive society was a privilege not available to everyone, and brethren avowed to keep certain aspects of their traditions and rituals private. Though this characteristic is often fodder for conspiracy theories on the association of America's founding faith with Freemasonry, every organization has its own sets of secrets and confidential business information that are considered private or executive privilege. Within the U.S. Government, for example, the Central Intelligence Agency (CIA) and the National Security Agency are tasked with the function of employing secretive means and classified information to safeguard the republic and the safety of American people. During the Revolutionary War, General George Washington and other Masonic brethren like Benjamin Franklin and Nathan Hale similarly used the Committees of Secret Correspondence (a precursor to the CIA), which were elaborately structured within a network of Freemasons reaching throughout the thirteen colonies.[15]

In modern times, Masons belong less to a "secret society" than to a "society with secrets." A pantheon of conspiracy theorists, authors like Dan Brown, and Hollywood movies—especially *National Treasure*—has recently gained a receptive and popular audience by creatively exposing Masonic tradecraft.[16] Yet the private aspects of modern Freemasonry in the twenty-first century are simply modes of recognition among members with certain degrees of hierarchy in leadership and within ritualistic components, which are often "public secrets."[17]

A fundamental aspect of Freemasonry is that members are not publicly recruited. By tradition, a potential candidate must ask to become a Freemason and the craft's motto is, "To be one, ask one," or, "2B1Ask1." Although a Masonic brother might feel that a non-Mason may be a welcome addition to the fraternity, the Mason is strictly prohibited from soliciting him to join. In this modern era of the Internet, solitary entertainment and social networks (i.e., Facebook and Twitter), Freemasonry is facing the declining of membership and increased difficulty in recruiting promising young candidates; therefore, the fraternity is becoming more open and less guarded.[18]

Of the Freemasons, Benjamin Franklin, grand master of the Grand Lodge of Pennsylvania, commented in 1730 that "their grand secret is that they have no secrets at all."[19] More than two centuries later, the grand master for Missouri and U.S. President Harry S. Truman underscored the fact that "the only thing new in the world is the history you don't know."[20] In fact, most of the so-called secret literature and rituals of Freemasonry are freely and openly available online, on television, and in other media.[21] Nevertheless, these revelations are somewhat deceptive as esoteric traditions and Masonic knowledge are exposed to only a few initiates and wisdom seekers. These initiates are more interested in the experiential-learning aspects of personal development and brotherhood than in being spectators of life or conspiracy theorists on the sidelines. Often, the human condition has historically been improved by the former and much less so by the latter.

Masons in Colonial America

Freemasonry was very popular in late eighteenth-century colonial America, and in the United States it has remained a fraternity associated with building communities.[22] Benjamin Franklin and Paul Revere served as heads of the Masonic lodges in Pennsylvania and Massachusetts respectively. Other Revolutionary War heroes and the founding luminaries—such as George Washington, John Hancock, the Marquis de Lafayette, Nathaniel Greene, John Paul Jones, and Joseph Warren— were illustrious Freemasons. Motivated by Enlightenment philosophies, they shared a common appreciation of the dignity of man, the liberty of individuals, the formation of democratic governments, the importance of public education, and the right of all people to worship as they choose. The fraternity gradually developed into a potent global organization dedicated to the fellowship of "brothers" who believe in a Supreme Being.[23]

In his well-researched novel with factual narrative, *The Lost Symbol*, Dan Brown accurately portrayed the core of Freemasonry when he wrote, "One of the prerequisites for becoming a Mason is that you *must* believe in a higher power. The difference between Masonic spirituality and organized religion is that the Masons do not impose a specific definition or name on a higher power" (italics original).[24] Unlike "definitive theological identities like God, Allah, Buddha, or Jesus," Brown added fittingly, "the Masons use more general terms, like Supreme Being or Great Architect of the Universe. This enables Masons of different faiths to gather together."[25] In the United States, Freemasonry has primarily evolved into two separate yet often mutually-inclusive[26] tradecrafts: the York and Scottish Rites.

York Rite Freemasonry descends from England—as opposed to the other concordant body of Scottish Rite Masonry that originated from France—and with the passage of time from the 1730s to 1801, it grew more common in colonial America than its counterpart.[27] However, after the first Supreme Council of the Scottish Rite established a headquarters in Charleston, South Carolina in 1801, its membership grew rapidly. Scottish Rite Freemasonry legitimately claims heritage from an English Lodge named la Loge Anglaise, which was founded in Bordeaux, France in 1732. An early offshoot of la Loge Anglaise was la Loge Française (the French Lodge), which was later chartered by the still-existing English Modern Grand Lodge. The French Lodge became very popular in France and began to confer the so-called "hauts grades," or high degrees. This form of Freemasonry worked its way through the Caribbean and New Orleans to the American colonies, and it later matured under the Grand Constitutions of 1786 that gave birth to "the Supreme Council of the 33rd Degree for the United States of America."[28] The Council was then referred to as the "Supreme Council at Charleston," and moved to Washington, D.C., once construction of the House of the Temple for "the Supreme Council, 33°, Southern

Jurisdiction" was completed in 1915. Another member of the Supreme Council was established in New York for the Northern Jurisdiction in 1813; ten years later, the Supreme Council granted jurisdiction of the fifteen states east of the Mississippi River and north of the Ohio River to the Supreme Council of the Northern Jurisdiction, which has its headquarters in Lexington, Massachusetts. The remaining thirty-five states are under the Sothern Jurisdiction.

As urban centers grew, greater numbers of Scottish Rite brethren congregated in major cities, while a slightly smaller body of York Rite members populated the more rural landscapes. The former, larger order merely required belief in a Supreme Being without religious affiliation and promoted individual freedom and good citizenship,[29] while the latter order championed defense of the Christian faith. Both bodies grew into a "gentlemanly establishment"[30] that inspired artisans and leaders in various occupations.

Overall, Freemasonry is a fraternal and elite organization as well as a philanthropic and social movement. Along with Shriners (or Shrine Masons, who are well-known for their Shrine Hospitals for Children and often participate in local parades riding comedy versions of cars, motorcycles, and two-wheeled vehicles) and a wide variety of appendant bodies for women and young people like the Order of the Eastern Star and DeMolay International, Freemasonry promotes "the cultivation of politeness and honor, mutual assistance, networking, and tolerance for differences in the delicate matter of religion"[31] through Masonic education. Enthused by the work of Paul Revere and the ideals of Freemasonry, a free African-American and leather-shop owner named Prince Hall and his Boston brethren founded their own Masonic lodge— an indigenous invention—during the American Revolution, inspiring a third American branch of Prince Hall Freemasonry.[32] It has also grown into have a parallel set of organizations with Scottish and York Rite tracts and their own blue lodges. While Prince Hall Masonry is separate and its lodges not considered regular, there is greater-than-ever recognition and mutual visitation between the related fraternities.

Together, these branches encouraged moral and ethical development while promoting the secret rituals of Masonic Brotherhood. Their knowledge was based on the ancient wisdom traditions covering the laws of nature and the European Enlightenment philosophies of science and reason, which guided American citizenry into an unfailing religious faith in what the Founding Fathers and Freemasons called the Great Architect of the Universe. Colonial America, which led the Revolution and established the new government, owed a great deal to Freemasonry and its role in creating a network of lodges in every colony and landmarks for the American civilization to prosper.

Revere as the American Mercury

As one of the first York Rite Freemasons in colonial Massachusetts, Paul Revere began to learn its tradecraft of rituals and traditions when he became a Royal Arch Mason and Knights Templar in 1769 and clearly understood the extensive system of symbolism in Freemasonry.[33] Of the various ranks within the organization of the York Rite—from a Royal Arch Mason to a Cryptic Mason and finally a Knights Templar—the Royal Arch degree epitomizes "the root, heart, and marrow of Masonry."[34] Membership in the Knights Templar, the highest order of the York Rite, was open to Revere who promised to defend the Christian faith. In her book *Paul Revere and Freemasonry*, Edith Steblecki chronicles Revere's thirty-four years as a Freemason, which culminated with his ascension to grand master of the Massachusetts Grand Lodge in 1794.[35]

During Revere's time, the fraternity was the place for aspiring leaders. Revere felt he had an obligation to pass on this history because he strongly believed the ancient teachings and practices made good men better. While serving as grand master, Revere distributed an official history of the ancient society, *The Constitutions of the Free-Masons*, written by Dr. James Anderson in 1723. Its revised edition, *The New Book of the Constitutions of the Ancient and Honorable Fraternity of Free and Accepted Masons* (essentially a compilation of Masonic history, rituals, and laws),[36] guided good men to refine their character by generating goodwill in the service of others, supporting philanthropic activities, and galvanizing the American cause for freedom.

Freemasonry was the primary catalyst of an intellectual and spiritual revolution within the thirteen colonies during the American Revolution.[37] By the 1730s, European Freemasonry had expanded overseas and eventually hosted a Masonic grand lodge in each North American colony. Under Revere's leadership, the Masons and Sons of Liberty met in the Massachusetts Green Dragon Tavern (on the first floor under the Saint Andrews Lodge) to organize and launch the Boston Tea Party of 1773. The principal driving forces behind the Boston Tea Party and other revolutionary efforts—including many other "tea parties" in Greenwich, New York, Philadelphia, Annapolis, Savannah, and Charleston—were the commercial interests of the colonies and the teachings of Freemasonry. These forces were successfully harnessed by Freemasons, who played a pivotal role as the organizers, messengers, and even financiers of the Revolution.

Masonic philosophy undeniably had a unique rallying power among the diversified colonies. Out of thirteen American colonies, the four New England colonies of Connecticut, Massachusetts, New Hampshire and Rhode Island had unique commercial motivations and characteristics founded in their religious affiliations, industries, and histories. These differed significantly from those of the Middle Colonies of Delaware, New Jersey, New York and Pennsylvania, whose inhabitants worked in shipyards and ironworks. The Southern Colonies of Georgia, Maryland, North Carolina, South Carolina and Virginia were almost all agricultural plantations with large slave populations. Freemasonry doctrines gave colonists a sense of unity, liberty, and goodwill toward fellow brethren that transcended localized and regional interests—as well as a shared purpose. In his book *Revolution and Freemasonry*, Professor Bernard Fay of the Collège de France confirms, "Freemasonry has been the main instigator of the intellectual revolution of the 18th century and the spiritual father of its political revolutions."[38] He further claims that American unity and liberty could not have developed otherwise as "without which there would have been no United States."[39]

At the same time, the financial viability of the colonists depended upon international trade and commerce. Both British merchants and colonial leaders recognized that their mutual economic survival would be jeopardized in the absence of peaceful international trade relations. Revere, a civic-minded business leader and later a Revolutionary War hero, was able to create a feeling of camaraderie through his flourishing silver business, which fostered the commercial success of a diverse group of New England merchants. To his fellow colonists everywhere, Revere epitomized commercial character, economic prosperity, and civic responsibility—qualities successive generations would replicate in order to create an ideal model for America's entrepreneurial archetype.[40] This might explain why America has come to "revere" him as a messenger of patriotism, a symbol of commerce, and the leader of the Masonic Brotherhood. Lesser known, however, is his designation as the "Mercury of the American Revolution."[41] The honorific title of "Mercury" was a reference to the Roman god of commerce. His mercurial personality and knowledge of closely guarded so-called "secret information" derived from esoteric Freemasonry elevated him to the status of a Renaissance man; one who understood the magical, mystical, spiritual, astrological, and allegorical literature of the enigmatic sect.[42] Revere integrated these unique characteristics with his commercial vision for personal success and national prosperity.

The Commercial Origin of America

Revere and his brethren also embraced the more "secretive" and esoteric teachings of Masonic Brotherhood, which included symbolic rituals and arcane traditions not only for the sake of social status, but also for the high-mindedness of morally-driven, fully-grown men. The philosophies shared amongst these men solidified a unity among them that was eternal. Famous Masonic brethren like Samuel Adams, Benjamin Franklin, John Hancock, and George Washington understood that their diverse interests, strong personalities, various leadership styles and religious orientations could not have converged seamlessly without common membership in the fraternity. Similarly, the unifying force of pervasive colonial commercial interests combined with the tenets of Freemasonry transcended prevailing religious, ethnic, social, cultural, and educational differences among all Americans. Not surprisingly, Masonic teachings helped regulate the colonists' commercial behavior through a uniform code of business. The ethical codes and traditions of Freemasonry initially served as a surrogate for the U.S. Constitution, governing the commercial and interpersonal relationships among colonies, settlers, Native Indians, and foreign traders.

When the Founding Fathers introduced the "commerce clause" into the U.S. Constitution, they were translating these Masonic teachings and Enlightenment ideas into a practical framework to govern commercial activities within the new American republic. More than any other in the Constitution, this clause has had the furthest-reaching implications for human and commercial behavior not only in the United States but also worldwide. This was because it gave the central government power to print money, pass laws for bankruptcy and monopoly, regulate weights and measures, and impose taxes and tariffs. The American ideals exemplified in Revere's life encompassed every aspect of his personal, political, economic, cultural, and social endeavors, and may have inspired the authors of the commerce clause to give it rightful prominence in the Constitution. Indeed, the clause was intended to replicate and nurture the likeness of more Revere-like business

personalities that were needed to develop the commercial republic and
guarantee its eventual destiny.

The Founding Fathers' membership in the fraternity was neither
merely nominal nor tangential. Besides being influenced by their shared
philosophies, the men were fully engaged in the tradecraft of ancient
rituals, ceremonial rites, and other perennial customs that took place at
Masonic lodges. They studied esoteric knowledge traditions and the
movements of planets and other celestial bodies, which were thought to
operate according to "Nature's God" and to be capable of influencing
human affairs on earth. (Thomas Jefferson first described the Creator as
"Nature's God." Though Jefferson was not a known Freemason, he
nonetheless exhibited a profound interest in celestial bodies and their
esoteric meanings). Franklin, provincial grand master of Pennsylvania,
openly applied similar knowledge and practices, including astrology and
zodiac symbols, to commercial enterprises and public affairs. For
example, Franklin enjoyed a great deal of popularity and wealth
generated by his famous publication *Poor Richard's Almanac,* in which
he used ancient astrological information and techniques to make weather
forecasts and prognosticate physical ailments of the human body (Figure
3.1). In *Benjamin Franklin: An American Life*, Walter Isaacson at the
Aspen Institute exemplifies this field of study with meticulous
illustrations of "the Anatomy of Man's Body" as governed by "the
Twelve Constellations."[43] Once taught at Harvard University, the study
of astrology was considered both a respectable profession and a valid
scientific examination of planetary movements throughout the eighteenth
century.[44]

Like Franklin, charter Master Mason George Washington at the
Alexandria Lodge in Virginia was also fond of celestial bodies and
studied how their movements, relationships, and meanings pertained to
terrestrial affairs. Starting from January 1, 1768, Washington used an
almanac to monitor celestial bodies and wrote in his memoirs of "the
Lunations, Conjunctions, Eclipses, the Sun and Moon's Rising and
Setting; the Rising, Southing and Setting of the Heavenly Bodies; true
Places and Aspects of the Planets . . . calculated according to Art."[45] This
language was arcane, but he enjoyed "Entertaining Observations for
Each Month, and other Pieces of Amusement."[46] As an astronomy and
astrology enthusiast and land surveyor, Washington applied this
astrological awareness to his business affairs as well as to benefit
seasonal harvests on his family plantation.

The Anatomy of Man's Body as govern'd by the Twelve Conftellations.

♈ The Head and Face.

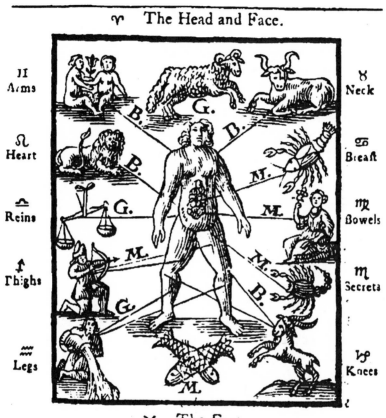

♊
Arms

♌
Heart

♎
Reins

♐
Thighs

♒
Legs

♉
Neck

♋
Breaft

♍
Bowels

♏
Secreta

♑
Knees

♓ The Feet.

To know where the Sign is.
Firft Find the Day of the Month, and againft the Day you have the Sign or Place of the Moon in the 5th Co umn. Then finding the Sign here, it fhews the Part of the Body it governs.

The Names and Characters of the Seven Planets.
☉ Sol, ♄ Saturn, ♃ Jupiter, ♂ Mars, ♀ Venus, ☿ Mercury, ☽ Luna, ☊ Dragons Head and ☋ Tail.

FIGURE 3.1: The ecology of Dr. Benjamin Franklin's astrological chart of man and the influence of celestial bodies. Each zodiac sign corresponds with various parts of the human body.

President Washington was also the primary architect of the nation's capital, and deliberately used methodology common in Freemasonry literature in his designs. Wearing full Masonic regalia (a triangulated ceremonial dress decorated with Masonic symbols) to the foundation ceremony of the Capitol, the president laid the cornerstone precisely at the time when Mercury aligned with the sun inside the Virgo constellation on September 18, 1783.[47] The date was momentous because on that day, Mercury—the planet that governs the nature of Virgo—held a significant measure of astrological importance to Masons. The sun symbolizes the source of life-giving power; the goddess Virgo is the sustainer of life; and Mercury is the god of commerce. This heavenly conjunction represents the harmonizing power of Mercury over the sun's enormity of power projecting both to and from the Capitol. The Capitol building, which consists of the House and Senate, lies directly below the Leo constellation—the planetary ruler of Regulus (which symbolically identifies Congress as the "Regulator"). Likewise, in Massachusetts, Revere placed the foundation stone for the new State House on the Boston Commons in a Masonic ceremony with Samuel Adams, Governor of the Commonwealth.[48] These actions demonstrate that Franklin, Revere, and Washington had no reservations about exploiting Masonic tradecraft, astrological calculus, and ceremonial rituals to depict the American ethos in both their public life and personal pursuits.

More importantly, these Masonic leaders fervently believed in the role played by Nature's God in the creation of celestial bodies, the earth, and our place in it. They also believed in the role and divine purpose of our nation within the Great Architect's grand design. President Washington confirmed, "When I contemplate the interposition of Providence . . . in preparing us for the reception of a general government, and in conciliating the good will of the people of America towards one another after its adoption, I feel myself . . . almost overwhelmed with a sense of the divine munificence."[49] With this in mind, Washington captured the embodiment of America's universal creed when he said, "We take the stars from heaven, the red from our mother country, separating it by white stripes, showing that we have separated from her, and the white stripes shall go down to posterity representing liberty."[50] Their public actions and writings collectively articulate the close association of early America with esoteric Freemasonry.

Although the rituals performed by Washington and Revere were public, other Masonic secrets were kept closely guarded as part of the fraternity's code of conduct. While today the body of Masonic knowledge may well be "public secrets" readily available on the Internet and other media, Masons themselves would not personally reveal their so-called secrets or esoteric knowledge (occasionally they have openly invoked the secretive nature of fellowship and ritualism, which are connected to the ancient stonemasons and master builders of the ages). Nonetheless, Masonic secrets are indeed an integral part of our nation's mystical heritage and remain our connection to both an ancient hope and future history. These powerful symbols and the ethos associated with them not only regulate the United States' commercial behavior and mercurial character, but have also had a catalytic effect on integrating our nation's colonial past with its rightful destiny.

Two great pillars—with celestial and terrestrial globes—in Masonic lodges illustrate the universal nature of the fraternal order and the duality of spiritual and material life.

FOUR

Worldviews of Colonists and Pilgrims

> My Fathers and Brethren, this is never to be
> forgotten, that New England is originally a plantation
> of Religion, not a plantation of Trade.[1]
>
> **Reverend John Higginson**, 1663
> Cambridge, MA

America is a human laboratory built to examine political experiments, personal rivalries, and innovative tensions. It all began with English settlers and their families, who arrived in the New World in the early 1600s to establish the first permanent colonial settlement in Jamestown, Virginia; the Pilgrims soon followed and settled in Plymouth, Massachusetts. Each group had a very different orientation, mission, and worldview. Colonists in Jamestown looked for economic opportunity and wealth creation, while the Puritans who founded the Plymouth colony sought religious freedom and spiritual happiness.

Given the two distinct purposes of the settlements, the combined originality and integrity of their respective missions was critical to each group. Sir Francis Bacon (1561-1626), a prophetic author, who penned the fictional *New Atlantis* (posthumously published in 1627), predicted a utopian-like commonwealth in America in which science and reason would prove better than religion in improving human civilization.[2] Influenced by Plato's *Republic*, which described an ideal commonwealth governed by a circle of philosophic guardians (i.e., elitists), Sir Bacon

visualized a perfect human society whose motivations would be guided
by scientific and collaborative investigation of the nature of man in both
the material and spiritual spheres.[3]

To establish such a utopian commonwealth, two kinds of harmony—
one with divine providence, the other with human reasoning—were
needed to reconcile divergent earthly and heavenly aspirations.[4] A devout
Christian and a man of the world, Sir Bacon characterized such thoughts
within a framework of dual emphasis on the supernatural (or
Providential) and scientific reasoning. This Baconian narrative resonates
with the American colonial experience; the mutually exclusive nature of
Puritan faith and economic aspirations paradoxically laid the critical
infrastructure for the commercial vision to germinate. As a result, the
"Cradle of the Republic" at Jamestown and the "Cradle of American
democracy" at Plymouth were born and flourished in Virginia and
Massachusetts.[5]

Ancient Philosophy in Action

Our political philosophy and human dichotomy illustrate the unique
nature of self-interest in commercial endeavors and moral sentiments in
religious pursuits. The politics of governance and the twin foreign policy
traditions—realism and idealism—that emerged from these two
settlements exemplify the dualistic tendency of human nature embedded
in our commercial republic. After twice serving as the first president,
George Washington reflected on these recurring themes, among other
matters, in his Farewell Address to the new nation delivered on October
19, 1796.

In his insightful book *To the Farewell Address: Ideas of Early
American Foreign Policy,* Professor Felix Gilbert at Princeton University
examines the background of President Washington's Farewell Address
and offers insight into the mindset of the former general and the
American experience.[6] According to Gilbert, the president explored the
geopolitical context of the late eighteenth century and the American
relationship with European powers. An early American distaste for Old
Europe and the desire for separation were clear. The president also
combined the nature of early foreign policy with the different
orientations of the settlers in Jamestown and Plymouth. In fact, these
settlers both collectively and separately formed a national character that
cultivated a unique and unified set of moral habits, civic virtues, and
commercial behaviors necessary for self-governance.

During his administration, President Washington had witnessed infighting between federalists and republicans who took opposite positions on foreign policy as if inspired, respectively, by the Jamestown colonists and the Plymouth Pilgrims. Wanting to unify the nation, the president called upon Alexander Hamilton to revise the draft of the Farewell Address. The document had originally been authored by Hamilton's rival, James Madison, who was a friend and political ally of Thomas Jefferson.[7] After several draft exchanges between Hamilton and Washington, the final speech retained Hamilton's worldview on foreign economic and trade relations.[8] The Farewell Address was viewed by many as a warning against isolationism and protectionism. However, the president pushed for the nation to pursue an effective balance of idealism and realism in foreign policy. In his analysis of the Address, Gilbert reflects on American politics with the following words:

Settled by men who looked for gain and by men who sought freedom, born into independence in a century of enlightened thinking and of power politics, America has wavered in her foreign policy between Idealism and Realism, and her great historical moments have occurred when both were combined.[9]

The president's message, calling for unity within the new nation, was indeed a collective reflection of America's colonial legacy, a fulfillment of Baconian prophesies, and the universal disposition of human behavior looking for compromise between the conflicting forces of greedy desires and moral sentiments. With the new nation's collective consciousness—a sort of "inter-being" of human personality—Americans were born again under the conviction that we are born free.[10] Influenced by Sir Bacon's prophetic writings, American philosopher Manley Hall wrote:

Wise men, the ancients believed, were a separate race, and to be born into this race it was necessary to develop the mind to a state of enlightened intelligence. The old philosophers taught that physical birth is an accident, for men are born into various races and nationalities according to the laws of generation; but there is a second birth, which is not an accident; it is the consequence of a proper intent. By this second birth man is born by enlightened intelligence out of nation and out of race into an international nation and an international race. It is this larger and coming race that will some day inherit the earth. But unless a man be born again by enlightenment, he shall not be a part of the philosophic empire.[11]

Unlike other national, religious, and racial groups in the world, Americans are defined by the measure of philosophic conviction. Hall argues that it has set them apart from other countries and nations.[12] The idea that freedom and equal opportunity are necessary to achieve human potential in life, liberty, and the pursuit of happiness—spiritual happiness—is a distinctly American invention. The duality of material prosperity and spiritual happiness is practiced daily in American life.

The American Manifestation of Human Duality

Unlike Washington's unifying theory, Alexander Hamilton and Thomas Jefferson each subscribed to his own preferred economic theories—realism and idealism, respectively—and this is reflected in Hamilton's affinity for Jamestown and Jefferson's inclination for Plymouth (Figure 4.1). Guided by their own personal experiences and ancient philosophies, the two men infused the early American experience with the nation's commercial destiny:

- The **settlers in Jamestown** were a community of secularists, opportunists, and realists. Their principal allegiance was to the Virginia Company of London. Nevertheless, they were also nominally faithful to the Anglican Church of England. For them, Jamestown was a purely economic venture based on extracting natural resources. The Virginia Company employed these colonists and actively traded in gold, silver, and tobacco. During the early years, Jamestown had a contentious relationship with Native Indians though mutual friendship was a stated goal of their Company charter. Hamilton's difficult upbringing, as well as his commercial philosophy and preferred trade policies (which bore similarities to mercantilism and to colonial economic ventures), may have moved him to identify more closely with the colonists. This group of 144 English settlers had landed first at Hamilton's birthplace on the Caribbean island of Nevis on March 24, 1607, before arriving at Jamestown. The experience of these colonists resonated with Hamilton's inborn ambition, illegitimate British ancestry, and determination for economic success in a chaotic new world.[13]

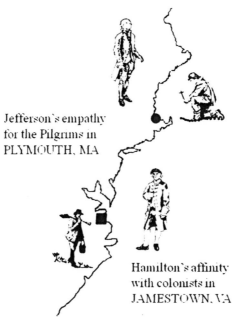

Jefferson's empathy
for the Pilgrims in
PLYMOUTH, MA

Hamilton's affinity
with colonists in
JAMESTOWN, VA

FIGURE 4.1: The views of Thomas Jefferson and Alexander Hamilton are associated respectively with the spiritually-minded Pilgrims and the profit-driven colonists.

- Fleeing the religious persecution of Archbishop William Laud in England, the Pilgrims were a Puritanical community committed to Calvinist principles. Following a brief stop in Holland, 102 like-minded people left Plymouth, England on September 16, 1620, aboard the famous Mayflower. These people became the **Pilgrims of Plymouth**, and successfully established a second English settlement on the west side of Cape Cod Bay in Massachusetts, in December of 1620. The Pilgrims maintained better, more peaceful relationships with Native Indians than the colonists did, trading glass beads for Indian furs that they then exported to England. The peace-loving settlers also engaged in commercial endeavors profitable to English venture capitalists known as Merchant Adventurers. In turn, the English provided the Pilgrims with investment capital. Although the Pilgrims sustained themselves with commerce and trade, their religious faith and idealism were more important. This purpose and vision have inspired Thomas Jefferson, whose wealthy upbringing afforded him the luxury of identifying and empathizing with the religiously motivated, freedom-seeking, and amiable Pilgrims.

Situated on the bank of the James River, Jamestown became without a doubt "the Cradle of the Republic."[14] Indeed, it is the birthplace of America's international commerce and trade. This does not make religiously-inspired Plymouth a less noteworthy foundation, however. Unlike Jamestown, neither the King nor any British trading entities were intimately engaged in the lives of Plymouth settlers who governed their own affairs independent of direct sponsorship from King James. In his book *The Mayflower Compact* (signed in 1620), William Bradford, second governor of Plymouth, described the Pilgrims' philosophy of self-government and God's plan for them:

> In the presence of God, and one of another, covenant and combine our selves together into a civill body politick, for our better ordering . . . to enacte, constitute, and frame such just and equall lawes, ordinances, acts, constitutions, and officers from time to time . . . for the general good of the Colonie (sic).[15]

As the foundation for principles of self-governance emerged in "the Cradle of American Democracy," two thousand newly-arrived Puritans established a second settlement near the Pilgrims under the charter of the Massachusetts Bay Company. Although by 1630 the Pilgrims had formed a system of self-government, they realized that the structure of their governance was extremely crucial in accommodating a growing number of new inhabitants.

After learning about the progressive nature of the Pilgrims, the Anglican Church of England decided to accommodate all Puritans under their Company charter, including the so-called "separatist" Plymouth settlers who had escaped England. Though the Anglican Church accepted the Puritan faith, Calvinist Pilgrims were particularly driven by spirituality, religiosity, and moral sentiments. By the middle of the seventeenth century, Puritan church leaders were reminding Calvinist Pilgrims arriving in the New World of their distinctly religious purpose. In his famous 1663 sermon delivered at Cambridge titled "The Cause of God and His People in New England," Reverend John Higginson said, "My Fathers and Brethren, this is never to be forgotten, that New-England is originally a *plantation of Religion*, not a *plantation of Trade*" (italics added).[16] Religious leaders made conscious efforts to distance themselves from the Jamestown colonists, whom they considered materially obsessed, wealth-seeking, greedy opportunists.

The parallel paths of the Pilgrims' spiritual orientation and the colonists' economic determinism resembled the foreign policy approaches favored by Thomas Jefferson and Alexander Hamilton. Professor Felix Gilbert differentiated between Jefferson's "idealist" approach and Hamilton's "realism," writing, "In all region[s] of the British settlements in North America, one could have found a strong feeling of material realism and a pervasive air of utopian idealism, consequently, two different attitudes regard the Old World: attraction and rejection."[17] Gilbert further explained that American foreign and trade policies entailed a "mixture or synthesis" of both orientations toward England and Europe during the colonial period.[18] This positioning and posturing has continued in one configuration or another since 1776.

The colonial experience drawn from the Jamestown and Plymouth episodes provided the basis for the emergence of America's two foreign policy traditions: realism and idealism. With this historical experience in mind, the Founding Fathers turned to Europe for further guidance on how to structure the nature of American foreign policy. To synthesize the Old World with the New, the Founding Fathers read extensively, studying the classical literatures of earlier civilizations along with colonial traditions. They celebrated the wisdom of Sir Francis Bacon who summarized, "As in the arts and sciences the first invention is of more consequence than all the improvements afterwards," and thus "in kingdoms, the first foundation or plantation is of more noble dignity and merit than all that followeth."[19] This practical precept is cleverly integrated into Washington's own foreign policy synthesis, in which he reflected on the distinct paths that were taken by the Pilgrims and the colonists—and the nation as a whole.

Like Washington, the other Founding Fathers—especially the authors of *The Federalist Papers*—clearly benefited from historical accounts of the colonial experience. Indeed, we have our own indigenous inventions similar to those classical concepts of Athenian democracy and the Roman republic: the birth of the republic conceived in Jamestown and the cradle of American democracy that blossomed in Plymouth. It is certainly possible that Thomas Paine had studied these astonishing parallels when he suggested "the United States of America" become a "Democratic Republic."[20] Of course, these affirmations are subject to further scrutiny; nevertheless, obvious similarities do exist as the Founding Fathers and others tried to draw upon various sources—

classical and colonial—for inspiration to unify the democratic nation through a commercial republic.

A Progressive Nation

The preceding exposition clarifies that the Founding Fathers were hardly submissive devotees of European ideas and Scottish Enlightenment thinkers alone. They were fully aware of early colonial America, and benefited from historical experience and the mercantile relations of Old Europe. For the most part, they relied on their individual experiences, which often reflected their ethnic heritage. They also drew wisdom from eclectic sources, such as the various esoteric traditions and intellectual persuasions of Greco-Roman and Egyptian thinkers and rulers.

In addition, it has already been noted that many of the most influential Founding Fathers were associated with Freemasonry and held important leadership positions within the fraternity. The Masonic lodges that transformed good men into better citizens were ideal recruiting places for entrusted positions of power. The commercial background, plantation ownership, intellectual drive, and involvement in military service and public affairs of these men prepared them well to take over leadership of the new nation: General George Washington's most trusted generals were largely Masons. Besides the first president's key cabinet members (and except for vice president John Adams and secretary of state Thomas Jefferson, neither of whom had any military experience), the governors of the thirteen states at the time of Washington's inauguration were also Freemasons.[21] The fellowship of brethren was an endowed social investment for them to find strength and encouragement in collectively addressing their immediate needs and to realize the potential of the United States and its future prospects. President Washington clearly confirmed the influence of Freemasonry in a letter to the Masonic Lodge in Rhode Island, writing:

> Being persuaded that a just application of the principles, on which the Masonic Fraternity is founded, must be promotive (sic) of private virtue and public prosperity, I shall always be happy to advance the interest of the Society, and to be considered by them a deserving Brother.[22]

The convergence of Enlightenment ideas, familiarity with Masonic knowledge, and personal experience was clearly reflected in the individual thoughts and independent actions of the Founders. These elements indeed shaped a unifying character of liberality, universality, and open-mindedness within the American people for greater progress. Benjamin Franklin elaborated:

> Freemasonry, I admit, has its secrets. It has tenets peculiar to itself. . . . They consist of signs and tokens, which serve as testimonials of character and qualifications, which are only conferred after a due course of instruction and examination. These are of no small value. They speak a universal language . . . act as a passport to the attention and support the initiated in all parts of the world.[23]

These universal characteristics made America an empirical, rational, and global nation. Many of the leading Founding Fathers who formed the new republic were Deists, although some of them (like Thomas Jefferson and George Mason) benefited from the experience of the religiously-motivated Puritans. The majority of these men, who distanced themselves from the faith of their Puritan Fathers, held the holy "trinity" (as Jefferson called them) of the English Enlightenment—Francis Bacon, Isaac Newton, and John Locke—in high regard. Influenced by the trinity, these leaders of American thought (John Adams, Benjamin Franklin, Alexander Hamilton, John Jay, Thomas Jefferson, James Madison, Thomas Paine, among others) were full of optimism about America's promise—promise realized through the use of scientific observation and logical reasoning to unlock the laws of nature for greater advancement. The *Age of Reason*, heralded by Paine's unkind critique of Christianity, triumphed over the prevailing *Age of Faith* once demonstrated by the Pilgrims. Given the historical abuses of Christendom and the religious tyranny to which the Pilgrims bore witness, the Framers of the Constitution made remarkable progress when they separated church from state, supporting no state-sponsored religion but protecting all religions. While this act resolved the issue of creating a Christian nation for the Puritans, greater human progress emanated from the entrepreneurial zeal and economic vision of the colonists who preferred an unrestricted flow of trade in the new commercial republic.

Thus, the Founding Fathers' most pressing need was to distance themselves from the bulwark of British mercantilism. Political and

economic theorist Adam Smith of Scotland—the most prominent
Western moral philosopher of any time—passionately opposed
mercantilism and monopolies such as the East India Company. Instead,
he championed free trade for the greater benefit of all. In his Farewell
Address, George Washington similarly advocated the "unrestrained
intercourse" of trade and commercial activities among all regions of the
thirteen colonies in order to "secure enjoyment" for the "indissoluble
community of interest as one Nation."[24] The president further promoted
international trade by affirming that the great rule of American conduct
with foreign nations is to extend our commercial relations, not political
entanglements and religious conversions. With this framework, he
envisioned unity by advocating "liberal intercourse with all nations," and
recommended devising a strategy through commercial "policy,
humanity, and interest."[25]

Alexander Hamilton, who had collaborated in drafting the Farewell
Address, embraced President Washington's vision for the nation's
commercial destiny.[26] Hamilton, who was pleased with the enduring
economic vision of colonists for a commercial republic (as opposed to
the Puritans' Christian nation) and helped Washington to guide the next
generation of wise American policymakers to advance the national
interest by ensuring American security through international trade.
However, as President Washington's secretary of the treasury, Hamilton
advocated protectionist trade policies to promote the domestic
manufacturing industry and to open up overseas trade opportunities for
American agricultural products. Hamilton had learned from the
experience of the economically powerful Dutch and British mercantilists
(whose policies and achievements Thomas Jefferson detested) that
national security was a top priority.

In general terms, the enlightened Founding Fathers selectively
integrated the finest prevailing progressive thinking with the best
practices in governance drawn from Roman and Greek civilizations, as
well as from the experience of early American settlers. In essence, they
were liberal in thinking, independent in action, and practical in
commercial endeavors. These elements have been the common threads of
America's progressive heritage, as Alexis de Tocqueville frequently
noted in *Democracy in America*,[27] and have fueled our economic and
commercial prosperity as an innovative nation.

PART II

A PHILOSOPHIC COMMERCIAL EMPIRE

"Europe was created by history. America was created by philosophy."

~ British Prime Minister MARGARET THATCHER

FIVE

Adam Smith on Founding America

It is not from the benevolence of the butcher, the
brewer, or the baker that we expect our dinner,
but from their regard to their own interest.[1]

Adam Smith
Author of *The Wealth of Nations,* 1776

As demonstrated by the colonial experience of the Pilgrims and colonists, our Founding Fathers inherited a natural conflict: How to resolve the two different yet innate motives for human behavior—economic self-interest and religious freedom—in drafting the U.S. Constitution. The Founders were fully aware of a group of New England Puritans who intended to establish a Christian commonwealth in 1639 with a draft constitution that affirmed their faith in God.[2] Governor John Winthrop of Massachusetts fervently believed that a Puritan commonwealth would create a "City upon a Hill"[3] for others to emulate as a model Christian nation. The most famous sermon of the former governor and president of Harvard University, also known as *A Model of Christian Charity,* inspired a successive chorus of writers and leaders to view the new nation's ethos as American "exceptionalism."[4]

Despite this glorious chapter in American history, our Founding Fathers purposefully distanced themselves from the founding philosophy of the Puritan Fathers and instead created a commercial republic under the Constitution of the United States. Delegates to the 1787 Constitutional Convention, for example, categorically refused to establish Christianity as a national religion. Moreover, the Constitution contained no reference to God or divine providence (and even the First Amendment stated, "Congress shall make no law respecting an establishment of religion").[5] In a congressional debate, the first House of Representatives again repudiated a Senate proposal to create a Christian nation, which would alienate Native Indians, Deists, and other non-Christians. Nonetheless, the Founding Fathers were highly receptive to the yearning of the Puritan Fathers' journey of faith and perpetual advocacy for religious freedom as the Founders were convinced that moral and ethical sentiments are innately human and politically sensitive.

To gain insight into these complicated issues, the founding generation resorted to the works of Scottish philosopher Adam Smith, the father of modern economics. New York University professor Roy Smith confirms this lesser-known aspect of American history in his recent book *Adam Smith and the Origins of American Enterprise*. Professor Smith (no relation to Adam Smith) states that the "Founding Fathers, including Washington, Franklin, Adams, Jefferson, Hamilton, Madison, and Jay" read Adam Smith's writings.[6] His principle ideas helped them to construct a commercial republic that would address both immediate and long-term survival. Once a wall of separation between religion and state was instituted, the framework for a commercial republic consisting of a free marketplace also accommodated their concerns. For them, the organizing principle of American government would then be self-interest and moral sentiments. The nature of American religiosity was itself well-preserved under Smith's framework; therefore, the Founding Fathers did not—and could not—keep religion out of the marketplace of American politics.

The Market as a Mechanism

According to Adam Smith, supply and demand was the natural mechanism by which a self-regulating marketplace system might produce societal provisions and prerequisites. In his *Wealth of Nations*, he applied the very same free market logic to churches—almost as if they were monopolistic corporations. Smith illustrated it this way:

The clergy of every established church constitute a great incorporation. They can act in concert, and pursue their interest upon one plan and with one spirit, as much as if they were under the direction of one man; and they are frequently, too, under such direction. Their interest as an incorporated body is never the same with that of the sovereign, and is sometimes directly opposite to it. Their great interest is to maintain their authority with the people; and this authority depends upon the supposed certainty and importance of the whole doctrine, which they inculcate, and upon the supposed necessity of adopting every part of it with the most implicit faith, in order to avoid eternal misery.[7]

When rival faiths offer opportunities to trade various religious teachings within a free marketplace, churches prosper by having to provide more choices. For Smith, such competition makes churches and clergies more industrious, opposes religious extremism, and eventually maintains social tranquility and equilibrium. In short, a religious marketplace without government sponsorship is better served when churches compete for worshippers. Smith noted that this had already been "established in Pennsylvania, where, though the Quakers happen to be the most numerous, the law in reality favours (sic) no one sect more than the other, and it is there said to have been productive of this philosophical good temper and moderation."[8] In the final analysis, Smith called for the removal of artificial barriers to trade, allowing individuals to pursue their self-interest in a free bazaar governed by the laws of supply and demand.

The Founding Fathers were naturally attracted to Smith's wisdom of choice and religious exchange for the promotion of freedom in the new Union, where religious faith varied from Puritans in Massachusetts to Quakers in Pennsylvania, Catholics in Maryland, Anglicans in Virginia, and Deists in almost every colony. More importantly, however, the universal nature of human diversity and religious faith is concordant with the ideals of Freemasonry, to which the Founding Fathers aspired as Masonic brethren. The freedom of religious choice was as fundamental for Masons throughout the thirteen colonies as it was for the United States.

Though Adam Smith principally integrated the European experience into his two classical works, the citation of Pennsylvania law and other documentations delicately referenced the colonial American experience.

His most well-known tome *The Wealth of Nations* (1776) outlined the primitive urge of "self-interest" in the survival, competition, and economic motivations of the colonists. His lesser-known *Theory of Moral Sentiments* (1759) drew attention to feelings of "sympathy" and the spiritual aspirations of the Pilgrims.[9] Smith described the complete nature of human morality in using the inherent emotion of sympathy. In doing so, he provided a history of ethical philosophy. In a more subtle way, these two theoretical formulations resonate with the dual experiences of colonial America's religious endeavors and economic enterprises.

Smith's two books had lasting influence over the Founding Fathers, albeit the intellectual polemic was not explicitly discussed in their writings (as a general norm of the era, they did not credit their sources). Nevertheless, the founding documents and their writings clearly reflected Smith's tone and meaning. With this kind of deep illumination, the Founding Fathers adapted a system that unified the two colonial traditions within Smith's framework of political economy (Figure 5.1). They shared Smith's vision of a good society that promotes personal freedom while harnessing the powerful forces of self-interest for greater public good. Smith writes, "By pursuing his own interest, he frequently promotes that of the society more effectually than when he really intends to promote it. I have never known much good done by those who affected to trade for the public good."[10] The emergence of free economic enterprise and its social system, which reverberates with the colonists in Jamestown and the Virginia Company of London, works through "invisible" market forces to create wealth and maintain tranquility.[11]

Wealth Creation and the Colonists

Adam Smith's *magnum opus* of political economy is prophetic and secular in its emphasis. The publication of *Wealth of Nations* actually converged with the most important human event of the century: the Declaration of Independence in 1776, followed by the most memorable commentary penned by American crusader Thomas Paine. In the "Birth of a New Nation," Paine characterized providential conviction in three beautiful phrases: "We have it in our power to begin the world again," "the birthday of a new world is at hand," and "these are the times that try men's souls."[12] As noted earlier, our colonial emissary in London, Dr. Benjamin Franklin, might have collaborated on the providential incidence as well.[13] Smith's masterpiece marked the dawn of modern economics, and had an enormous impact on commercial unity and individual liberty in the United States.

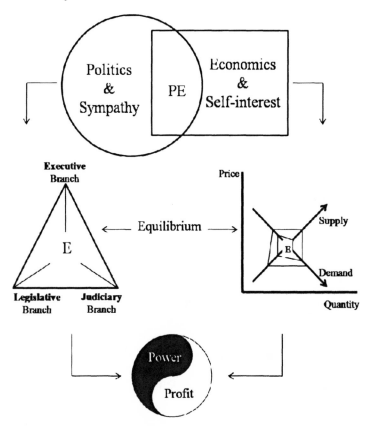

FIGURE 5.1: A framework of political economy (**PE**) within which Adam Smith's marketplace and James Madison's political system interact for American innovation, freedom, and eventual equilibrium (**E**).

The 1776 publication of his book was a direct and symbolic reaction to the heavy hand of government authority, explicitly intended for the British Empire's interference with the right to economic and political self-determination and to the mercantilist controls of business monopolies. Hence, the manuscript stresses the importance of individual liberty within a society. Altogether, Smith and the Founding Fathers addressed the greater challenge of building an institutional framework for governance that would transform their vision into reality.

In this book, Smith expounded on the laws of political economy and provided a comprehensive analysis of the nature of *homo economicus* and *homo politicus*. Drawing upon the book's three key concepts—the division of labor, the pursuit of self-interest, and freedom of trade—the Founders laid the needed intellectual groundwork for a commercial society of merchants, manufacturers, shipbuilders, planters, and landowners. Of the three concepts, the two most important features are Smith's "invisible hand" and the economic realities of "self-interest."[14] Together, they formed the guiding framework for advancing commercial progress and individual freedom through a system of free-market economics and a government of representative democracy. This framework cultivated a fertile environment within the United States for economic progress, individual freedom, social harmony, and opportunities for all in a manner unprecedented in world history.

Moreover, *Wealth of Nations* set the course for unifying the global economic system. Smith's insightful interpretation of the workings of "self-interest" and the "invisible hand" has illuminated a dynamic engine that drives every aspect of economic behavior from investors to producers and consumers, regardless of religious, racial, social, and cultural identities. These two concepts are more likely to promote human equilibrium, social equality, and economic prosperity for the community as a whole than those of any other alternative theory or explanation (i.e., Marxist theories). Smith's notions expounded on the natural motives for economic integration and political cooperation (e.g., the European Union) similar to the American idea of union or unity, and different from segmentation or Balkanization. For the Birth of a New Nation, his ideas offered powerful arguments that reaffirmed realism and the secular human experience rather than dwelling on theoretical constructs that had no value in the practical affairs of men. The Virginia Company of London in Jamestown, for instance, remains an important example within which economic gain, social unity, and self-improvement motivated each colonist.

Moral Sentiments and Pilgrims

In his relatively unknown book *Theory of Moral Sentiments*, Smith argued that individual self-interest includes the interests of the greater community and sympathy for others. Therefore, members of the community should make decisions that are socially beneficial to everyone in the group.[15] This *modus operandi* seemed to provide the basis for the Pilgrims in Plymouth, whose sympathy, moral sentiment, and religious orientation created a sense of community and belonging.

In her brilliant and compelling book on Smith's literary works titled *Economic Sentiments*, Professor Emma Rothschild of King's College in London suggests that emotions are just as important and influential as self-interest. She meticulously interprets Smith's various forms of trade in terms of freedom and liberty. To highlight her point that the totality of enlightened human nature is beyond self-interest—like the selfless and charitable acts of the saintly Mother Teresa of Calcutta—Rothschild asserts Smith's basic precept. The professor explains, "Economic life is difficult or impossible to distinguish from the rest of life . . . one's freedom to buy or sell or lend or travel or work is difficult to distinguish from the rest of one's freedom."[16] To balance this proposition, the function of Smith's "invisible hand" and self-serving human nature must be considered within a larger scheme of human behaviors and altruistic endeavors. This is because in the end freedom matters most in individual, spiritual, moral, and collective decision-making. Evidence suggests that the Founding Fathers understood this proposition in their deliberation on and drafting of the U.S. Constitution.

For the Founding Fathers, the dictum "unity in diversity" was the primordial theme of the American experiment. In search of this, they gained particular insight from *Theory of Moral Sentiments*, which Adam Smith developed as a theory of human psychology. The theory states that an individual can expect sympathy and equality in seeking approval from an "impartial spectator."[17] Smith's direct influence on George Washington was evident after the president used Smith's language in different contexts, referring to the "invisible hand"[18] in his Inaugural Address and the "impartial hand"[19] in his Farewell Address. More importantly, President Washington applied Smith's ideas to campaign against the monopolies and political influence disrupting social harmony. Smith emphasized that self-interests, moral sentiments, and the ability to sympathize with others would bond the community—eventually leading to social stability and perpetual peace.

Smith also viewed the twin psychological tendencies—self-interest and sympathy—as important in commercial unity and economic decision-making. As economic beings (*homo economicus*), people tend to oscillate between innately influential "passions"—sex, hunger, anger, fear, and greed—and internal "voices of reason"—ethical and moral ramifications beyond one's own feelings and gratifications.[29] Our learned Founders obviously understood this natural conflict between self-interest (passion) and morality or sympathy (a voice of reason) in primordial human behavior, decision-making, and self-governance. For society as a whole, Smith's *Theory of Moral Sentiments* concluded that justice and moral reasoning are necessary conditions for social harmony and stability.

A Secular and Providential America

These apparently opposite forces of primal human nature and moral sentiment were at the center of the political debate among the Founding Fathers. The authors of *The Federalist Papers* dwelled heavily on these issues to find unity in diversity. Their discourse was not just limited to balancing the interests of states with those of the federal government, the northern entrepreneurial class with the southern plantation owners, or the civilian authority with the military command. They also incorporated individual character as they understood it in human nature—i.e., a universal conflict between greed and morality—in considering diverse ethnicities, religious faiths, and various other special interests for collective governance and unity. Reconciling these human tendencies was not an easy task. *Atlantic Monthly* editor Robert Kaplan wrote, "The American people have been optimists for 225 years, precisely because by good fortune their institutions were founded on pessimism."[21] The Founding Fathers, especially James Madison and Alexander Hamilton, "always thought in terms of a worse-case scenario of human conditions," and that "men were creatures of passions, not rationality."[22] Kaplan then argued, "The job of government was to channel their passions toward positive ends. Because the founders thought tragically and pessimistically, their worst nightmares never came true."[23] They then devised a system of checks-and-balances to act as a means for addressing disparate political and economic interests, religious and self-identities, moral imperatives and spiritual needs, and the geographic and demographic diversities of the thirteen colonies.

Smith's *Theory of Moral Sentiments* had an enduring impact on James Madison as well. In *The Federalist Papers,* Madison suggested a mechanism that would establish a structure of checks-and-balances between different parties. Madison argued that:

Ambition must be made to counteract ambition. The interest of the man must be connected with the constitutional rights of the place.

It may be a reflection on human nature, that such *devices should be necessary to control the abuses of government.* But what is government itself, but the greatest of all reflections on human nature? *If men were angels, no government would be necessary.* If angels were to govern men, neither external nor internal controls on government would be necessary. In framing a government, which is to be administered by men over men, the great difficulty lies in this: you must first enable the government to control the governed; and in the next place *oblige it to control itself.* A dependence on the people is, no doubt, the primary control on the government; but experience has taught mankind the necessity of auxiliary precautions (italics added).[24]

Both Smith and Madison believed that people have a limited capacity to control themselves, and they act virtuously when their self-interests compete with each other. Such competition could neutralize or modify opposing forces. When virtues are different but not compatible, however, they could also bring about disaster and social instability. Therefore, Smith's notion of an internal "impartial spectator" fascinated Madison, who was interested in how to resolve public disputes among factions. Madison used the concept as a second-best alternative to virtuous superiority and confirmed, "No man is allowed to be a judge in his own cause."[25] He then argued in favor of an impartial judiciary and envisioned a system of legislative and judiciary branches that would work separately and competitively.

As wise and venerated bodies, the Senate and the Supreme Court were his choices for impartial actors that could resolve disputes among passionate congressional representatives, divided communities, and special interest groups. Madison wrote that these impartial "umpires" should prevent the "violent factions" from undermining the enduring union and dissolving the "state to pieces."[26] Smith paralleled this principle in *Wealth of Nations* by advocating that the central government should restrain state governments from fighting with each other, and that the impartial judge should resolve conflicts before they erupt into violence. Madison clearly drew from Smith's basic arguments on human nature and moral sentiments to formulate a system that addressed the nature of conflict resolution in governance.

Having devised a new model of self-governance, the Founding Fathers wanted the Birth of a New Nation to evoke the story of the Exodus of the Hebrew people—who gained freedom from bondage in

Egypt—and their journey to the Promised Land in Israel. The evocation would also draw awareness to the plight of the Pilgrims of Plymouth, who had escaped religious persecution in England. This religious society believed it had a special mandate from God to create a holy community in Massachusetts. Their inspiring history and system of self-governance—not necessarily the notion of a Christian nation—had been a model for the Founding Fathers. The Founders felt obligated to make this new nation an "exceptional" one owed to the Pilgrims, whose beacon of light would inspire freedom-loving people from every corner of the world. The Pilgrims had maintained a modest level of commercial activity and trade relations for their sustenance. As a community, however, their sympathy, moral sentiments, and spiritual happiness were still supreme. In this sense, the Plymouth model permeated Smith's *Theory of Moral Sentiments* to explain the sources of motivation for religious freedom and charity.

Manifest Commercial Destiny

The idea of the United States—either by birth or by design, or both—was a human experiment, originating from creative tensions between self-interests and moral sentiments. It featured neither a domineering ideology nor a particular religious creed. The wisdom of our Founding Fathers was clear in purposeful departure from European religious tyranny, the imperial power structure, and the colonial mentality both in political governance and in the mercantilist economic system. In the United States, they decided, people would govern themselves; indeed, there has never been an American religious hierarchy or royal ancestry. Professor Christian Fritz at the University of New Mexico's Law School describes the crucial difference between the new style of American government and the known systems before the Civil War:

Government was no longer something that happened to people. In America, it now became something that the people—by their consent and volition—brought into being. The people gave their consent through their conduct and their active participation reinforced the message that the people were America's new sovereign.[27]

The *Mayflower Compact* of 1620, the first governing document of the Plymouth Colony, may have inspired Abraham Lincoln in his Gettysburg Address when he characterized post-Civil War American governance as "government of the people, by the people, for the people, [which] shall not perish from the earth."[28] This statement further solidified the commitment of the United States to continue the best of its colonial heritage, which had given our Founding Fathers the needed basis for a "united nation" of "one people" under Nature's God.

Adam Smith held equal influence over Thomas Jefferson, who called *Wealth of Nations* "the best book extant" on political economy.[29] A champion of religious freedom, Jefferson empathized with the plight of the Pilgrims. He also embraced the Pilgrims' idea of the pursuit of spiritual happiness—the kind that connected Nature's God with His creations. Jefferson's agrarian pursuits in Virginia were similarly part of his own happiness, because the land and its agricultural uses connected directly to the Creator. Jefferson's notion of the pursuit of happiness had its origin in "moral sentiment," the idea of an "impartial spectator," and the virtue of empathy. Jefferson thus desired to infuse the hearts of Americans with unity over economic greed. In this approach, the influence of the Pilgrims' *Mayflower Compact* on Jefferson was clear. In fact, he authored documents appealing for religious freedom to reconcile greedy human endeavors and allow for greater human progress and happiness. Nevertheless, deist Thomas Jefferson, drafter of the Declaration of Independence, was inspired more by the philosophies of Enlightenment thinkers (especially John Locke's notion of human rights) than Protestants (or Puritans) for achieving independence, equality, and autonomy in the name of Nature's God. Jefferson facilitated the passage of statecraft more for greater commerce than in honor of the Christian faith. This may explain the removal of the divine nature of Jesus in his *Jefferson Bible* and his support for free trade: "Commerce with all nations, alliance with none, should be our motto."[30] Yet excessive greed, for Jeffersonians, diminishes America's founding vision, and the undisciplined pursuit of wealth demoralizes the hope for an egalitarian nation. On this account, both Smith and Jefferson shared a preference for a system of good institutions and governance to foster greater equality within economic progress, and to inspire virtuous citizenry.

Indeed, the (secular) invisible hand or (moral) providential agency may have had some influence on the intention of the United States to strive for its "manifest commercial destiny" globally (the term derives from Manifest Destiny, which meant Westward expansion, but manifest commercial destiny refers here to global outreach through international trade). The Founding Fathers subtly combined Smith's theories with their own colonial heritage—both material and spiritual—to inspire unity within a common denominator (i.e., commercial interests) to reach America's global manifest commercial destiny.

Creative Tensions for Innovation

Adam Smith was not the only Scottish Enlightenment philosopher who influenced the Founding Fathers. John Locke—who coined the phrase "life, liberty, and the pursuit of property"—also greatly affected the Founders and even Smith himself. From Locke's concepts of life and private property, Smith developed his maxim of an "innate desire" for property ownership and human motives of "self-interest" in a capitalistic marketplace that lead to the creation of greater wealth and harmony among nations.[31] Jefferson adapted his favorite author's axiom "life, liberty, and the pursuit of property,"[32] which Thomas Paine had inscribed in his book *Common Sense* (1776). Fearful of excessive greed finding its way into the pursuit of property, Jefferson changed Paine's language to "life, liberty, and the pursuit of happiness" when drafting the Declaration of Independence. Jefferson's language was crucial. In the pursuit of happiness, he included "spiritual happiness" of the kind that emanated from the colonial experience of religiously-motivated Pilgrims. Their primary consideration was the highest realm of spiritual motivation and human contentment—not material pleasure.

In Jefferson's view, single-minded pursuit of material wealth hardly achieves human happiness, let alone the welfare of a nation. In reference to the fortune seekers of Jamestown and in agreement with Locke and Smith, Jefferson declared that "the selfish spirit of commerce . . . knows no country, and feels no passion or principle but that of gain."[33] Like Smith, Jefferson generally admired capitalism but distrusted capitalists, especially those who were unruly and greedy. Both felt that excessive greed—as demonstrated by those charted mercantilists of the British and Dutch East India Companies and the Virginia Company of London— had been destructive to the welfare of the nation and to human progress in general. However, Alexander Hamilton and John Adams disagreed. Instead, the two men vigorously advocated the development of commercial activities and policies to promote manufacturing enterprises for the new nation. Jefferson would later concede to his rival Hamilton in this respect, writing, "Great truth that industry, commerce and security are the surest roads to the happiness and prosperity of a people."[34]

The comparison of Hamilton and Jefferson shows that while the traditional archrivals agreed on the nation's commercial mission as a unifier and a wealth creator, they disagreed on the preferred approach to reach Paine's commercial vision. As a Stoic, Jefferson reasoned that a virtuous life, as demonstrated by the Pilgrims, is harmonious, unified, and providential. He recognized that the innate desire for life, liberty, and happiness (not property) would precede the pursuit of power and wealth, which is a distraction that requires regulation for social harmony and tranquility.

As both Scottish Enlightenment philosophers and our Founding Fathers wrestled with the conflict between human "self-interests" and "moral sentiments," Jefferson was inclined to side with the latter. He wanted to minimize the importance of securing wealth and property in order to pursue "happiness," as the Pilgrims considered the blessings of providence. Hamilton's Epicurean approach, on the other hand, aligned with natural human instincts that have often been associated with the fortune-seeking adventurers of the Jamestown colony. These perspectives contributed to creative tensions that in turn inspired innovation. For the nation of innovators, each of these Founding Fathers also developed unique visions for America and its foreign policy and trade promotion in agriculture, manufacture, and most importantly, the orientation of American ideas and ideals.

The obscure but elegant statue—in comparison to the pantheon-like Thomas Jefferson Memorial on the shore of the Tidal Basin of the Potomac—at the south entrance to the U.S. Department of the Treasury signifies Secretary Alexander Hamilton's enduring commercial and financial foundation for the nation and its superior economic power around the world.

Six

Hamiltonian Means to Jeffersonian Ends

There is nothing to fear in difference;
that difference, in fact, is one of the healthiest and
most invigorating of human characteristics without
which life would become lifeless. . . . Where opinions
clash, there freedom rings.[1]

Ambassador Adlai E. Stevenson
American Statesman

Thomas Jefferson and Alexander Hamilton continued the early colonial heritage of the Pilgrims and colonists. As illustrated by the spiritually and religiously motivated Pilgrims, Jeffersonians reasoned that all nations would naturally share the ethical and moral sentiments of the "voices of reason" so that every citizen might be free and happy (Adam Smith made a similar argument with the human emotion of "sympathy" toward this end in *Theory of Moral Sentiments*). Jeffersonians have a greater appreciation for uplifting less fortunate people, promoting democracy, and advocating liberal internationalism than Hamiltonians and aristocracy. For example, when Jefferson learned of the French Revolution, he wrote an enthusiastic letter to Colonel Joseph Fay of Vermont on March 18, 1793, assuring that the Revolution would "produce republics everywhere" and "at least soften the monarchical governments."[2]

Unlike Jefferson, Hamilton was preoccupied with commercial destiny as a pathway to national security and world peace. Philosophically, Hamilton was more inclined to associate with the ideas postulated by Smith in *Wealth of Nations* and the chartered intentions of the Virginia Company of London. Hamilton once remarked, "The spirit of commerce has a tendency to soften the manners of men."[3] This Hamiltonian realism, set in motion within the Jamestown settlement and by the rationale of Smith's "self-interest" and "invisible hand," seems to have had a more pervasive, enduring and practical effect on solving the problem of economic survival and other tribulations than Jefferson's utopian approach to human security.

As in the ancient Stoic and Epicurean traditions, Jefferson and Hamilton represented the American replica of human nature: idealism and freedom vs. realism and greed. The conflicting nature of these deep-seated schools of Epicureanism and Stoicism—understood through the prisms of the Hamiltonian and Jeffersonian visions—is essentially the bedrock of our freedom. As Governor Adlai Stevenson believed, "Where opinions clash, there freedom rings."[4]

The "realistic" Hamiltonians continued to believe in the conduits of commercial activities and global trade relations. The "idealist" Jeffersonians envisioned an "Empire of Liberty" through statecraft that promotes freedom, equality, human rights, and moral values.[5] Yet in practice, the Hamiltonian vision seemed to embrace the cause for freedom, as epitomized by Paul Revere's survival instincts and the economic motives behind his patriotic involvement in the Boston Tea Party. Thomas Jefferson likewise placed life before liberty in his famous dictum—"Life, liberty, and the pursuit of happiness"—to suggest the sequential importance of natural human priorities. As the Revolutionary War attested, Jeffersonian liberty was a result of Hamiltonian action. Without Hamilton, there would be no Jeffersonian statecraft. Without either, there would be no United States (Figure 6.1).

The Republic of Creative Tensions

The United States is a union by definition; in fact, it is a chaotic re-public of opposing viewpoints. This was the American colonial experience and the founding legacy as well. Pilgrim-inspired Jefferson was an idealist sage from the commonwealth of Virginia, which later aligned with the Confederacy during the Civil War. Jamestown-inspired Hamilton, on the other hand, was a realist visionary from the empire state of New York, which sided with the Union. Human nature is such that "idealism gave way to realism," and "worldliness replaced heroic optimism."[6]

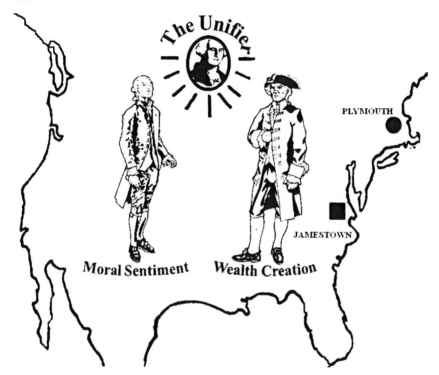

FIGURE 6.1: The tradition of creative tensions began with Thomas Jefferson and Alexander Hamilton, who were inspired by Adam Smith's *Theory of Moral Sentiments* and *Wealth of Nations* respectively. Influenced by the Pilgrims in Plymouth and colonists in Jamestown, the team of founding rivals served under George Washington, the Unifier.

Each Founding Father largely championed a complex array of competing approaches—reflective of the very nature of humankind—to politics and economics. These diverse frontiers eventually formed the basis for dynamic equilibrium in the commercial republic and foreign policy traditions, as well as our two political parties. This is surely paradoxical and disruptive in nature but healthy and harmonious in the end. The Founding Fathers explicitly disagreed on many issues, for example, the worst instance resulting in the Civil War during the presidency of Abraham Lincoln; yet, the union emerged even stronger.

American history is contradictory, but it is our guiding post—a beacon for national unity and human security. On this point, Patrick Henry and John Adams could not have proven more wrong in their thoughts on national unity. Henry once warned during the early years, "United we stand, divided we fall. Let us not split into factions which must destroy that union upon which our existence hangs."[7] In the same way, Adams worried that a republic divided into two great parties would be the "greatest political evil under our Constitution."[8] Jefferson disagreed and remarked about Hamiltonian federalists, "If I could not go to heaven but with the party, I would not go there at all. Therefore, I am not the party of Federalists."[9] Though it may seem oxymoronic, the Jefferson and Hamiltonian divide actually illustrates that the nation has been better off *without* consensus and unity.

In fact, the boundary between the Jeffersonian world of immutable moral laws and the corruptive Hamiltonian world of material profits has actually worked relatively well throughout the American experiment. The genius and creative energies unleashed by each perspective have serendipitously helped both democracy and capitalism to not only succeed, but also sustain their inherent wonders. While these learned constitutional authors owed their political philosophies to the European Enlightenment writers, it was their childhood experiences, personal circumstances, and visions of grandeur for the infant nation that set them apart. Diversity, it seems, was enshrined in Providence; creative tensions were good for the nation's health, growth, and innovation. In his *Federalist Papers*, James Madison concluded, "It is impossible for the man of pious reflection not to perceive in it [but] a finger of that Almighty hand . . . has been so frequently and signally extended to our relief in the critical stages."[10] It is certain that Providential Agency has undeniably favored the diversity of human spirit and public opinion that radiates to and from the center of the human heart and mind, just as the Great Architect of the Universe intended.

Both Jeffersonians and Hamiltonians kept the Union together. Jefferson, the Romantic "Sage of Monticello," as he was known during his golden years in the agrarian commonwealth, envisioned an egalitarian and loosely confederated union. Hamilton wanted to extend the capitalism of the manufacturing and trade-based empire state of New York to the rest of the union through a strong federal government. This earned him the titles of the "patron of Wall Street" and the "father of American capitalism." The Jeffersonian Social Gospel inspired millions of people throughout the world, even as America became a Hamiltonian nation driven by the Prosperity Gospel. In the United States, certain money-driven Christian congregations and wealthy preachers readily accept the latter, while elitist liberal activists champion the former. Whether conservative or liberal, these seemingly divergent perspectives eventually gravitate toward the center cautiously—as long as freedom reigns.

The American Machiavelli

The political genius of Niccolo Machiavelli may have ostensibly influenced both Hamilton's realist vision as well as Jefferson's political thoughts on idealism. Machiavelli's classic work *The Prince* has dominated the realist perspective of a political world associated with power within which the evil motives ingrained in human nature influence behavior for self-preservation and personal gratification. Despite popular belief, however, Machiavelli was neither evil nor saintly.[11] The renaissance strategist wrote on the acquisition of power in the absence of morality and once declared, "[It] cannot be called virtue to kill one's fellow-citizens, to betray one's friends, to be treacherous, merciless and irreligious; power may be gained by acting in such ways, but not glory."[12]

For some reason, however, Machiavelli is a mystical and fascinating figure in the American consciousness, and typically thought of as a heartless, amoral, and power-hungry strategist. The manner in which Hamilton conducted himself in personal relationships and formulated his economic policy instruments as a nation-builder bears broad similarities to Machiavellian practices. In *American Machiavelli: Alexander Hamilton and the Origins of U.S. Foreign Policy*, Johns Hopkins University professor John Harper contends that Hamilton governed as a Machiavellian. This was not so much due to the accordance of Hamilton's style of government with the original description offered up in *The Prince*, but to Hamilton's connection with nation-building and the manner in which his quest for fame and glory acted as a passionate driving force.[13] Harper also draws explicit parallels between Hamilton's thoughts and life story, and Machiavelli's strategies for accumulating power. The similarities do not derive from Hamilton's illegitimate birth in the West Indies or his immigrant status in colonial America, but rather from his path to becoming a policy advisor, military strategist, and finally, the first U.S. secretary of the Treasury. Evidently, Hamilton searched for Machiavellian-type views and strategies in international politics and trade relations—the same views that had once made the Roman Republic a powerful state—to become the father of American realist statecraft.

Nonetheless, Machiavelli bears a general reputation for being a teacher of evil, while Hamilton is known to have a greater affinity for American founding principles. Hamilton's thoughts could have easily derived from Hume, Locke, Montesquieu, or Smith. However, the central thesis of *The Prince,* "the ends justify the means," falls far closer to evolved Hamiltonian tradecraft and foreign policy tradition than that of the idealist Jeffersonians.

Contrary to popular opinion, however, Machiavelli's descriptive analysis was neither immoral nor motivated by self-interest. Instead, he provided a realist interpretation of the human propensity to accumulate, sustain, and expand sources of power within an amoral framework. Hamilton realized the value of such power in overcoming the prevailing social and economic challenges confronting the nascent nation. His less-fortunate personal circumstances in the mid-eighteenth century—an illegitimate childhood under colonialism in the West Indies, the early death of his mother and the bankruptcy of his father, poverty, war, slave uprisings, and communicable diseases—were all important factors in his formative years.[14] When destiny ushered him to American leadership under the tutelage of General George Washington, Hamilton was driven by a mounting desire to create wealth and order as a way to generate social stability and harmony.

Perhaps surprisingly, Jefferson may have equally profited from the wisdom of Machiavelli's realist views. As a man of culture, Jefferson modeled his literary thinking based on the writings of classical Athens and Rome, which had been updated and interpreted by Machiavelli. As the Founding Fathers sought after a democratic republic to regenerate the human spirit, uplift moral sentiments, and organize new governance, *The Prince* offered valuable insights. Without embracing Machiavellian thoughts, however, Jefferson continued to live and dream in a world of idealism and classical literature at his Monticello plantation.

The Sage of Monticello

The enormity of Jefferson's decency and gentleness was on display when he declared to "a horseman" on his way to the White House, "May I never get too busy in my own affairs that I fail to respond to the needs of others with kindness and compassion."[15] In a similar tone, Saint Francis of Assisi once affirmed, "Remember that when you leave this earth, you can take with you nothing that you have received—fading symbols of honor, trappings of power—but only what you have given: a full heart, enriched by honest service, love, sacrifice and courage."[16] With his affinity for Nature's God and His creations at his Virginia plantation, Jefferson bore a remarkable resemblance to the Christian patron saint of animals, birds, and the environment. The Sage of Monticello could have easily been "the Assisi of Monticello" given his enduring love for nature and human ideals.

This is not to imply that the visions of these two Framers of the Constitution were reincarnations of Italy's best-known icons, whose worldviews in fact differed significantly. Rather, these human personalities represent the very essence of human nature, self-interests, and power orientations that Adam Smith expounded upon in *Wealth of Nations* and more importantly in *Theory of Moral Sentiments*. In his book on wealth creation, Smith argued that self-interests deriving from human selfishness, greed, or fear naturally work themselves out in the "invisible hand" of the marketplace.[17] Hamiltonians could have easily collaborated with this notion of capitalism. In his book on moral sentiments, Smith rationalized that an internal "voice of reason" or "impartial spectator" constantly modifies less moral, human "passions" for sex, wealth, and power."[18] Therefore, the calculus of ethical and moral responses has a tendency to contribute more to the greater public good than do narrower, personal interests, and self-indulgence. Thus, in order to advocate greater social welfare, Jeffersonians would have naturally championed this moral worldview and sympathized with humanitarian efforts that might minimize social costs to the greater community.

Hamilton seemed to have been more than merely influenced by *Wealth of Nations*. He applied some of Smith's ideas, especially Smith's critique of mercantilism and monopoly, to his realistic policy formulation and implementation. As secretary of the Treasury, Hamilton also incorporated many of the ideas of Jean-Baptiste Colbert, then former French minister of finance, in his *Report on Manufacturers* to Congress. Hamilton was convinced that the state ought to acquire enough power to introduce policy measures in the marketplace through the workings of government, just as Colbert's dirigisme policies fostered manufacturing enterprises that enriched France's wealth by trade and commerce.

After returning from France in 1789, Jefferson served as the first secretary of state and opposed many of Hamilton's policies. Fiscally, Hamilton preferred all states to share the Revolutionary War debts equally and the central government to play a greater role in banking. He supported an alternative vision of corporate and elitist commercial development, and held a large-scale industrial vision for America. Looking towards Great Britain for policy inspiration and commercial success, Hamilton advocated greater power for the central government and its support for the industrial might of the young nation. Conversely, Jefferson believed each state responsible for only its own war debt since his home state of Virginia had not accumulated much of it during the American Revolution. Jefferson also considered Hamilton's idea of a national bank unconstitutional, and favored state's rights as opposed to centralized power in banking. The Virginian imagined an agrarian society comprised of small, self-sufficient, harmonious hamlets of happy citizens that relied on small-scale production for essentials. Jefferson's Romanticism of the French ideas of *liberté, egalité, fraternité* (liberty, equality, and fraternity) sustained a more egalitarian vision of social and democratic development within the United States.

These examples illustrate that self-interest and moral sentiments in complex mechanisms govern the affairs of people. Like Machiavelli and Saint Francis of Assisi, these two American leaders demonstrated the very nature of human tendencies and ethical orientations. Those who made up George Washington's first Cabinet—primarily Hamilton, Jefferson, and secretary of war Henry Knox—differed in their worldviews on almost all issues and prescribed alternative policies. This disunity hardly led to the dissolution of the Union. Instead, it enriched the transformational leadership of Washington. The first president was fully mindful of constant dialogue over contrasting ideas on earthly desires and heavenly aspirations, which manifested themselves in cabinet discussions, policies, and actions. For Washington, these conferences were part of a grand providential design to create a "more perfect Union."

As Hamilton became a New England leader of the Federalist Party of Paul Revere and John Adams, Jefferson empathized with the Republican Party that he helped establish. It is ironic that Adams, who warned that division of the republic was "evil,"[19] later championed the Federalist Party. The Federalists preferred centralized national power, while Jeffersonian Republicans (then the Democratic-Republican Party) supported states' rights on issues related to interstate commerce, foreign relations, international trade, and military affairs. These two strong personalities and their philosophies—fermented by the experience of the flight of the Pilgrims and the adventurous colonists—paved the way for the development of two distinctive worldviews and sets of party politics, as well as the dual traditions of foreign policymaking: realism and idealism.

The Genius of Rival Traditions

Wise American leaders have recognized that authentic and patriotic sentiments from dissenters are as uniquely American and nationalistic as those of nominal party loyalists. These loyalists conform uncritically on national matters of importance, and raise the American flag instead to compensate for their genuinely patriotic duty to be independent. George Washington, who had the ability to lead with ambiguity and decide independently, understood servant leadership best, wherein he benefited from the diverse viewpoints of everyone—including rivals like Jefferson and Hamilton.

Like Washington, Benjamin Franklin realized the importance of considering the best available advice, experience, and wisdom of others. Distinguished historian Doris Kearns Goodwin describes Abraham Lincoln displaying characteristics similar to those of Washington and Franklin.[20] Their integrative thinking—a unique leadership sign of fully-grown men who have equally developed their rational and intuitive mindsets—has been influenced by the teachings of Freemasonry, which excels at unifying themes of duality and diversity.

Unlike Washington and Franklin, Lincoln was not a known Mason. However, he "came into contact with many Masons" and "possessed and displayed all the important qualities of Freemasonry: faith, hope, and charity, belief in God, the equality of all people, and the ability of each person to improve."[21] In his famous 272-word Gettysburg Address delivered on November 19, 1863, President Lincoln majestically unified the sublimity of the Declaration of Independence, the oratory of Daniel Webster, Shakespeare, the Bible, and the ideals of Freemasonry.[22]

As Pennsylvania's provincial Masonic leader, Franklin seemed to combine the best mix of American traditions—realism with rationality and idealism with intuitive knowledge—in foreign and commercial relations. Franklin realized the importance of Jefferson's virtues and the grammar of the human heart in addition to Hamiltonian powers of reasoning and logic. The prudent Founding Father's case for unity is less important, but competing visions are most likely to produce greater public goods through creativity and constructive dialogue in a nation of innovators. Such creative tensions, while not necessarily the unity advocated by Patrick Henry and John Adams, are the lifeblood of a vibrant and open democracy.

SEVEN

The Commerce Clause as the Force for Unity

> Peace is the natural effect of trade. Two nations
> who traffic with each other become reciprocally
> dependent; for if one has an interest in buying,
> the other has an interest in selling; and thus their
> union is founded on their mutual necessities. But
> if the spirit of commerce unites nations, it does
> not in the same manner unite individuals.[1]
>
> **Charles de Montesquieu**
> Author of *The Spirit of the Law,* 1748

The United States began as an idea; ideas are contagious. The search
for freedom from religious tyranny led the escaping Pilgrims to sanctuary
in Plymouth; the freedom to search for economic opportunity attracted
colonists to Jamestown. Like colonial settlers in Massachusetts and Virginia, the Founding Fathers disagreed on a chorus of public policy issues
of the era, with the exception of trade and commerce.

European philosophers ingrained the idea of freedom and the moral
rationale for trade into the American psyche from the very beginning.
David Hume led the founding generation to conclude that the confluence

of trade and freedom is a natural ally of peace and stability. Hume argued convincingly:

> Commerce and manufactures gradually introduced order and good government, and with them the liberty and security of individuals, who had before lived almost in a continual state of war with their neighbors, and of servile dependency upon their superiors. This, though it has been the least observed, is by far the most important of all their effects.[2]

A century before Hume, Thomas Hobbes had revealed the intrinsic nature of trade and human desire in his *Leviathan* (1651). Hobbes observed, "The passions that incline men to peace are fear of death, desire of such things that are necessary to commodious living, and a hope by their industry to obtain them."[3] In his well-known *Perpetual Peace* (1795), Immanuel Kant also maintained that "the spirit of commerce" is a driving force in human nature and since commerce and war were "incompatible;" the forces of commerce can be viewed as working by nature toward "peace."[4] He also underscored the importance of having commercial republics, which are governed by representatives rather than monarchs, and that such republics do not fight with each other.[5] A legion of other Enlightenment writers—like Charles de Montesquieu and Adam Smith—also held similar views on trade effecting peace and unity.

Since Montesquieu first developed a moral rationale for trade in his seminal 1748 book *The Spirit of Laws*,[6] the Enlightenment writer was highly regarded within colonial America. As a champion of the notions of liberty and freedom, Montesquieu greatly influenced many of the Founding Fathers, especially Alexander Hamilton, Thomas Jefferson, and James Madison. The moral argument for the opposite of plundering and robbery, as Aristotle often reasoned, is that "the spirit of trade produces in the mind of a man a certain sense of exact justice."[7] Such sentiments of justice tend to overcome the private "self-interests" and innate human desires of individuals. Montesquieu argued that, "the spirit of commerce unites nations."[8] His affirmation, however, differs from uniting individuals as opposed to nations, because the spirit of commerce does not work in the same manner. This seemingly trivial philosophical gambit was relevant to the colonial experience; hence, it was important to the founding vision.

Adam Smith distinguished the nature of "self-interest" in *Wealth of Nations* from that of "self-love" in *Theory of Moral Sentiments*. For the latter Smith insisted, "Every man is, no doubt, by nature first and principally recommended to his own care" out of self-love, sympathy, and even mutual gratification as in the ancient Stoic tradition. Although the Pilgrims were somewhat less commercially-inclined than the colonists, these Puritans identified themselves more with the self-love (*amour propre*) that united them as a faithful Christian community. Their religious belief was related to self-emptying (*kenosis*) through compassion for their neighbors and contemplation of the majesty of the universe. Their religious and spiritual confinements were surely limited to their own community, a distinctive commonwealth in the wilderness of a new land.

Colonists driven purely- by self-interest (and less sympathy for the Native Indians, for example) were more open to trade relations and the search for economic wealth anywhere in the world as multinational corporations do. Given the spirit of commerce with such self-interest, the commonwealth of those colonists seems more likely to have united with other nations as Epicureans (or the contemporary Chinese do in Africa, Asia, Latin America, and elsewhere with less appreciation for human rights and religious freedom).

In the final analysis, commerce is not only mutually inclusive but also it has greater power for all-encompassment. For instance, self-interested colonists bonded more with others in order to maximize profit than self-loving Pilgrims did in their quest for spiritual contentment and personal happiness within their own locale (like the traditional Bhutanese do in their Himalayan kingdom).

Markets Integrate Nations

Just as Smith's analysis slightly discounted the importance of the individual, Montesquieu maintained that moral virtues such as sympathy (for hunger from famine, for example) could be collectively traded for money—and eventually exchanged for mutual benefits (foreign aid and food assistance). Montesquieu concluded, "The people move only by the spirit of commerce"[9]—a collective reference to nations and free markets. This kind of moral and natural argument convinced the Founding Fathers to lionize Smith who postulated, "The invisible hand of the marketplace guides this self-interest into promoting general economic well-being."[10] This invisible hand works through the signals of market mechanisms.

The price mechanism determines the ideal quantity of production and consumption. For example, when the demand for a product is greater than the supply, a shortage occurs and the price of the product increases to create a profit margin for the seller. Large profits then create an incentive for others to enter the marketplace, thereby producing more and fulfilling the shortage created by excessive consumer demand. Supply increases as more producers join the market, which eventually drives the price of the product down. This then stabilizes the marketplace and allows the community to find happiness from market equilibrium (Figure 7.1). The community of stakeholders—ranging from investors, producers, suppliers, laborers, retailers, and consumers—enjoys the accompanying economic prosperity and social order through the wondrous invisible hand of price mechanism.

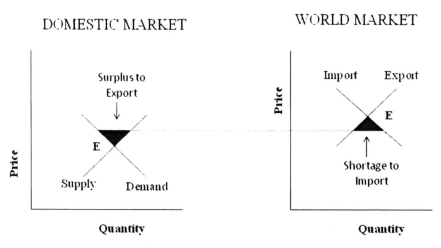

FIGURE 7.1: A simplified framework extended to illustrate domestic export (i.e., surplus) and world import (i.e., shortage) for market equilibrium (**E**) in the both situations.

The nature of the amoral marketplace, in which a multitude of buyers and sellers determine the price of products and services, rests on the principles of democratic freedom as opposed to a dictatorial, totalitarian, or religious authority. In open and free societies, trading regimes decide prices and self-interests steer personal decisions. Then markets actually become social equalizers. For the most part, various religious persuasions, socio-economic backgrounds and cultural imprints drive the nature of decision-making and policy actions by government officials and political leaders. Market signals, however, are neutral to all human affiliations, racial identities, and other backgrounds. In essence, human self-interests drive these market forces.

Impressed by enlightened viewpoints, the Founding Fathers upheld the notions of self-interest and competition as part of human nature. Therefore, the general feeling of common good among all stakeholders harnesses collective human action, even as it appears people are acting freely without external interference. In liberal economic thought, the interests of the public good may not be the driving force for individuals. Instead, individual self-interest may serve as a catalyst for each person to reconcile diversity in varied backgrounds, consolidating their common interest from a general pool of possible choices. In other words, it is the pursuit of self-interests that causes people—and private corporations—around the world to promote overall economic efficiency and social harmony without even realizing it.

Smith believed that free markets foster such behavior (as well as human emotions like happiness and satisfaction) more effectively than other alternatives as the marketplace does not discriminate between participants based on nationality, ethnicity, occupation, religious faith, or any other social or sexual orientation. In *Theory of Moral Sentiments*, Smith concluded,

> When Providence divided the earth among a few lordly masters, it neither forgot nor abandoned those who seemed to have been left out in the partition. . . . In what constitutes the real happiness of human life, they are in no respect inferior to those who would seem so much above them. In ease of body and peace of mind, all the different ranks of life are nearly upon a level, and the beggar, who suns himself by the side of the highway, possesses that security which kings are fighting for.[11]

Thus, markets can provide certain virtues and a sense of moral justice, both of which are vital to commercial progress and societal happiness. Self-interest is a common denominator shared by every type of group and as a result, trade is often the most convenient path of least resistance to penetrate other cultures and nations. In this respect, the Hamiltonian approach (primarily with manufacturers and merchants during his time) to achieving peace and stability might be a more viable option than the Jeffersonian instrument of promoting democracy to create an Empire of Liberty. Montesquieu concluded, "Peace is the natural effect of trade,"[12] which Jefferson supported in 1774, saying, "Free trade with all parts of the world" is a "natural right."[13] Jefferson reiterated this in a letter to John Adams in 1785: "I think all the world would gain by setting commerce at perfect liberty."[14] Though they rarely concurred, trade interconnected both Hamiltonians and Jeffersonians.

Politics for War; Trade for Peace

The constitutional authors were fully aware of the perennial assertions of Enlightenment philosophers that politicians cause war while traders cause peace. In 1750, for example, Benjamin Franklin described the population of the thirteen colonies as a contented bunch: "Abundance reigned . . . and a more happy and prosperous population could not perhaps be found on this globe."[15] Long before the Revolutionary War, a combination of restrictive trade policies, money supply, and taxation by British Parliament frustrated otherwise happy merchants and colonial inhabitants. As a colonial representative in London, Franklin was asked why British America did extremely well while the motherland remained less self-sufficient. "That is simple," the diplomat replied. He then added:

> In the colonies, we issue our own money. It is called Colonial Scrip. . . . We make sure it is issued in proper proportion to make the goods pass easily from the producers to the consumers. . . . In this manner, creating for ourselves our own paper money, we control its purchasing power.[16]

After learning of the economic genius of the colonies, English bankers successfully lobbied the British Parliament to prohibit the thirteen colonies from issuing their own legal tender. The Currency Act of 1764 not only forbade the colonies from printing notes, but it also forced them to pay future taxes to England in gold and silver. Within a year, this political fiasco had reduced the circulation of colonial money supply by half. Franklin later observed, "[T]he streets of the colonies were filled with unemployed beggars, just as they were in England."[17] The belief that taxation on tea triggered the Boston Tea Party and the Revolutionary War is a popular one. In fact, deteriorating economic conditions resulting from the Currency Act were the primary causes for war, because the New Englanders did not have adequate gold and silver to pay the British tax. Franklin exposed the real reason for the Revolution, saying: "The Colonies would gladly have borne the little tax on tea and other matters, had it not been that England took away from the colonies their money, which created unemployment and dissatisfaction."[18] Yet, the tax on tea was an easier and more popular rallying force than convincing inhabitants with the political and economic consequences of currency.

With this historical episode, Thomas Paine, Hamilton, and Jefferson realized that trade must be the protector of the new country if it were ever to establish itself as a sovereign and independent nation. Nevertheless, the nature of the international political environment at that time forced them to pursue a set of protectionist, rather than liberal, trade policies. Hamiltonian realism and Jeffersonian idealism converged out of this necessity for the protection of domestic industry. After the British crackdown on the supply of money through the 1764 Currency Act, Hamilton strongly advocated a robust national banking system as the first treasury secretary of the United States. He favored protectionist trade policies and deliberately imposed tariffs on imports as well as campaigned for domestic subsidies (i.e., "bounties") for manufacturers.

President Jefferson similarly introduced trade sanctions in 1807 against France and Britain—a diplomatic innovation in world politics at the time. The goal was to safeguard American ships from attack by these two warring nations. The sanctions were unsuccessful in modifying the behavior of the aggressors, and instead endangered New England business interests. Jefferson's embargo failed within fifteen months and led the United States into the War of 1812, which finally settled the issue of British hostility at sea.

Nevertheless, Jefferson, Hamilton, John Adams, and James Madison adamantly believed in free trade. Franklin concurred:

> Freedom of commerce . . . is the right of all mankind. . . . To enjoy all the advantages of the climate, soil, and situation in which God and nature have placed us, is as clear a right as that of breathing; and can never be justly taken from men but as a punishment for some atrocious crime.[19]

Madison agreed. Corresponding with Jefferson in 1785, he wrote, "Much indeed is to be wished, as I conceive, that no regulations of trade, that is to say, no restrictions on imports whatever, were necessary. A perfect freedom is the system which would be my choice."[20] The relatively peaceful colonial commercial existence, the collective devotion to free trade by the Framers of the Constitution and the implications of British policy clearly illustrate that trade did not cause the two British-American wars (the Revolutionary War of 1775 and the War of 1812). As history attests, politicians did.

The Commerce Clause, the Modifier of Human Behavior

Notwithstanding human flaws and politics, the enlightened Founding Fathers designed the U.S. Constitution to provide the framework for our commercial republic. The Constitution operates in a way that protects both property and liberty within a secular society made up of diverse groups with special interests ranging from slave ownership to navigational rights in the thirteen colonies. It was an unlikely enterprise. For these men, the "Birth of a New Nation" had indeed been a miraculous undertaking. John Adams believed that the task of forming a plan for the new government was "the divine science of politics" because "the blessings of society depend entirely on the constitutions of government, which are generally institutions that last for many generations."[21] Since the Framers and Ratifiers of the Constitution fervently believed in the guidance and blessing of Providence, such a massive undertaking did not discourage them. In 1781, the Articles of Confederation acknowledged that a "Great Governor of the World"[22] had been involved in orchestrating this birth. George Washington himself said "the hand of Providence"[23] had been at work in the precipitous events that led to America's founding and its commercial mission.

While the Constitution was seen by some as a sacred document, it primarily addressed the most important earthly endeavors related to interstate commerce and foreign trade—two imminent concerns for industrialists, planters, and traders. The Founding Fathers recognized the necessity of a uniform system of commercial regulations. This uniformity was expressed in twenty-one words: "The Congress shall have power . . . to regulate Commerce with foreign Nations, and among the several States, and with the Indian tribes."[24] This compact language in Article I, Section 8, Clause 3 of the U.S. Constitution is known as the commerce clause (Figure 7.2). It is one of the most far-reaching grants of power to Congress for "foreign" trade relations. Interstate commerce covers the movement of all people and things across state lines as well as every form of communication and transportation, including interstate prostitution and slavery. Hence, the commerce clause permits a wide variety of federal laws ranging from the regulation of business to the outlawing of racial segregation. The "Indian commerce clause" has become the main source of power for congressional legislation dealing with Native Americans and tribal lands. It also presented "the remarkable instance of a national power" [25] because it radically transformed the emergence of the new American commercial republic. Through this clause, the federal government was granted the power to coin money, institute uniform laws of bankruptcy, establish post offices and postal roads, regulate weights and measures, control patents and copyrights, and manage taxation

FIGURE 7.2: U.S. Congress has the power to regulate trade and commerce among states as well as with foreign nations and with Indian tribes.

The commerce clause resulted from much deliberation. In the draft of the Constitution submitted to the Convention on May 29, 1787, for example, South Carolina delegate Charles Pinckney proposed using the words "all nations," instead of "foreign Nations," as it stands now.[26]

Northern and southern states had great difficulties with issues related to the slave trade and navigational privileges. They compromised to include the words "several States," instead of "all states." This was reportedly "the first great compromise of the Constitution."[27] The resulting clause on commerce essentially expresses the economic contours of both the nation and its legal framework. Constitutional authors and many subsequent policy leaders and legal scholars widely debated this definitive clause.[28] It not only outlines the balance of powers between the federal government and the states, but also foreshadows the Constitution's eventual influence on regulating the commercial behavior of the American people—and the world (through the World Trade Organization). Even contemporary legislators have argued intensely over the president's fast track negotiating authority, also called the Trade Promotion Authority.[29] In all, by way of Congress or the president, the United States' original commercial vision and the constitutional device have had global influence on trade agreements and international relations.[30]

To understand this significant historical debate, it is important to define the meaning of the word "commerce" as the founding generation understood it. Expanding well beyond its current connotation, the term "commerce" then referred to all affairs of human life including non-economic relations and trade transactions. In his well-researched book *America's Constitution*, Professor Akhil Reed Amar at Yale Law School defines the broader meaning of commerce in 1787 as extending "to all forms of intercourse in the affairs of life, whether or not narrowly economic or mediated by explicit markets."[31]

In a traditional sense, the all-encompassing constitutional clause on commerce has become one of the primary instruments for regulating human behavior in every nation. The embedded regulating mechanism is not confined to merely commerce, but it directly and indirectly extends to all social, economic, financial, cultural, and political aspects of American life as well as our diplomatic and trade relations with other nations.

PART III

ANNUIT COEPTIS, PROVIDENCE (GOD) FAVORS OUR UNDERTAKINGS

"The stage is set, the destiny disclosed. It has come about by no plan of our conceiving, but by the hand of God who led us into the way. . . . America shall in truth show the way. The light streams upon the path ahead and nowhere else."

~ President WOODROW WILSON
July 10, 1919

EIGHT

The Pythagorean Potomac Delta

> It is sometimes called the City of Magnificent
> Distances, but it might with greater propriety be
> termed the City of Magnificent Intentions; for it is
> only on taking a bird's-eye view of it from the top
> of the Capitol, that one can at all comprehend the
> vast designs of its projector.[1]
>
> **Charles Dickens**
> Victorian Novelist

Ancient philosopher Pythagoras once proclaimed the word "Eureka!"
to mean, "I have found it" in Greek. For the most famous Masonic
Founding Father, the discovery of the Pythagorean Y-shaped Potomac
delta region for the location of the new Federal City was a true Eureka
moment. Inspired by the esoteric meaning contained in the Pythagorean
Theorem, President George Washington announced on March 30, 1791
that he had chosen a hallowed ten-mile square of land and two rivers—
Potomac and its eastern branch Anacostia—which naturally formed a
Pythagorean Y with the adjacent borders of Maryland and Virginia (Figure 8.1). The Pythagorean Theorem, or the Forty-seventh Problem of
Euclid, is the sum of the squares of the legs of a right triangle is equal to
the square of the hypotenuse: $a^2 + b^2 = c^2$ (see Figure 8.2). The Pythago-

reans believed that everything in the universe could be represented by numbers and that nature is a huge mathematical process. According to Masonic and Hermetic traditions, this is expressed in the saying, "As above, so below."[2] Appreciative of the wisdom traditions and Freemasonry, Washington bypassed two already well-established and flourishing capital cities of New York (population 33,000 in the first census of 1790) and Philadelphia (42,000) in favor of placing the new capital on the banks of the malaria-ridden, marshy landscapes of the Potomac delta.[3] Historically, all seats of power—from the early Egyptian, Roman and Greek civilizations and their capital cities of Memphis, Rome, and Athens, respectively—have prospered commercially near waterways.

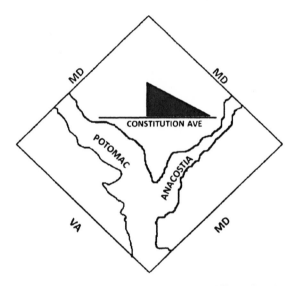

FIGURE 8.1: The Potomac delta and its namesake Tiber Creek, which flowed beneath the east-west running Constitution Avenue. The original Goose Creek, an estuary of the Potomac River, was renamed for Rome's Tiber River.

The symbolic association of the Pythagorean Y, which represents dualities such as the sacred versus the secular and self-interest versus moral sentiments, was important to the Founding Fathers. Pythagoras, who established a religious and mystical system of philosophy in the sixth century B.C., described the fixed heavenly stars as moving "through courses in the rational order and harmony of the universe."[4] He believed that the universe has a supremely intelligent mind, which is omnipresent, omnipotent, and omniscient. As if Providence (God) perpetually connected to the stars above, Pythagorean followers used the

Greek letter Y to represent the sacred triad formed by the dyad originating from the monad. That monadic supreme mind encompasses everything. Pythagoras understood everything as divided into three components. These three compartments must be viewed as triangular and as archetypes of the universe. The forking paths signify the duality of life: vice and virtue (earthy desires and divine wisdom). The bottom of the Y symbolizes uncertainty—the real mundane path of life. The fork of the letter characterizes accountability; the path that leads upward to the right ends in divine wisdom, while the path heading leftward arrives at earthly desires (Figure 8.2).

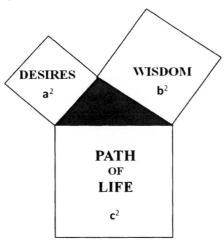

FIGURE 8.2: The sacred Pythagorean Y denotes the Divine Trinity: The masculine (the perpendicular line), the feminine (the base), and the offspring (the hypotenuse) segments of a triangle.

For Freemasons, the Pythagorean Y implies the primordially unified triad that illustrates the power of choice. The responsibility entailed on the right-hand path leads to virtuous living to gain divinity; the liability contained on the left passageway leads to earthly desires and vices. Those persons stationed in positions of authority and government power ought to take the virtuous right-hand path, as is demonstrated by taking the oath of public office with the right hand upheld. Symbolically, the Pythagorean Y denotes the search for perfection—through integrity, industry, and sincerity—in a purpose-driven life, as George Washington did. (Thomas Jefferson, Benjamin Franklin, and Alexander Hamilton had personal challenges in balancing the two paths outlined by Pythagoras).

The comparative advantage of the Potomac delta over the two previous capitals was neither geographical nor economical (nor even limited to the political compromise between Hamilton and Jefferson as we knew it), but rather the direct providential connection between the stars (and other celestial bodies) and the new real estate. The delta was an uninhabitable, steamy, and foggy wasteland—especially the lowland area surrounding Tiber Creek (originally Goose Creek), which flowed beneath the east-west running Constitution Avenue.[5] The Pythagorean location also had its own infamous political history apart from the mysterious traditions of antiquity. When debate arose over the new location for the nation's capital after Congress voted to create a permanent Federal City in 1790, President Washington maintained his "Washington the Unifier"[6] position through good will, natural calm, and a strategic vision for the capital city. American history textbooks tell us that the debate began with the president's Secretary of the Treasury, Hamilton from New York. As a financial wizard and Machiavellian strategist, Hamilton argued that northern states should necessarily oppose a southern capital. The northern states had accumulated a huge portion of the Revolutionary War debt and wanted the central government to assume their burden. Secretary of State Jefferson from the Commonwealth of Virginia offered a political compromise: the south would assume the debt incurred by the north if the northerners would support the "Potomac solution"[7] to build the nation's capital in the south.

Several years before the Congressional vote, the location of a future capital was intensely discussed. In 1783, Virginia and Maryland delegates in Congress suggested building the prospective seat of federal government on the Potomac. In their letter to Governor Benjamin Harrison of Virginia, the delegates wrote that Maryland and Virginia might offer "a small track of Territory . . . in the neighborhood of George Town on Potowmack, [which] might meet with the acceptance of Congress, in preference to [the one offered] by New York."[8] These delegates believed that a governmental complex with federal buildings would create a prosperous commercial and cultural center in their own region similar to those of Boston, New York, and Philadelphia.

When the issue was finally resolved, the president had chosen a swampy marshland as the new location for the nation's capital, as stated in the Residence Act of 1790.[9] After the capital site moved to the mosquito-flying "foggy bottom" on the banks of Potomac and Anacostia Rivers, the futuristic Washington correctly anticipated the Federal City becoming a vibrant political capital, while New York prospered as the financial center of the nation and the world. The purposeful distance between economic wealth and political power not only seemed to typify the separation of "absolute power" (i.e., the nexus between Wall Street bankers and federal government officials), but to signify the earthy desires of northern Hamiltonians and the lofty ideals of the Jeffersonian south. Other alternative southern locations like well-established Richmond in Virginia, Annapolis in Maryland, and Charleston in South Carolina were apparently on neither Jefferson's nor Washington's mind.

With his keen interest in numerology and astronomy, Washington used his self-taught esoteric knowledge and skill to identify and design a unified Federal City that astronomically and symbolically reflected the commercial vision of the nation and the wisdom traditions of the past. As the most prominent Freemason of his time, Washington was a highly capable surveyor and cartographer who understood the meaning of the southernmost Y-shaped Potomac delta and its prime real estate value for the new capital.

The "Square Deal" for the Nation

The unified Federal City—first known as the Territory of Columbia and later the District of Columbia (D.C.)—is a perfect ten miles on each side; it rotates 45 degrees to bear a resemblance to the Masonic symbol of a square and compass. The four corners of 100 square miles (260 km^2) of land area between Maryland and Virginia point to each of the cardinal directions.[10] At the southern turning point of the diamond-shaped capital city at Jones Point (where the district began its official boundary at the Hunting Creek on the south side of Alexandria in Virginia), a Masonic ceremony took place exactly at three-thirty in the afternoon of April 15, 1791. Dr. Elisha Cullen Dick, grand master of Alexandria Masonic lodge, laid a marker on the ground with those involved and other Freemasons who understood the significance of the time and location. Christian author Cisco Wheeler writes:

> The astrological reason for starting the ceremonial ritual at preciously 3:30 PM had everything to do with Jupiter. Jupiter in all its glory had begun to rise over the horizon. It was within 23 degrees of Virgo—he seized on the moment when the zodiacal Virgo was exerting an especially strong and beneficial influence.[11]

The zodiacal power of Virgo was able to "stamp her benign influence on the building of the federal city," as she was *"linked to the future destiny of America itself"*[12] (italics original). Moreover, President Washington wanted to symbolize the city with a square—a philosophical and Masonic statement that brings to mind the straightforward nature of "square" dealings (dealings of honesty, fairness, and equality) amongst the thirteen former colonies and their inhabitants, and with other nations. The square also signifies the physical and spiritual world. These worlds include the four elements of life (air, earth, fire, and water) essential to physical existence as well as the four spiritual components. Air represents the power of thought; earth corresponds to the principle of solidarity; fire indicates the power of intention; and water relates to the power of creative emotions.

With this duality in mind, the president appointed two illustrious Freemasons—Dr. David Steward and Daniel Carroll (brother of first Catholic Bishop John Carroll)—and Thomas Johnson to serve as commissioners to make final recommendation for "a district or territory of the permanent seat of the Government of the United States."[13] Andrew Ellicott, who impressed Washington with his proficiency in astronomy and experience as a surveyor in the colonies, was "appointed to survey the district lines,"[14] the president wrote in his diary on March 28, 1791. Ellicott's associate Benjamin Banneker, the astronomer and mathematician of free African American ancestry,[15] worked closely with the surveyor-engineer. To demarcate the boundary of a 100-square-mile diamond, for example, Ellicott placed forty stone markers at one-mile intervals,[16] for which Banneker decided the exact locations "based on celestial calculations."[17] Banneker observed the positions of stars constantly at Jones Point in Alexandria and maintained a clock to monitor heavenly bodies appearing over the Federal City.[18] As the ancients believed, these city planners led by Washington accepted that the movement, conjunction, and positioning of celestial bodies held influential power over the destiny of America and the public affairs of the new nation.

The Capital City

After identifying the benedictory location, the enterprise of constructing a Federal City was an intimate task for the first president. President Washington indicated to Thomas Jefferson that he reserved the right to locate the main federal buildings in the city:

The enlarged plan of this agreement having done away the necessarily, and indeed postponed the property, of designating the particular spot on which the public buildings should be placed, until an accurate survey and subdivision of the whole ground is made, I have left out that paragraph of the proclamation.[19]

His focal point was the Capitol—the symbol of American democracy that is essentially a figurative embodiment of the U.S. Constitution. The building complex itself lies over Jenkins Heights as if inspired by the heavens. Atop its dome, the Statue of Freedom points toward the skies above. The figure stands on a cast-iron globe encircling the national motto, *E Pluribus Unum*. It projects the universal nature of America's founding conviction and its global outreach. The Capitol, which identifies with the representative nature of the republic, is truly a symbol of national harmony and human freedom.

For the colossal undertaking of designing and constructing the city and federal buildings, President Washington assembled a highly talented group of learned men. When the French-born military engineer and city planner Pierre Charles L'Enfant wrote to his former Revolutionary War commander, Washington commissioned him to devise a plan for the physical layout of the city.[20] The fabled designer was a multi-talented loyalist whose father had exposed him to European architecture and city planning. Having worked in the palaces and gardens of Versailles in Paris, the younger L'Enfant was significantly influenced by his father.[21] His unique background (seemingly divinely ordained) genuinely impressed Washington, especially after L'Enfant expressed an earnest desire to build a capital "magnificent enough to grace a great nation."[22] President Washington described his former soldier and admirer as "not only a scientific man but one who aded (sic) considerable taste to professional knowledge; and that, for such employment as he is now engaged in; he was better qualified than any one who had come within my knowledge in this country."[23] When L'Enfant arrived in the city of Washington in 1791, he enthusiastically remarked that Jenkins Heights, the current location of Capitol Hill, appeared to be "a pedestal waiting for a monument."[24] Washington knew of the Frenchman's commitment, enthusiasm, eloquence, and expertise from their time together in the Revolutionary War. L'Enfant naturally gained the president's trust and respect.

With his French upbringing and solid understanding of the elaborate design of Versailles, L'Enfant sketched the original plan for the district.

In some ways, it resembled Paris.[25] Thomas Jefferson had intimate knowledge of and admiration for the architecture of the French capital.
Working closely with L'Enfant, Jefferson offered advice to the team involved in the planning process and even provided European maps.[26]
Under Washington's direct guidance, L'Enfant remained fully occupied
with his team that consisted of Andrew Ellicott from Pennsylvania (a
close friend of Benjamin Franklin) and Benjamin Banneker from Maryland. Like Franklin and Washington, Ellicott and Banneker were highly
informed on the subject matters of astronomy and astrology, and in the
esoteric teachings of Freemasonry and antiquity. These men subsequently designed a fully accorded architectural blueprint for their ideal
metropolis intended to symbolize not only America's national unity but
also a harmonious connection to the divine powers positioned above the
city.

Edward Savage's famous 1796 oil painting of the Washington family—Washington, his wife Martha, and her granddaughter Nelly pointing
to the triangle of L'Enfant's map while her grandson Washington Curtis
rests his right hand on a celestial globe—projects a powerful message of
symbolism and imagery, and connects Washington's terrestrial endeavors to their celestial counterparts.[27] Thanks to the collective and
conscious efforts of those involved in the grand design, the structure of
the nation's capital is a striking example of a harmonious layout. The
layout begins with a grid pattern of radial and axial streets, and a broad
range of diagonal avenues dotted with major landmarks. These landmarks present a set of orderly groupings of circles (like DuPont, Logan,
and Scott) and squares (such as Benjamin, Farragut, and McPherson)
decorated with beautiful sculptures to memorialize important events and
leaders in American history.

The city expresses perfect unity, stability, and authority with smaller
and larger scale monuments to the extent that successive architects, astronomers, and writers found inspiration in L'Enfant's original blueprint.
For example, legendary Victorian novelist Charles Dickens, who wrote
critically about America in 1842, had a surprisingly different outlook of
the nation's capital. Dickens described, "It is sometimes called the City
of Magnificent Distances, but it might with greater propriety be termed
the City of Magnificent Intentions; for it is only on taking a bird's-eye
view of it from the top of the Capitol, that one can at all comprehend the
vast designs of its projector."[28] The Victorian critic was quite right when
he called it the "City of Magnificent Intentions." In fact, President Washington first announced "the City of Magnificent Distances," from which

Dickens substituted the word "intentions" for the word "distances." Of course, the Founding Fathers intended for the capital to be a portrait of American unity and order in diversity—as a providence-driven endeavor in perfect alignment with constellations in the sky.

The Mother of the National Symbol

A vast array of astrological images and symbols—including Virgo and Mercury—project the commercial origin of the nation, but the pinnacle of the Capitol represents the mother of national symbolism: the Statue of Freedom pointing toward the heavens. A testament to the Union after the Civil War, the statue was finally hoisted to the top of the Capitol dome with a thirty-five-gun salute (for each of thirty-five states) in the middle of a grand celebration at twelve o'clock on December 2, 1863.[29] Thomas Crawford, who completed the plaster model in Rome, Italy, finally cast it in bronze at the Mills Foundry in Bladensburg, Maryland under the supervision of Philip Reid, an African slave. The elevated allegorical female figure represents Virgo reaching out to the celestial world.

When Capitol architect Thomas Walter drew the structural outline for the great Statue of Freedom, he chose to clothe the figure with a Phrygian cap—a head covering traditionally worn by freed Roman slaves.[30] Secretary of War Jefferson Davis, who was appointed by President Franklin Pierce to supervise the Capitol expansion project, objected to the sculptor's intent to include a liberty cap. The secretary of war asked to replace it with a crested Roman helmet.[31] Secretary Davis remarked that "a helmet with a circle of stars" would be "expressive of endless existence and heavenly birth."[32] Thus, her helmet is encircled with a wreath of thirteen stars to represent the original colonies and features a crest composed of an eagle's head, feathers, and talons to represent all Native Americans (Figure 8.3).

Besides the centrality of the statue on the Capitol dome (modeled after domed Saint Peter's Basilica in Vatican City), the building complex itself symbolizes the divinity, democracy, and centrality of the Federal City. For its part, the city divides the District of Columbia into four distinct quadrants: Northwest, Northeast, Southeast, and Southwest. Streets are marked by a numbering and lettering system that begins at the Capitol. As a whole, the massive building signifies the integrative nature of the U.S. Constitution with a trinity of main porticos that lead to the Senate chamber on the north side, to the House chamber on the south side, and to the Rotunda in the center.[33] This is a symbolic and deliberate expression of unity. The secretary of war quite noticeably captured the essence of all symbols employed in Washington—including those of Mercury, Venus, and Mars—in a unified manner to represent the first President's intended celestial connection to terrestrial matters.

FIGURE 8.3: The Statue of Freedom on the Capitol dome represents a "heavenly birth" and all Native Americans.

In the Capitol, an assortment of ancient symbols, sculptures, and paintings has come to life in a subtle but purposeful manner. One of the nation's greatest murals is the *Apotheosis of Washington,* which adorns the Rotunda. The inner circle around President George Washington depicts thirteen maidens (representing the thirteen original colonies), two of whom hold a banner inscribed with the legend *E Pluribus Unum.*[34] To his left is the goddess of Victory (draped in green and using a trumpet-like horn) and to his right is the goddess of Liberty. The outer ring of the canopy is adorned with six allegorical clusters representing various national themes: war (Columbia), science (Minerva), marine (Neptune), commerce (Mercury), mechanics (Vulcan), and agriculture (Ceres). At the center, directly above the president and next to *E Pluribus Unum*, is Mercury, the god of commerce. Mercury, with his winged cap, sandals and caduceus, is illustrated giving a bag of money to Robert Morris, financier of the Revolutionary War. The caduceus symbolizes "heralding and peaceful interactions."[35] In the midst of all these metaphoric groupings, Italian artist Constantino Brumidi amusingly decided to identify himself with the god of commerce (i.e., "C") by signing his masterpiece with the inscription "C. Brumidi 1865" on the box below Mercury.[36]

Another important astrological reference in the Capitol is *The Car of History* in the Statuary Hall, which was created in 1819 by Florentine sculptor Carlo Franzoni[37] (Figure 8.4). The raised relief sculpture of *The Car* depicts Clio standing on George Washington's winged chariot in honor of the first president.[38] The wheel of the chariot is a clock. It rests on a marble globe marked with three zodiac signs[39] that symbolize the passage of time, eternity, and the indestructible nature of the Capitol. The female represents Virgo, protector of the city. This masterpiece is not well-recognized but highly significant in esoteric Freemasonry.

The Car of History

FIGURE 8.4: Italian sculptor Carlo Franzoni's *Car of History* in the Statuary Hall of the Capitol rests on a marble globe upon which three zodiac signs are carved into an arc-like relief panel. Starting left to right with Sagittarius (ruled by Jupiter for prosperity), the chariot travels in the direction of Aquarius and Capricorn (both governed by Saturn) to signify the eternity of the Capitol and its deliberations. Clio (the Muse of History), who stands on the winged chariot with the bas-relief portrait of George Washington and the clock, symbolizes Virgo and the passage of time.

The city builders and architects clearly understood the sacred wisdom and continued veneration of Virgo and its zodiac signs. Symbols of Mercury, the governor of the capital city, vividly affirm the Virgoan nature of Constitution Avenue, which laid the foundational and spiritual cohesiveness for national unity and American identity. The nation's Capitol itself presents an array of unifying symbols, purposeful images, and meaningful themes (be they temporal or esoteric by nature). The learned Founding Fathers, subsequent architects, and city planners concealed no secrets. Instead, study of ancient traditions and esoteric knowledge reveal their intentions for the commercial mission of the nation. Even if there were secrets, there is nothing to hide; the architecture of the nation's capital manifests this information and is available to all who seek to find it.

Washington, the Unifier

While other Founding Fathers creatively focused on ideas of the Enlightenment Age, ancient symbols, and the American colonial experience in order to design a Great Seal of the United States and draft the Constitution, George Washington reflected intensely on ways to express constitutional unity through symbolism. He discretely organized a way to accomplish this mission. His designs incorporated the earliest symbols of Egyptian and Greco-Roman origin—as well as Masonic traditions—that have become American icons of hope, growth, and opportunity.[40] In his application, however, the symbolism seems to have expressed the power of unification. This unity is observable in the successful assimilation of a diverse American populace and in the balance of the duality between material happiness and spiritual pursuits.

For the Founding Fathers, the operative word was unity. Highly immersed in classical philosophies, these men fully understood the difference between two familiar systems of political governance: the Roman republic and Athenian democracy. The Founders combined the practical aspects of both civilizations. In this respect, the concepts expounded on in the Pythagorean Y and in Adam Smith's *Wealth of Nations* and *Theory of Moral Sentiments* were influential in guiding the commercial character and unity of the new republic.

Some of the concepts ambiguously visible both in physical structures and in ancient symbols seemed to reflect the temporal dialogue between human nature and "self-interest," and the higher level of "moral choices" in the sacred sphere and public affairs. The Founding Fathers commonly believed that the Great Architect of the Universe and heavenly bodies in various constellations served as guarantors of "morality and civil order," as well as judges who would "reward the good and punish evil in the afterlife."[41] Such ideas of social harmony through divine power were part of the classical writings of Rousseau, Kant, and others. Their literary works held a great deal of weight with the Founding Fathers.

These ideas in symbolism reveal the nation's commercial mission to the enlightened, while simultaneously concealing it from the uninformed. Nevertheless, there is neither controversy nor conspiracy to Washington's grand vision and the divine-like portrayal of him in the Capitol dome. The Christian Bible tells us, "For nothing is secret, that shall not be made manifest; neither any thing hid, that shall not be known and come to light."[42] Those with inquiring minds and inquisitive eyes may easily observe the symbolism adorning the arts and architecture of the capital and bear witness to its Mercurial nature and unity.

Both Gemini (male) and Virgo (female) are ruled by Mercury, Roman god of Commerce.

NINE

The Anatomy of Commercial Providence

> Astrology interested us, for it tied man to the system. . . . [For] an isolated beggar, the farthest star felt him, and he felt the star.[1]
>
> **Ralph Waldo Emerson**
> American philosopher

The European Enlightenment thinkers and other "natural scientists" (as those philosophers were then called) like Sir Isaac Newton, Galileo Galilei, and Johannes Kepler upheld the view that there is unity and order in the universe. The natural system included the orderly movements of celestial bodies, such as the constellations of fixed stars and planets. Sir Francis Bacon, father of modern science, wrote about universal order as a "celestial hierarchy," and spoke of "celestial bodies" and their relation to the "terrestrial" affairs of people.[2] Sir Bacon, whom Thomas Jefferson considered one of his "trinity" along with Isaac Newton and John Locke, further explained, "Whoever despises the imaginary separation between terrestrial and celestial things . . . may receive a clear information of what happens above from that which happens below."[3] These natural philosophies were not contradictory to scientific, philosophic, or rational minds—especially among the Founding Fathers and those who subsequently followed them as enlightened and scientific thinkers.

Like Sir Newton, who wrote in 1692 to Reverend Richard Bentley that the "Motions which the Planets now have could not spring from any natural cause alone, but were impressed by an intelligent Agent,"[4] Dr. Albert Einstein defended the belief that all impersonal events and movements operate in deterministic universal laws, and that intelligence is manifested in nature. The Nobel Laureate in Physics, writing to his old friend Maurice Solovine in 1952, explained this order as an unexpected event and regarded it as a miracle or a mystery:

> You find it curious that I regard the intelligibility of the world as a miracle or an eternal mystery. Well, *a priori* [reasoning from cause to effect] one should expect that the world would be rendered lawful only to the extent that we intervene with our ordering intelligence. It would be a kind of order like the alphabetical order of the words of a language. . . . [T]he success of such an endeavor presupposes in the objective world a high degree of order that we were *a priori* in no way authorized to expect. This is the 'miracle' that is strengthened more and more with the development of our knowledge (italics original).[5]

In the midst of the chaos and complexity of the universe, human and natural events in Einstein's view were most likely arranged like words in a dictionary. For him, the detection of that intelligence and order was a "miracle or an eternal mystery." In his famous 1937 lecture on *Religion and Natural Science*, Einstein's German colleague and Nobel Prize-winning physicist Max Planck also asserted that "a certain order prevails" in the universe, and that the universe itself is governed by an "all-powerful intelligence."[6] Indeed, the complexity and simplicity that coexist in the universe demonstrate the creative handiwork of an "Intelligent Agent," as Sir Newton described. In the twentieth century, Einstein understood the reverence and wondrous nature of this universal mind, which the Founding Fathers called the Great Architect of the Universe. In his book, *Einstein: His Life and Universe*, Walter Isaacson describes the genius scientist as "the mind reader of the creator of the cosmos, the locksmith of the mysteries of the atom and the universe."[7] It is remarkable that not only did the Founding Fathers express such ideas in their writings, but they also applied them in practice—particularly George Washington and Benjamin Franklin.

As Above, So Below

The celestial-terrestrial maxim can be traced back to the Greek god, Hermes Trismegistus, and the Egyptian god, Thoth. The dramatic opening lines of *The Emerald Tablet of Thoth* declare, "Look thee above, or look thee below, the same shall ye find, for all is but part of the Oneness that is at the Source of the Law. The consciousness below thee is part thine own, as we are a part of thine."[8] George Washington's arcane knowledge of Freemasonry seemed to have enabled him and others to fully realize that the macrocosm of Nature's God is the same as the microcosm on earth. Acting on that ancient knowledge, the designers of the Federal City constructed two reflecting pools on the west side of the Capitol and the Washington Monument to signify the heavenly-earthly connection. As the sun rises from the east (or the full moon), this connection makes a reflective image on the water of the pool as a reminder of the continuity of wisdom traditions. The sophisticated philosophy of Hermes[9] (or his Roman counterpart Mercury) has been a part of Western esoteric traditions that evolved with the so-called secret teachings of Masonry.

With the development of science and astronomy, these Freemasons advanced their own understanding of astrology and the calculation of planetary movements to clarify their significance on human events. Sir Bacon wrote, "A man shall find in the traditions of astrology some pretty and apt divisions of men's natures, according to the predominances of the planets."[10] American philosopher Ralph Waldo Emerson agreed: "Astrology interested us, for it tied man to the system. . . . [For] an isolated beggar, the farthest star felt him, and he felt the star."[11] This helps explain why astrology has been an important field of scientific study able to attract the interest of prominent Americans including Franklin, Jefferson, Revere, and Washington.

Unlike Washington and Jefferson, the famous grand master of Freemasonry, Benjamin Franklin, openly employed the names, characters, symbols, and techniques of astrology for twenty-five years. These were in evidence when he wrote his famous *Poor Richard's Almanac*, printed in 1733. By the time he was twenty-seven, Franklin had developed a keen interest in astrology and astronomy. He used this obscure scholarship to make astro-meteorological weather forecasts for farmers and diagnose ailments of the human body as governed by the twelve zodiac signs and arcane symbols of planets.[12] His almanacs brought him wealth and fame throughout the American colonies, France, and in England.

Sales of *Poor Richard* were second only to the Bible for the quarter century following its first publication in 1733.

In *Franklin: The Apostle of Modern Times*, Professor Bernard Fay at the Collège de France writes, "Astrology was very much in vogue. . . . It occupied an important place in business, agriculture, and private life. Astrology was [even] employed in determining the future of newly born children."[13] As the popularity of Freemasonry grew in the seventeenth century, institutions of higher education discussed cryptic and heavily guarded knowledge associated with Freemasonry. Fay, a Harvard alumnus, explains, "Wise, serious, and pious people also believed in astrology, for as late as 1728 candidates for Harvard discussed such topics . . . [and] on the eve of the American Revolution in 1777, the faculty proposed such subjects."[14] The intellectual discourse and the practice of astrology played a traditional role during the early years in American society—a role similarly found in earlier Roman, Greek, and Egyptian civilizations. The French author concludes, "Everybody turned to the astrologers, and the publishers of almanacs had an immense public. These little books were the faithful mirrors of the preoccupations of the times."[15]

Since the Babylonian and Egyptian civilizations, rulers and even Popes and bishops have employed astrologers in special ceremonies such as coronations, and consulted with them on expanding their empires and on other personal affairs. Professors Christopher Knight and Robert Lomas write, "Freemasonry and astrology are two traditions which best preserve that belief that the position of the heavenly bodies affect the actions of individuals on Earth. At first sight these two belief systems are very different, but our research was showing that each has retained different elements of the 6,000-year-old ideas."[16] Benjamin Franklin clearly reminded Americans and their leaders of this, writing:

COURTEOUS READER, Astrology is one of the most ancient Sciences, [held] in high Esteem of old, by the Wise and Great. Formerly, no Prince would make War or Peace, nor any General fight a Battle, in short, no important Affair was undertaken without first consulting an *Astrologer*, who examined the Aspects and Configurations of the heavenly Bodies, and mark'd the *lucky Hour*" (emphasis original).[17]

As the elderly sage among the relatively young Founding Fathers, Dr. Franklin surely exercised an enormous influence on the timing of all major landmark events ever conducted in the infant nation.

Celestial and Terrestrial Triangles

With his fellow Freemasons, President Washington and his learned architects collectively integrated both traditions—Freemasonry and astrology—for aligning key landmarks with celestial bodies and the design of the Federal City.[18] Professor Robert Lomas uncovered Washington's personal diaries and concluded that the previously unsuspected secret science of Masonic astrology was behind his actions.[19] With the president's guidance, Pierre Charles L'Enfant, Andrew Ellicott, Benjamin Banneker, and other commissioners designed a Federal City that connects the three principal structures with three stars visible in the sky above the nation's capital. Here, the president's intimate involvement was clear according to his diary on March 30, 1791 where he inscribed:

> This business being thus happily finished & some directions given to the Commissioners [Steward, Carroll, and Johnson], the Surveyor [Ellicott] and Engineer [L'Enfant] with respect to the mode of laying out the district—Surveying the grounds for the City & forming them into lots—I left Georgetown—dined in Alexandria & reached Mount Vernon in the evening.[20]

With his esoteric and geometric understanding of the Masonic initiation experience (especially the Master Mason degree) and the meaning of symbolism, President Washington clearly had his hands on approach to the application of that knowledge via the blueprint of the Federal City. In his book *The Secret Architecture of Our Nation's Capital*, David Ovason demonstrates that the location of primary landmarks (the White House, the Capitol, and the Washington Monument) corresponded to the three stars—Arcturus, Regulus, and Spica—that rose from the east at sunset and formed a celestial triangle in the darkened skies over Washington, D.C., on August 10, 1791 (Figure 9.1). This heavenly geometry of fixed stars partially enclosed the Virgo constellation (Figure 9.2). The constellation itself inspired city planners to devise a parallel layout, almost as if the physical creation of the new capital were an act guided by Providence or the Great Architect of the Universe.

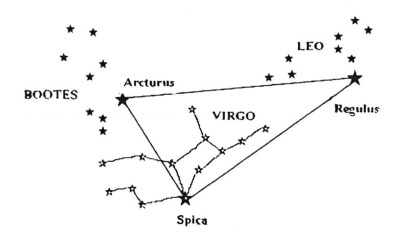

As Above

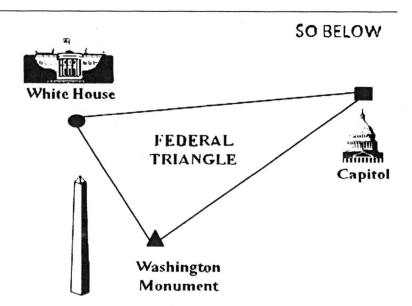

FIGURE 9.1: Celestial and terrestrial triangles connecting the Washington Monument (Spica), the White House (Arcturus), and the Capitol (Regulus) in Washington, D.C.

In Freemasonry, the five-pointed blazing star symbolizes both the constellation of Virgo and the idea of regeneration.[21] The iconic star—also known as the Dog Star, morning star, or Sirius—graces the architecture of the city and firmly underpins the city's design as if it belonged to a science of stars that guides human affairs.[22] Moreover, the city architects, especially the Masonic brethren, believed that Virgo—ruled by Mercury—would help the American people bond with the newly created nation and foster their commercial success.[23]

FIGURE 9.2: Virgo constellation within the celestial triangle, which corresponds to the terrestrial replica of the Federal Triangle, is ruled by Mercury, the Roman god of commerce and communication.

The Arcturus-Regulus-Spica triangle is a spiritual statement to the founding purpose with no particular religious affiliation. Despite the religious overtones of early Christian traditions, the forces of ancient and esoteric knowledge were pervasive in colonial America and in the new republic. As illustrated earlier, the Founding Fathers were very familiar with these wisdom traditions, associated astrology, and symbolism. Evidence further suggests that even Thomas Jefferson, who was not a known Freemason, studied the ancient knowledge, including the works of the most influential Egyptian astronomer of his time, Claudius Ptolemy (circa 100-178 AD).[24] In his *Tetrabiblos* (Four Books), Ptolemy described the meaning of stars, the planetary movements, and their earthly associations.[25] The new Federal City was dedicated to, and baptized by, Virgo—and nurtured by Regulus and protected by Arcturus. Ultimately, the city was glorified by the heavenly-directed, phallus-like Washington Monument. Ovason and other observers describe the multiplicity of the esoteric, astrological, and Freemasonry significance of this divinely conceived plan and its purposeful celestial-terrestrial connection:

- The brightest star in the Leo constellation is **Regulus**—the "prince" or "little king" in Latin—and corresponds to the Capitol (U.S. Congress). It represents the center of the kingdom that "regulates" power, freedom, and independence.

- The brightest star in the Bootes constellation is **Arcturus**, which means "Bear Guard" in Greek. A "guardian" of hope, the fixed star directly corresponds with to the White House.

- The most powerful star in the Virgo Constellation is **Spica**. In Latin, *spica virginis* means the "Virgo's ear of grain." This star corresponds to the Washington Monument and represents the advancement, future prosperity, and heavenly ascendance of the enlightened American people.

The exposition indicates that the original city planners led by President Washington held a strong belief in ancient knowledge, and that the Federal City had a providential birth. Ovason explains: "A city that is laid out in such a way that it is in harmony with the heavens is a city in perpetual prayer. It is a city built on the recognition that every human activity is in need of the sanctification of the spiritual world, of which the symbol is the light of the living stars."[26] For the Founding Fathers and Freemasons, there was no explicit need to reveal the mystery of American power and the wonders of freedom derived from the Great Architect of the Universe. The visionary L'Enfant even wrote to Washington and Jefferson that the nation's capital was not merely to devise a system of streets and avenues suited to the needs of a city that was to be the capital of a small country, but to meet the needs of the United States should become populous and most powerful.[27] This shared prophetic vision was part of predestiny and free will of the American nation.

The Anatomy of Divine Providence

Washington, L'Enfant, and Ellicott—the "trinity" of the nation's capital architecture—sought to design the city knowing that the power of symbols would radiate throughout every American state, inspiring na tional unity, order, and freedom. The arcane symbols of astrology and astronomy were treasured traditions in the mystery school of Pythagoras. These traditions are generally known, or revealed, to those who are privy to the esoteric traditions of Masonry. To others, however, they often remain unknown or concealed. Referring to Washington, Banneker, and L'Enfant, British author Ovason writes:

> After all, the three Brothers, while drawing this earthly triangle, are also forming a triangle above their own heads, in the realm of the stars, and no doubt recalling the Trinity in the spiritual world. Their gesture was designed to unite the celestial realm of the stars with the Earth, through the medium of the human body.[28]

History professor John Young at Howard University in Washington, D.C., independently confirms that the layout of the city clearly reflects the constellation of Virgo and its intended providential connection to the city.[29]

Similar to the spatial dimension, the element of timing was equally important to the Founding Fathers and city architects. Ovason provides a clear description of how the builders coordinated time and space in their purpose-driven scheduling of significant events. The Freemasons ensured that the laying of the cornerstones for each of these prime landmarks correctly corresponded with the timing of planetary movements, which aligned with Virgo in the most traditionally auspicious manner.[30] Ovason explains that L'Enfant's meticulous layout of the nation's capital was executed by using astrological terms and arcane language that only Franklin, Revere, Washington, and a few others could comprehend:

- The Masonic brethren of the Georgetown Lodge and the commissioners of the District of Columbia set the cornerstone for the **White House** on Saturday, October 13, 1792, when the moon had entered the same degree as the Dragon's Head (a sort of "shadowy planet" in astrology, as explained below), which was situated within twenty-three degrees of Virgo.

- George Washington laid the **Capitol** cornerstone during a Masonic ceremony on September 18, 1793, when Mercury, the Dragon's Head, and the sun were all within the constellation of Virgo. This historical ceremony is enshrined on the bronze doors of the U.S.

Senate, which feature a plate of President Washington wearing a white Masonic apron and using a trowel to lay the cornerstone. (The actual apron is publicly displayed at the George Washington Masonic Memorial in Alexandria, Virginia).

- The Masonic time scheduled for the laying of the foundation stone for the **Washington Monument** was at noon on July 4, 1848, when the moon and the Dragon's Head were in the Virgo constellation. After a 30-year hiatus surrounding the Civil War period, the construction of the phallic monument officially began again at exactly 11:59 on the morning of August 7, 1880 when the star Spica—a joyful, radiant star in Virgo—was rising over the eastern horizon. For astronomical and astrological reasons, the dedication ceremony took place on February 21, 1885—one day before President Washington's actual birthday—when Jupiter, the esoteric icon of prosperity, was in the Virgo constellation.[31]

Benjamin Franklin used the term Dragon's Head, *Caput Draconis* in Latin, in all of his almanacs.[32] In astrology and ancient astronomy, as in Franklin's almanacs, the Dragon's Head—opposite to the Dragon's Tail (*Cauda Draconis*)—is formed when the ecliptic, or the course of the sun, intersects with the moon's visible path in the sky as seen from earth. This was believed to be the time when the moon wielded the greatest influence over human affairs. These architects acted on the belief that a beneficial period for angelic affairs on earth occurs when the Dragon Head aligns with Virgo.

The Dragon's Head and Tail are not planets in the astronomical sense. Rather, these obscure head and tail creations are the "shadowy planets" that naturally formed from the overlap of beaming rays when the moon crosses the sun.[33] The Dragon's Head, also called the North Node, is the ascending node when the moon crosses the ecliptic from the southern to northern celestial latitudes in Washington, D.C. In all astrological and other esoteric traditions, this conjunction (as compared to that of the Dragon's Tail) is considered by far the most auspicious and significant in directing human destiny.

Both western and eastern cabalistic traditions—that is, those found in Greco-Roman and Chindian (Chinese Confucian and Indian Vedic) cultures—respectively invoke the images of a serpent-like demon (or Satan) and the Dragon to describe the malefic nature of those two mystical parts of the creature: the Head and the Tail. The former (also known as Rahu in Sanskrit and Hindu mythology) encloses the brain of the serpent, which behaves like a demon of animistic intelligence and displays an insatiable worldly desire for pleasure and material happiness. The latter (Ketu, in Sanskrit) has no brain, so the tail acts compulsively and unconsciously in the pursuit of spiritual happiness and asceticism. Unlike other celestial bodies, these two shadowy planets are more like a formation of the masses of powerful energy than the stationary forces of traditional stars and planets. The shadowy planets' radiating force is more influential on human activities and in predicting events than the power associated with other celestial bodies. (Employing the science and art of astrological techniques, Franklin accurately predicted the death of his dear friend Titan Leeds at 29 minutes after 3'o clock on the afternoon of October 17, 1733).[34]

The Genesis of American Mercury

In Benjamin Franklin's astrology, the Dragon is neither masculine nor feminine; each gender is exalted in the signs of Mercury (Mercury in Gemini or Mercury in Virgo). Mercurial characteristics—both material and spiritual happiness—are associated with the mystical personalities of these shadowy planets. The idea of a "better angel" in human nature comes with the consciousness of the Dragon's Head rather than the "mindless acts" of Tail, or so-called "tail biting." Therefore, the builders of the nation's capital believed that the movements of heavenly bodies would have a divine effect on the mercurial affairs of the commercial republic when the Dragon's Head, not the Tail, lay in Virgo. The common thread among the ceremonies for laying the foundations of the White House, the Capitol, and the Washington Monument is now clear: the Founding Fathers acted on ancient knowledge to lead the Mercurial nation toward peace and prosperity. (President George H. W. Bush revived the American consciousness many years later when he referenced "ancient knowledge" in his acceptance speech for the presidential nomination at the Republican National Convention in New Orleans on August 18, 1988).[35]

All of these purposeful actions, designs, and symbols associated with ancient knowledge suggest that the presence of Virgo graces the nation's capital and the nation as a whole. The exaltation of the Dragon's Head in Virgo is not only beneficial, but the "shadowy planet" symbolizes the formation of the American "soul" in association with Virgo's ruler Mercury. This mythical Roman god of commerce advances America's

evolutionary process and sustains undertaken enterprises with dignity
and prosperity (the commercially-oriented federal city is just one such
metaphysical and physical endeavor; for the Ford Motor Company, Mercury vehicles symbolized the genesis of America commerce). Over
twenty-four major Masonic zodiacs emphasizing Virgo decorate the
capital city, and more than 1,000 similar astrological images have been
systematically added over the past 200 years.[36] Ovason describes:

> From the very beginning, the city was intended to celebrate the
> mystery of Virgo—of the Egyptian Isis, the Grecian Ceres and
> the Christian Virgin. This truth—and this truth alone—explains
> the structure of the city, and the enormous power of its stellar
> symbolism. Washington D.C. is far more than merely a city of
> zodiacs—it is a city, which was built to celebrate a massive cos-
> mic symbolism, expressed in stars. Its three main buildings—
> Capitol, White House and Washington Monument—mark on the
> Earth the annual renewal of that magical pyrotechnic display in
> the skies, which occurs on the days around August 10.[37]

Virgo is glorified as a divine icon in early Christian traditions, as
well as in hermetic principles and cosmological ideas. Ovason argues
that many individuals involved in building the city—besides being architects, planners, and artists—happened to be Freemasons as well, and
concludes by writing that "these individuals were also committed Christians."[38] In fact, the primary mission of York Rite Freemasonry is to
defend and protect the Christian faith.

Contrary to this observation, however, various forms of Deism and
non-Christian beliefs existed in the minds of Franklin, Washington, and
others. (Scottish Rite Freemasonry is open to those who believe in God
in any religious and faith traditions). In his *Faiths of the Founding Fathers*, Professor David Holmes at the College of William and Mary
carefully examines the religious culture of late colonial America.[39] He
offers evidence that Deism had a profound influence on the intellectual
movement of the founding generation. Acknowledging the existence of a
few agnostics, Holmes also reveals that some—like Samuel Adams, Patrick Henry, John Jay, Jefferson's daughters, and Martha Washington—
held orthodox Christian views. Many of the most influential Founding
Fathers and their spouses—including Franklin, Washington, John and
Abigail Adams, Jefferson, James and Dolley Madison, and James Monroe—were believers of a different ilk, if not believers of Deism or

nothing at all. They respected Christianity, admired the ethics of Jesus, and believed in the beneficial role of religion in society. Professor Holmes finally argues that the first five presidents tended to deny the divinity of Christ and follow a path of reason.[40]

It is more or less true that the Founders attended Baptist, Roman Catholic, Episcopal, or Presbyterian churches and adhered to a set of simple Christian virtues and morals. For them, the unity of all ancient traditions, religious faiths, and self-interests was important. In one form or another, Virgo is common to all these elements. It is conceivable that the unifying strategy culminated in the following great American projects: the auspicious conceptualization of laying the foundations for the Capitol, the White House, and the Washington Monument.

To honor Virgo, Bishop John Carroll of Baltimore (again emphasizing his brother Daniel Carroll as an illustrious Freemason, a Founding Father, and a close friend of Franklin), the first Roman Catholic bishop in America, consecrated the newly created United States under the protection of the Blessed Virgin Mary in 1790. In his *Episcopate in America,* William Perry writes that the major American undertakings have an immaculately Virgin origin and were blessed by the Virgin Mary—the founding Patroness of the United States—years before the three landmarks (the Capitol, the White House, and the Washington Monument) were conceived.[41] The "Vatican" of the United States—known officially as the Basilica of the National Shrine of the Immaculate Conception—is located on a hilltop just north of the Capitol as if it were constantly watching over the affairs of the legislative body. This is the largest Roman Catholic Church in North America and one of the ten largest churches in the world.[42]

America's Ancient Future

Vatican leaders and rulers throughout the ages have claimed that celestial bodies influence not only people but also the notions of national unity, order, and purpose. The Catholic Church publicly disapproved of astrology; however, "many of the cardinals maintained private astrologers"[43] and some discretely remained as Freemasons. Roman Emperor and philosopher Marcus Aurelius once said, "The world is either a medley of atoms that now intermingle and now are scattered apart, or else it is a unity under law of order and providence."[44]

Many centuries later, President Ronald Reagan, considered one of the great presidents, reportedly believed in the forces of planetary movements and their impact on leadership and greatness. In his 1988 memoir *For the Record*, President Reagan's chief of staff Donald Regan confirmed that the president was continuously devoted to astrology and even scheduled important events according to the movements of heavenly bodies.[45] Caspar Weinberger, President Reagan's long-time friend and his eventual defense secretary, wrote that Reagan moved his 1967 inauguration as the thirty-third governor of California from noon on January 2 to just after midnight on January 3 for astrological reasons.[46] Interestingly, Fred Kleinknecht, the thirty-third degree Masonic leader in Washington, D.C., pointed out the importance of ancient knowledge when he wrote, "Not only have the stars guided the traveler on earth and the seas, but their constellations are archetypes that have been viewed as guides for the lives of men and nations."[47]

Evidence indicates that Presidents Truman, Reagan, George H. W. Bush, and George W. Bush subtly integrated the wisdom, language, and traditions of continuity, believing that earthly order is governed by some kind of universal rhythm and purpose. This recurring theme is implied in classical ideas of duality—like self-interest and moral sentiments, heaven and earth, and good and evil—which were expounded on by Enlightenment thinkers, Freemasons, and other esoteric fraternities like the Rosicrucian Order.

Modern leaders like Ronald Reagan and George W. Bush have also recognized the duality of human nature as evidenced by expressions like good versus "the evil empire" and "the axis of evil." As nature governs human behavior, many realistic observers believe that integration is necessary in order to fulfill the "ancient hope" as the Great Architect of the Universe intended and to bring about unity, order, and providential grace to the United States and the world.[48] As seen in this chapter, the United States was meant to realize this vision through commercial providence and American Mercury.

TEN

The Mercurial Ruler and Sacred Constitution Avenue

> The Sacred Rights of Mankind are not to be
> rummaged for among old parchments or musty
> records. They are written, as with a sunbeam, in
> the whole volume of human nature, by the Hand
> of the Divinity itself; and can never be erased or
> obscured by mortal power.[1]
>
> **Alexander Hamilton**
> First U.S. Secretary of the Treasury

President George Washington's Federal City is a Hamiltonian masterpiece; however, the American project is a triumph of intentional concealment. Compared to the massive pantheon-like national memorial for Thomas Jefferson on the south side of the Tidal Basin, Alexander Hamilton is marginalized in a small but majestic statue located obscurely at the southern end of the U.S. Treasury Department building as if he were an afterthought.

As their opposing backgrounds and visions reflected in constitutional and other debates, Jefferson preferred a decentralized, agrarian democracy with a modest capital city, while Hamilton envisioned a magisterial, centralized capital like London. When Pierre Charles L'Enfant's grander blueprint won over Jefferson's own plan (of just expanding the city of Georgetown in Maryland), the Federalists and Hamilton, who advocated a strong central government with an entrepreneurial spirit and a competitive manufacturing base, believed their vision of a commercial republic would become omnipresent in everyone's daily life.[2] Hamiltonians—who today benefit from his national banking system and ATM services—hardly need a gigantic national memorial to draw attention to Hamilton's ubiquitous legacy. After Jefferson left the White House for Monticello in 1809, the disappointed third president never returned to the Federal City. Nevertheless, he has inspired millions of people who yearn for political freedom and religious rights everywhere.

Yet, they all live in a Hamiltonian world of commerce and finance. Though it may disappoint Jeffersonian-inspired congressional leaders and other vocalists today, the Hamiltonian city acts more like an imperial metropolis motivated by the politics of money and power. The check-and-balance system devised in the Constitution seems to content Jeffersonians as the scheme works through a cycle of dynamic equilibrium in governance. In essence, it is a constant balancing act between Hamiltonian and Jeffersonian instincts. For this very purpose, the legislative and executive bodies watch over each other as the Constitution dictates. This gambit is symbolically expressed through the unobstructed view of the mile-long Pennsylvania Avenue that connects the Capitol to the White House. With their grand design, both Washington and L'Enfant hoped that unhindered passage by way of the "Avenue of the Presidents" might keep members of Congress and the chief executive open and honest about their decisions and actions.

The construction of the oldest cabinet-level building of the Treasury Department became an infringement upon the original plan. According to legend, President Andrew Jackson—who detested legislators but tired of delaying the exact location for the building—stood at a site on the diagonal axis of Pennsylvania Avenue and commanded, "Build it here!" while ignoring the founding intention of maintaining a clear line for watchful eyes between the White House and the Capitol.[3] For some reason, many presidents like Jackson have acted more like "the great architect of the universe" than congressional representatives have, though the power of the republic was vested in Congress. In reflection of human nature, the Hamiltonian republic is more a centralized system than Jefferson's egalitarian democracy. This is why even Jefferson himself acted like a Hamiltonian once he was elected president. For the American system to work effectively, it needs both Founding Fathers: Jefferson to inspire and Hamilton to conquer from each end of Pennsylvania Avenue. Half-way through the avenue on the front of the Old Post

Office Building, a statue of Dr. Benjamin Franklin symbolizes the wisdom of compromise for American progress and freedom.

The conquering spirit of the master is overshadowed by the colossal monument to Jefferson. The effective architectural design has had its own purpose in concealing the esoteric meaning of Hamilton's commercial republic and the Roman god Mercury from normal eyes. The center of the Federal City—which forms the Federal Triangle within the larger triangulation of the Arcturus, Regulus, and Spica constellations that correspond to the White House, the Capitol, and the Washington Monument on earth[4]—is the inner sanctum of the Hamiltonian world.[5] The compact seventy-acre Federal Triangle includes a centralized university of more than twelve massive government buildings bordering Fifteenth Street NW, Pennsylvania Avenue, and Constitution Avenue. The concept of "Providential Agency,"[6] as President Washington often described it, radiates from the heavenly bodies to grace America's founding purpose from the altar of this triangular city. Ancient philosopher Paracelsus wrote:

I make it abundantly clear that everything in which man is subject to the light of Nature comes from the stars. All natural arts and human wisdom are given by the stars, we are the pupils of the stars, and they [are] our teacher. God has ordered everything in the light of Nature, so that we may learn from it.[7]

A relatively hidden display of ancient symbols related to Mercury depicting the celestial bodies prominently epitomizes the providential connection to the center of the Federal City.[8] Renaissance philosopher and physician Paracelsus defined Mercury as "divine wisdom," or "knowledge of the soul" that realizes "the truth, and which has nothing to do with the action of the intellect, that consists in collecting and comparing ideas. All things are hidden within all things. . . . All things are revealed within this vehicle;" as a physical manifestation of the "spirit."[9] The philosopher further clarified, "The whole of Nature is a vehicle and visible manifestation of the wisdom of God; but God Himself cannot be described. He is the universal life, the root of all consciousness and knowledge, and the will of divine wisdom."[10] In light of Paracelsus' description, the Federal Triangle and the city encapsulates such a vehicle— a grand vessel for commerce—for the founding architects to reveal the intention of Nature's God and the commercial mission of the republic.

The Ruler: Mercury

To reflect stellar power in federal government, the buildings of the central campus—among many other triangles in the nation's capital—bear subtle architectural impressions of unity and order through a myriad of Mercurial and other symbols. These zodiac signs and Greco-Roman images are on display to both reveal and conceal the power of Mercury, the ruling planet for the astrological houses of Gemini and Virgo. According to Susan Miller's *Planets and Possibilities*, the feminine Mercury (Virgo) represents analytical skills and critical thinking,[11] which are two of the most useful attributes for a forward-looking nation. The masculine Mercury (Gemini) illustrates the energy and entrepreneurship necessary for material prosperity and human health. Collectively, Mercurial activities are likely to generate entrepreneurship in economic affairs, arouse human passions in arts and literature, and nurture loyalties and bonds in political entities and personalities. These complicated relationships are utterly chaotic and often unhealthy, but the symphony of activities in the nation's capital remains serenely calm beyond rational explanation, almost as if the mythical Mercury invoked therapeutic power with his magic wand, the caduceus. That is the caring and calming nature of American Mercury expressed in the Latin dictum, *Ordo ab chaos*, "Order out of chaos." Interestingly, Freemasonry uses the same expression as its motto.[12]

Familiar with Masonic and esoteric traditions, the founding generation—especially the founding mothers, sisters, and daughters—no doubt appreciated the twin feminine and masculine representations of the Mercurial ruler and its neutral nature (in astrological traditions, Mercury is the only ruling planet that has both feminine and masculine power). The harmonious combination discreetly projects a divine quality upon the Roman god of commerce, who is astrologically a divinity of unity, or the unifier, between not only the sexes but also other divisions like race, ethnicity, and religion.

The Founding Fathers lived in a distinctly masculine and racially-divided world; however, they symbolically expressed a hope for unity within the commercial republic especially in terms of gender. In the male-dominated eighteenth century, women (and slaves) were considered property and had no right to vote until the adoption of the Nineteenth Amendment in 1920 (and the Twenty-fourth Amendment in 1965 for African-Americans). In a compensatory tone, city architects deliberately included a greater number of images and sculptures of beautiful women (typically holding bundles of harvest or involved in domestic affairs) than those of muscular men in the Federal City. In a forceful letter to her husband on March 31, 1776, the brilliant and devoted Abigail Adams cleverly warned, "I desire you would remember the ladies . . . We are determined to foment a rebellion, and will not hold ourselves bound by any laws in which we have no voice or representation."[13] In her book *Founding Mothers*, veteran journalist Cokie Roberts recognizes that the founding mothers, wives, sisters, and daughters were noticeably left behind by history.[14] The remarkable women of that time—Abigail Adams, Mercy Warren, Deborah Franklin, Eliza Pinckney, Martha Washington, and others—made enormous personal sacrifices during the Revolutionary War and provided valuable intellectual contributions in other affairs of the infant republic.[15] Striking a balance between the feminine and masculine, the portrait of a virgin as a feminine archetype of Mercury (the only female figure in the entire zodiac) signaled gender equality within the new nation. This was at least an attempt by the architects to inject an impartial equilibrium into city planning to project American destiny.

The racial issue was more troubling. Nevertheless, a number of free slaves fought in the Revolutionary War and worked closely with the Founding Fathers; among the most noted was Benjamin Banneker. By no means were these enlightened men—including plantation and slave owners like Thomas Jefferson and George Washington—racists. The inherited socio-economic system and prevailing culture prevented them in acting otherwise for the benefit of the slave population and mutual economic survival. Indeed, the writings of Jefferson and Washington support this historical fact. On a limestone relief on the Federal Trade Commission building, there exists a white trader exchanging a pot of money with an African merchant for an ivory tusk. The other accompanying image is an exchange of a bundle of grain between a female and her mate to depict the natural order of a commercially-constituted world that binds people together. Slavery and gender issues were then an accepted fact of colonial life; nevertheless, the forces of commerce seem to have closed the gap between the powerful and the powerless.

President Washington and his other Masonic brethren understood, from the teachings of the mystic school of Pythagoras, that the Federal Triangle is a cosmic connection to the three fixed stars that triangulate Virgo,[16] whose blessings unify the city, serve as its celestial protector, and most importantly, sustain its commercial vision through Mercury the Unifier. These facts demonstrate that the founding "intentions" are eternally powerful as they were also the intentions of the Creator. The symbolic portrayal of the Pythagorean Y on the Potomac delta, the square-shaped Federal District, and the mythical images of Mercury (both Virgo and Gemini) were deliberate acts. The convictions of the Founding Fathers collectively transcended diversity to forge unity as best they knew given the actionable knowledge and intelligence they acquired as mostly self-taught men.

When the architectural plan of the capital by Washington, L'Enfant, Banneker, and Andrew Ellicott was conceived, the commercial destiny embedded in the U.S. Constitution was figuratively born. In affirmation of the "commerce clause" in the Constitution, the celestial triangle sanctified the physical manifestation of the commercial republic. It reveals that these purpose-driven Founding Fathers employed the power of ancient symbols to conceal America's Hamiltonian vision, which is shrouded in Commercial Providence. These secrets are revealed only to those who actually seek them. As an associate of Masonic brethren in both America and France, the versatile Thomas Jefferson was fully aware of the grand scheme of Mercurial activities and endorsed the commercial mission.[17] Understanding the secret intentions of symbols, Jefferson said, "Commerce with all nations, alliance with none, should be our motto."[18] After he magnanimously accepted the rejection of his plan for the city, Jefferson worked closely with Washington and his other architects to crystallize their vision.

Using the instrument of arcane language, commercial symbolism was embodied in Constitution Avenue as a modern-day communiqué to "brand" the commercial republic (or to "market" American Mercury like a product, in the nomenclature of contemporary marketing management). The cooperative workmanship is further exemplified by the balancing nature of designing commercial institutions for both regulatory and trade promotion, as well as in the message of unity put forward by advancing the American idea that trade is a critically important tool for world peace. These ideas are reflected in America's cause for freedom, which began with the Boston Tea Party and the Revolutionary War.

When Jefferson realized himself that he was a natural Hamiltonian like other Founding Fathers whose commercial interests mattered dearly to them, the third president promoted "peace and commerce" as an integral component of the nation's business model. In a letter to William

Short, who was his protégé or "adoptive son"[19] in New York, Jefferson described the country's 1790 commercial emblem as "a Columbia (a fine, female figure) delivering the emblems of peace and commerce, to a Mercury, with a legend 'Peace and Commerce' circumscribed, and the date of our republic, IV July MDCCLXXVI, subscribed as an exergum."[20] Jefferson's meticulous inscription confirms the elaborately protracted depiction of Mercury as the messenger of peace and commerce, as well as the nation's celestial patron. This providential connection is openly hidden as a "public secret" in the nation's capital architecture.

A Sacred and Celestial Avenue

The prime denominator of the city on the south side of the Federal Triangle is Constitution Avenue NW, which runs from the northern side of the Capitol property westward toward the Potomac River through Foggy Bottom near the U.S. State Department and the new home of U.S. Institute of Peace (Figure 10.1). The mid-point is the intersection of the east-west and north-south axes at the south end of Ellipse Road of the White House campus. This is the zero-mile marker of the square District, where L'Enfant proposed an equestrian statue in honor of George Washington.[21] Instead of erecting another statue next to the Washington Monument, however, a momentous Masonic obelisk was constructed in Alexandria, Virginia.

The north-south axis begins at the northern center of Lafayette Park, adjacent to the White House. The park has five major statues of illustrious Freemasonry war heroes. Legendary General Andrew Jackson stands at the heart of the rectangular park while four foreign generals are positioned at each corner: the Marquis de Lafayette, Friedrich Wilhelm von Steuben, Jean Baptiste de Rochambeau, and Thaddeus Kosciuszko, who fought the Revolutionary War (Figure 10.2). The horse-riding Jackson raises his hat to salute the regiment at the victorious Battle of New Orleans during the war of 1812; he later became a lionized U.S. president. General Marquis de Lafayette was a French nobleman and a close friend of George Washington. German-born Major General Friedrich Wilhelm von Steuben established the military training program for the Continental Army. After the Revolutionary War, French Major General Jean Baptiste de Rochambeau served as the Marshal of France and established a friendship between the two nations. Polish Brigadier General

Thaddeus Kosciuszko was an engineer in the Revolutionary War and built fortifications at Saratoga and West Point in New York and along the Delaware River. These leaders were the most notable among the thirty-three generals under Washington's command.

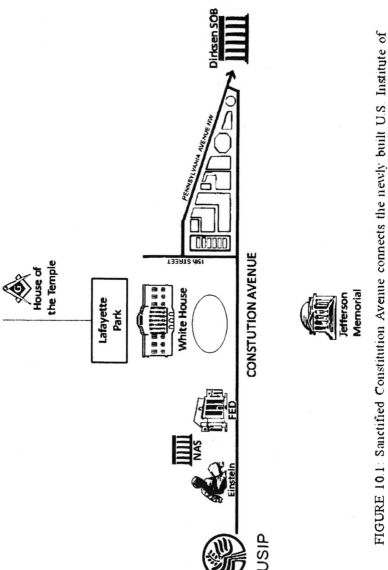

FIGURE 10.1: Sanctified Constitution Avenue connects the newly built U.S. Institute of Peace with the Andrew Mellon Zodiac Water Fountain and the Dirksen Senate Office Building.

The emblematic terminus of Sixteenth Street, which delineates a hidden power structure, creates a type of meridian that aligns with the White House at 1600 Pennsylvania Avenue and elevates northward through Meridian Hill Park. This is a major feature of L'Enfant's initial plan, as the original architects had intended for the longitudinal line to replace the Prime Meridian in London. In his *Egypt on the Potomac*, historian Anthony Browder notes that the city correctly aligns with the heavens so that specific celestial bodies may properly orient and favorably influence the corresponding streets, buildings, and landmarks.[22]

FIGURE 10.2: The famous Lafayette Park, also known as President's Park, immortalizes a group of Masonic war heroes (clockwise from top left): Friedrich Wilhelm von Steuben, Thaddeus Kosciuszko, the Marquis de Lafayette, and Jean Baptiste de Rochambeau surrounded by President Andrew Jackson.

In fact, many of the buildings on the symbolically, spiritually, and mythologically powerful Meridian corridor feature a wide range of meaningful Greco-Roman, Italian, and Egyptian-style architecture. The beautiful headquarters of the Supreme Council of the Southern Jurisdiction of the Ancient and Accepted Rite of Freemasonry is located just thirteen blocks north of the White House.[23] The entrance of the Masonic Temple exhibits a pair of sphinx-like sculptures of lion bodies bearing the heads of men (Figure 10.3). The twin monuments represent the symbols of "wisdom" and "power" in a perfected man, whom Plato described as a "philosopher-king" in his ideal republic.[24] Architect John Russell Pope modeled the Temple after the tomb of King Mausolus at Halicarnassus, one of the seven wonders of the ancient world (located in modern Bodrum, a southern seaport of Turkey).[25] Directly south of the White House, an imaginary Sixteenth Street extends to the Jefferson Memorial, which was also designed by Pope. The astronomical significance around the vicinity of the park and the street—along with the supernatural powers of the ancient symbolism contained in the architectural designs—reinforces a mythological tradition of power linked to the Federal City and the Meridian corridor.

FIGURE 10.3: Two solid limestone sphinxes guard the Sixteenth Street, NW entrance to the Masonic Temple symbolizing Wisdom (with eyes half-closed on the right) and Power (with eyes open on the left).

Similar to the Constitution itself, the east-west running Constitution Avenue symbolically unifies all conflicting and complex interrelations of the federal government. The Constitution and its namesake avenue are both a literal and figurative manifestation of a "grand central station" of self-interests and moral choices, as reflected in the Pythagorean Y. The avenue was Pierre L'Enfant's *Via Sacra*. The roadway was meant to represent the sacred or spiritual source of the Constitution in which the United States is not governed by a lineage of hereditary families or tyrannical powers, but by the idea of a democratic republic led by meritocracy. The sanctified avenue—a conglomerate of very special zodiac signs and prominently placed Virgoan and Mercurial images displayed from east to west[26]—underscores the purpose of the commerce-bestowed republic.

Similar to Rome's *Via Sacra*, the hallowed avenue in the Federal City is "cosmologically sacrosanct—confirming that it is a sacred road, linked with the stars,"[27] according to British author David Ovason. The consecrated avenue parallels the European-like, spacious boulevard of the Washington Mall. In his original design, L'Enfant called it the blessed "Grand Avenue."[28] However, after studying L'Enfant's plan, President Washington named the narrower avenue that connects the Federal House (the Capitol) to the President's Palace (the White House) Pennsylvania Avenue, and suggested that this mile-long corridor be developed into a thoroughfare called Grand Avenue.[29] For directly linking the two branches of government, the president described Pennsylvania Avenue as the "most magnificent and most convenient."[30] The revitalized "Avenue of the Presidents,"[31] as the late Senator Daniel Patrick Moynihan called it, forms the hypotenuse of the Pythagorean triangle of the Federal City center. It is the commercial and ceremonial heart of the capital, while Constitution Avenue remains the nation's *Via Sacra*.

Celestial Constitution Avenue has functioned as a sort of public foyer for the cathedral-like city, along with a significant number of zodiac signs at its east and west ends. Capital architects purposefully integrated a vast array of astrological symbols along the east-west passageway to reflect the position of the nation's capital under the dominion of Virgo and her planetary ruler, Mercury. The Capitol itself displays a considerable number of esoteric symbols—including sculptures like the Mithraic zodiac, *The Car of History*. The Library of Congress also contains many astrological symbols, including the radiant zodiac in the Great Hall. Historian Ovason identifies an impressive collection of more than 23 complete zodiacs and over 1000 astrological and planetary symbols in government buildings and other less noticeable landmarks, like the Andrew Mellon "Zodiac" Water Foundation.[32]

One of the most noteworthy is a statue of President James Garfield, erected in 1887 by John Quincy Adams Ward, who appears as if watching over Constitution Avenue. Not too distant from the corner of Pennsylvania and Constitution Avenues, the colossal bronze statue stands atop a circular granite pedestal installed near the southwest face of the Capitol, at First Street and Maryland Avenue. Beneath the twentieth president, three heroic reclining figures also cast in bronze symbolize the important phases of his life: scholar, soldier, and then leader. This is not just an elaborate memorial to the martyred president (the second president to be assassinated after President Abraham Lincoln); it is an embodiment that illustrates various aspects of his most gifted and tragically shortened life (after six months in office), and which points to his Masonic background.

To honor this distinguished Master Mason, the sculpture's pedestal features both astrological signs and planets. Just above the head of the scholar is a bronze relief that displays the earth (a map of the Americas) encircled by the orbits of multiple small rings. A larger ring of zodiac symbols borders the outer area, which is decorated with acacia leaves and a compass. Drawn from Isaac Newton's astronomical language, the "Planetary Globe"[33] depicts certain planets that signify the ascendancy of Virgo, according to Ovason.[34] In Freemasonry, the acacia plant symbolizes death, the compass points to a measured direction, and Virgo signifies the birthing of new life. The esoterically-meaningful symbols ingeniously connect the president's life and the ruler of Virgo, while the ruling Mercury demonstrates the significance of the nation's commercial vision. From this elevated location, the commanding executive has a watchful eye—reminiscent of providential influence—on Constitution Avenue, as if from an altar of a cathedral.

From East to West: The Dirksen Senate Office Building

On the east side of Constitution Avenue NW lies the Dirksen Senate Office Building—one of the points on the grid originally outlined by L'Enfant and dedicated to former Senator Everett McKinley Dirksen from Illinois. Dirksen was an illustrious 33° Freemason who attended the University of Minnesota and built a distinguished, 36-year political career that culminated as Senate Minority Leader and champion of the Civil Rights Bill in the 1960s.[35] There are six uniquely designed conference rooms in his seemingly Masonic-inspired building, each adorned with ornate ceiling panels containing thirty-eight astrological images. Altogether, this congressional hall bears more than twelve full zodiacs as well as a number of beautiful signs and depictions of virgins and other arcane sculptures to total 228 zodiacal and Virgoan images.[36] As home to the Senate committees on budget, finance, banking, commerce, energy and the environment, among others, the Dirksen building is itself a powerful cosmic statement in honor of Masonic brethren.

For a regular visitor, the cryptic symbols in the Dirksen Building seem to have been either concealed or dismissed as having no apparent meaning at all. When novice Senator Joe Biden from Delaware (who would be elected as vice president to Barack Obama thirty-four years later) officially inquired about the symbols in 1974, a researcher on the Art and Research Staff in the Capitol responded that the symbols "were just decorative devices that have been in use for many years in the Capitol Hill buildings."[37] The inquisitive Catholic senator was misinformed. Without an integrative understanding of the Masonic symbolism and other esoteric knowledge, these arcane images indeed appeared meaningless "decorative devices" for the uninitiated. The "unseen" power of the building is present, however, in depictions of American industry—shipping, farming, manufacturing, mining, and lumbering—on bronze spandrels in the third and fourth-floor windows of this seven-story mystical building, which bears the following inscription beneath the west pediment on the First Street facade: "The Senate is the Living Symbol of Our Union of States." Overall, the integrative power of the zodiacs seems to narrate what is seen for the normal eye.

Besides the Dirksen Senate Office Building, the four major landmarks along Constitution Avenue west of the White House form a range of similes derived from ancient archetypes of heavenly harmony and national unity. They include the Federal Reserve Bank, the National Academy of Sciences, the celestial statue of Albert Einstein, and the latest addition of the U.S. Institute of Peace building on the western end of Constitution Avenue. These landmarks are bookends to the ecliptic—the path of America's sacred avenue, which itself is a testament to the fact that the United States is governed by the Constitution and not a monarch or hereditary ruler. Indeed, it is certain that the city planners emphasized the importance of our Constitution in universally symbolic language.

The Federal Reserve Bank

The outwardly austere-looking, mysterious Federal Reserve Bank (generally known as the Fed and established in 1913) building between Twentieth and Twenty-first Streets has an elegant interior design. The four-story H-shaped building forms east and west courtyards on either side of the crossbar of the H facing the two streets. (A fifth story was added to the center section of the crossbar in the 1970s). The Art Deco building, designed by architect Paul Philippe Cret in 1937, was named after former Fed chairman Marriner S. Eccles by an Act of Congress in 1982. In her column for the *Washington News* on February 3, 1938, First Lady Eleanor Roosevelt commented on the building:

> I think the building exterior is very beautiful and have admired it often, but I was equally impressed by the interior. . . . I gathered they had, perhaps, been criticized for thinking too much about beauty and too little about utility. Surely, this country had learned that we must meet both needs in public buildings. . . . Unless we satisfy our sense of beauty in a public building, we have failed in one of its most important functions. . . . When Mr. [Adolph] Miller [chairman of the Fed's building committee] told me he felt there was a fine esprit de corps among the people [Freemasons] who work in the buildings, I was not at all surprised, for I think our surroundings have a great deal to do with our mental attitudes and I believe they affect our characters and dispositions more than we think.[38]

The statues on the exterior, at the north entrance of C Street and the south entrance to Constitution Avenue, reflect Mercury's magical power. Inside the Bank's north and south entrances to the atrium, a black and white checkered floor replicates the traditional design of Masonic lodges. The beautiful starry sky glass of the domes of two ceiling lamps at each entrance are etched with the twelve signs of the zodiac. These images, which were designed by American sculptor Sidney Waugh in 1937, signify the all-encompassing nature of the independent institution that is associated most often with Alexander Hamilton, architect of the commercial republic and the nation's financial system. The images of maidens wearing halos imply a divine ordination—an overtly Christian overtone perhaps intended to evoke association with the Virgin Mary.

There are a number of other Mercurial signs on the windows as well. Virgo, the feminine figure of Mercury, who holds a wand—the sacred caduceus—in her left hand while her right rests on the seal of the Federal Reserve Board, highlights this wondrous power. If Mercury is the planetary ruler of Virgo who in turn rules the nation, the Fed is an all-encompassing power embedded in money—and a Mercurial representation of the independent agency of U.S. monetary (and interest rate) policy. The monetary system, which is synonymous with the evermore powerful Fed, is the lifeblood of national prosperity. The exploitation of the caduceus, which is often used as an emblem of medicine, figuratively denotes the perfection of economic health.

The image of Virgo traditionally represents the seven fields of the liberal arts and sciences: arithmetic, astronomy, dialectic, geometry, grammar, music, and rhetoric.[39] In classical literature, these are all considered the branches of any national economy, and are represented by the integrative power of Mercury's intellectual and enterprising personality. The etched-glass ceiling of the Eccles Building atrium has an abstract image of the official seal of the Federal Reserve System that includes twelve regional branches. The official seal depicts an eagle and its shield encircling 48 stars for each state in the Union (Alaska and Hawaii were added in the 1950s). These icons collectively symbolize the productivity and stability of the all-inclusive but diverse American economy.

The National Academy of Sciences

On the west side of the Federal Reserve Bank building is the National Academy of Sciences. The entrance to the Academy features an illustration of Aristotle and his student Alexander the Great. Aristotle, who was a pupil of Plato, favored a scientific and rational approach to understanding the laws of nature (as compared to Plato's tendencies toward the mystical).[40] A brainchild of President Abraham Lincoln, the National Academy searches for evidence-based, scientific approaches to the country's problems. With the influence of Western philosophy, the Academy is holistic in its approach to resolve issues, as depicted by three zodiac signs on each of the four bronze doors inside the main foyer. The apex of the dome in the Great Hall is a conventional sun encircled by the zodiac symbols of eight planets and the inscription: "Ages and Cycles of Nature in Ceaseless Sequence Moving."[41] The ancient images in the eight diamond-shaped figures represent anthropology, astronomy, botany, chemistry, geology, mathematics, physics, and zoology. The comprehensive outlook—history, science, and a universal approach—highlights the nation's rational, logical, and scientific orientation.

The Albert Einstein Memorial

At the southwest corner of the Academy building stands a memorial to the eminent scientific figure of the twentieth century: Dr. Albert Einstein. Unveiled on April 22, 1979 to celebrate his centennial birthday, Einstein sits on a semi-circular bench contemplating a diagram of constellations and the arrangements of major stars and planets at his feet.[42] More than 2700 metal studs inserted into the ground replicate the sun, moon, planets, stars, and other heavenly bodies positioned on the dedication date.[43]

Marveling at the zodiacal map, Einstein holds a paper on which three mathematical equations are inscribed: the photoelectric effect, the theory of general relativity, and the equivalence of energy and matter.[44] He was the genius who unlocked some of the great mysteries of the universe and its natural order; what the Founding Fathers described as the Great Architect of the Universe.

The U.S. Institute of Peace

The newest addition to the National Mall is the U.S. Institute of Peace located next to the U.S. State Department at the northwest corner of Constitution Avenue and Twenty-third Street NW. As the western entrance to Constitution Avenue from the Commonwealth of Virginia, the Peace headquarters occupies some of the most prominent real estate in the nation's capital. The congressionally-mandated institute has a five-story edifice and an impressively curved roof shaped like the wings of a dove.

The idea of a Peace Academy goes back to President George Washington, who called for a "proper peace establishment"[45] for the training of the militia in a letter to the Confederation Congress in 1783. Seven years later, Dr. Benjamin Rush, a signatory of the Declaration of Independence, proposed a Peace Office similar to the War Office and the appointment of a "secretary of peace" for humanitarian purposes.[46] Obviously, their purposes differed; however, the nominal intention continued in various formulations over the years.

In 1955, President Dwight Eisenhower, for example, appointed former Minnesota Governor Harold Stassen as his "secretary of peace."[47] In order to establish a permanent institution, Senators Jennings Randolph,

Mark Hatfield, and Spark Matsunaga created a U.S. Commission on Proposals for the National Academy of Peace and Conflict Resolution in 1978. Under the motto "Peace through Strength," Congress formed the Institute in 1985. The circular- and square-shaped architecture of the soft-looking, white building signifies the terrestrial-celestial connection. The deliberate location at the sun-setting corner of Constitution Avenue also communicates figuratively America's ultimate purpose: eventual world peace by way of the U.S. Constitution.

A Commercial Empire

In a global community of sovereign nations, America's Manifest Destiny derives not from acquiring more lands, but by expanding and promoting trade as dictated in the commerce clause of the U.S. Constitution. The arcane images intentionally carved on stones and sculpturally embedded in these landmarks are purpose-driven esoteric ornaments in the commerce-like cathedral of sanctified Constitution Avenue. Borrowing language from the first president, Victorian novelist Charles Dickens wrote an epithet of "intentions" for George Washington's "distances" in the Federal City that proved truly prophetic. With America's exceptionalism, the nation has always endeavored to build "a territorial and commercial empire"[48] for the United States; however, that exceptionalism radiates from Providence to build an Empire of Commerce—not necessarily an expansion of territory as understood in a traditional Manifest Destiny view.

Toward this end, Constitution Avenue is more symbolically expressive than the literal language of the U.S. Constitution. The distinguished British visitor further acknowledged that the planners of the city—Washington, L'Enfant, Ellicott, and Banneker—aimed for "greatness," like that of the Roman Empire.[49] That greatness started from trade with other nations. America's Roman Empire then presents a direct mirror image of Jefferson's Empire of Liberty through a blueprint of the Hamiltonian playbook for Jeffersonian ends.

In addition to the celebrated Constitution Avenue, the actual mechanism to implement the Jeffersonian "vision" and the Hamiltonian "mission" is subtly entrenched in the Federal Triangle. The Founding Fathers believed that a mantle of celestial protection for the commercial republic to achieve its permanent peace was fixed within the hovering

Virgo constellation, which is locked in the triangulated sky by the stars
Arcturus, Regulus, and Spica. The earthly replica of this celestial triangle
is the seat of mystical power that intends for an invisible commercial
empire to succeed globally as God's crucible nation. The absence of
obvious Hamiltonian symbolism in the nation's capital stands in direct
contrast to the omnipresence of the Founding Father's influence on our
day-to-day lives, resonating relentlessly beneath the radars of Jefferson's
inspiring idealism.

ELEVEN

Altar of Empire: The Virgoan Federal Triangle

A city with free ports that hummed with commerce and
creativity . . . if there had to be city walls, the walls
had doors and the doors were open to anyone with
the will and heart to get here.[1]

President Ronald Reagan

The founding conviction for a commercial empire is physically expressed in the Federal Triangle. As indicated before, the triangle is a
residual of an outer triangle created by the three fixed stars—Arcturus,
Regulus, and Spica—and superimposed over the hypotenuse of Pennsylvania Avenue; its adjacent denominator, Constitution Avenue; and its
opposite denominator, Fifteenth Street (Figure 11.1). This altar of commercial power is dedicated to the American Mercury who represents the

Roman god of commerce—the ruler of Virgo that is triangulated by the stars in the sky over the nation's capital.

Pierre L'Enfant's terrestrial plan for the capital as conceived has been modified over the years. Nonetheless, the *original intention* carved in the stones and depicted in the arts and architectural designs of the federal buildings had far *greater significance* than the modifications that ensued years later. The plan was said to have a divine DNA to replicate cosmic order on earth. Such a belief system was associated with the Great Architect of the Universe, who operates as a generic divinity common to all religions and universally shared by Freemasons. The genetic codification of ancient religious and wisdom traditions in Freemasonry has acted as the high priest of America's national religion, which amalgamates every religious tradition to make the United States an inclusive nation safe for commerce and democracy.

FIGURE 11.1: The Federal Triangle includes a web of building complexes and monuments: **A.** Department of Commerce, **B.** Wilson Building (District Building), **C.** Ronald Regan Building, **D.** Environmental Protection Agency (Labor Building), **E.** Andrew Mellon Auditorium (Departmental Auditorium), **F.** Environmental Protection Agency (Interstate Commerce Commission Building), **G.** Ariel Rios Building (Post Office Department Building), **H.** Old Post Office Pavilion, **I.** Internal Revenue Service Building, **J.** Department of Justice Building, **K.** National Archives, **L.** Apex Building (Federal Trade Commission), and **M.** Andrew Mellow Zodiac Water Fountain.

Despite times of change and progress, the original concept remained intact as the foundation; thus, it continued to be more important than the American odyssey for its eventual destiny. For instance, the compact area now known as the Federal Triangle has also evolved over time. Until the Civil War era, the Central Market at the east end of the triangle was famous for its slave trade (the institution of slavery was abolished from its corridors in 1850). The western portion was a popular red light district; the word "hooker" derived from General Joseph Hooker and his men of the Union Army who reportedly frequented neighborhood brothels.[2] The vicinity was for a long time a place for congregating prostitutes and slave auctioneers. Still, these historical facts did not tarnish the nation and its reputation; subsequent architects continued to find inspiration in the power of the founding intention, the moral imperative, and the cause for freedom.

The construction of the Federal Triangle has noticeably changed the personality, status, and human character of the place. The original design has three precise geometric angles that make up the Virgoan campus:

- The first lies to the east, formed by the twenty-degree angle created by Constitution and Pennsylvania Avenues at the Andrew Mellon Memorial "Zodiac" Water Fountain.

- The second corner points to the northwest, which is formed by the seventy-degree angle created by Pennsylvania Avenue and Fifteenth Street.

- To the south, the ninety-degree junction of Constitution Avenue and Fifteenth Street creates the third and final angle.

With respect to the inner and outer triangles, author David Ovason describes the city as positioned in "such a way that it is in harmony with the heavens . . . a city in perpetual prayer. It is a city built on the recognition that every human activity is in need of the sanctification of the spiritual world," symbolizing "the light of the living stars."[3]

First appearing on the American flag in 1777, the five points of the pentagram were chosen as "living stars" to indicate the five cardinal limbs of man—the head, two legs, and two arms—as depicted in Leonardo da Vinci's *Vitruvian Man* (Figure 11.2). These also represent the five elements of the material world that provide creative energy—earth, water, fire, wind, and ether. The five-pointed star symbolically links earthly matters (in da Vinci's square) with celestial bodies (in his circle) and blesses the commercial affairs of the American Mercury within the Federal Triangle. In the minds of the original architects, this purpose-driven design—part of the ancient mystery school of Pythagoras—was a meaningful reflection of their own collective belief.

EARTH

FIGURE 11.2: Leonardo da Vinci's *Vitruvian Man's* five cardinal limbs represent the five elements of earth, water, fire, wind, and ether.

The federal workforce in this commercial campus-like building complex set the original intention in motion to eventually form a "united states" of America (beginning with the former thirteen colonies), and expanded it to forge a globalized community through international trade and commerce. Though the construction of the Federal Triangle took a number of phases and several modifications, the elaborate design of L'Enfant's plan has remained relatively unchanged in order to depict America's founding commercial mission to the world. The seemingly unseen (occult) connection between the celestial design and its reflective Mercurial workforce also appears to signify a perpetual contention between private interests and public goods (that parallels the human desires and the divine wisdom of the Pythagorean Y, as well as Adam Smith's notions of self-interest and moral sentiments). Andrew Mellon, renowned financier and philanthropic leader of the Federal Triangle's renovation efforts, characterized the original scheme as a "beautiful harmonious building" that expresses "the soul of America."[4] That sentiment by Mellon, an illustrious Freemason, is the essence of American Mercury and national harmony.

The McMillan Plan

The inspiration that gripped the city's original planners began to languish over time. L'Enfant's initial plan had been immediately adapted somewhat by his successor, Andrew Ellicott. After that, however, the plan was "mutilated by successive generations of scheming speculators and ignorant politicians."[5] By the late 1800s, the triangle was known more as a place of infectious diseases and for its many bars, brothels, and theaters than as a center of federal government offices, prestigious banks, and luxury hotels.

During the Civil War, the city grew enormously. President Ulysses Grant appointed Alexander Shepherd to manage the newly established Board of Public Works to beautify roads, construct bridges, and convert Tiber Creek into drainage for waste. Throughout this period, engineers used landfills to create more space for the Jefferson, Lincoln, and other war memorials in the artificially-expanded Mall region.

On the eve of the centennial anniversary of the nation's capital in 1901 during the Theodore Roosevelt administration, Senator James McMillan of Michigan formed a committee—famously known as the McMillan Commission—to complete the design of the Federal City as envisioned by L'Enfant and President George Washington.[6] The Commission was determined to maintain the original design and purpose with federal patronage.

Supported by President Roosevelt, a fellow Mason, McMillan's plan harmoniously integrated the original architectural concept that had included a wide range of freestanding monuments, diverse sculptures, classical architecture, and esoteric and allegoric themes.[7] Masonic in nature, these themes edified the mindsets of the three original designers. They elegantly fit into the whole Plan, which may be summarized by this equation: "Washington + Planning = L'Enfant 1791 + McMillan 1902."[8] The equation reflects the sum of its parts to convey a more unifying and powerful message; likewise, subtle yet overtly manifested symbolism has remained in the nation's capital architecture. In particular, the Federal Triangle projects the universal and expansive power of the United States government, and the potential to use this power for greater public good and commercial success. Like Senator McMillan's own Scottish heritage—born in Canada and successful in Michigan industry, commerce, and eventually in American politics—the triangle presents a cross-cultural unity and continuity for successive generations to assume ste-

wardship of advancing American destiny through commercial endeavors.[9]

The construction that began with the McMillan Commission halted
during the Great Depression. President Franklin D. Roosevelt used his
Works Progress Administration (WPA) to put unemployed workers back
to work on public projects, including federal buildings, in the 1930s. The
WPA also hired a number of artists and sculptures to paint and beautify
these buildings. A commercial campus of government buildings was finally completed when the Ronald Reagan Building and International
Trade Center officially opened in 1998, just before the bicentennial celebration of the capital.

Drawing on material from James Wasserman, David Ovason, and
various government documents, a descriptive analysis of the major building complexes in the Triangle is presented below to illustrate the
commercial nature of the Federal City.[10] To that end, the following section starts with the Mellon Memorial Fountain on the eastern side of
Constitution Avenue NW, runs westward to Fifteenth Street, and finally
ends up at the Reagan Trade Center (see Figure 11.1).

The Andrew Mellon Memorial "Zodiac" Water Fountain

Situated across from the National Gallery of Art, the congressionally-mandated memorial fountain is a welcome sign for visitors to the
Federal Triangle. Designed by American sculptor Sidney Waugh and
dedicated in 1952, it is one of the most elegant of the capital's prized
possessions. Its namesake was yet another prominent Freemason, who
was also one of the wealthiest and most powerful men in America: the
late Scottish industrialist Andrew Mellon. In addition to his eleven years
as U.S. Treasury secretary and a brief stint as ambassador to the United
Kingdom, Mellon donated $15 million and a personal collection of art,
including the famous "Washington Family" portrait of "a plan of the new
Federal City."[11] To recognize his public service and philanthropic endeavors, Congress passed legislation to build the memorial bowl in his
honor.

The Mellon Water Fountain has twelve prominently marked, zodiacal relief signs etched into its base. The eastern focal point of the
fountain's bowl clearly depicts Aries—the first astrological sign—facing
the sunrise, symbolizing a source of energy and daily renewal for the

Federal City. The masculine symbol of Libra—a pair of scales balancing from horns representing justice, the Greek goddess Themis—adorns the west side of the fountain directly opposite the Federal Trade Commission (FTC) building. Libra projects the city's commercial purpose, suggesting government regulate commerce to avoid the excessive greed and hubris of Wall Street, to advance social prosperity, and to maintain economic equilibrium. Both the Pennsylvania and Constitution Avenue sides of the fountain bowl are precisely calibrated to signify a meaningful connection to the zodiac signs: the image of Virgo is oriented toward the northwest-running Pennsylvania Avenue (which links the White House to the Capitol), while the Aries-Libra nexus of the Mellon zodiac faces the domineering east-west Constitution Avenue. Though it may seem arcane, the symbolic symmetry of the Mellon Water Fountain, also known as the "Zodiac Fountain," acts as an obscure, yet purpose-driven, metaphysical "Grand Central Station" of the Virgoan Federal City (Figure 11.3).

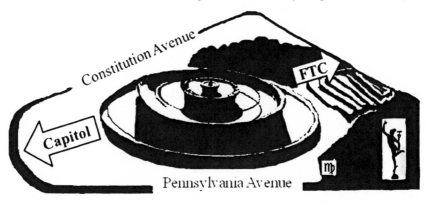

FIGURE 11.3: The Andrew Mellow Zodiac Water Foundation is the mystical "Grand Central Station" that diverts the morning sun rays from the Capitol to the Federal Triangle through the Federal Trade Commission (FTC).

In a *Washington Post* article, Paul Richard describes the fountain as "veiled by the trembling translucent sheet of water that falls from its rounded rim. . . . It's also astrological."[12] Richard further elaborates on the nature of this celestial-terrestrial landmark:

Behind its shimmering veil, in bronze in high relief, are the twelve signs of the zodiac. Each March at the vernal equinox (when one straight line connects the First Point of Aries, the fountain and the center of the Sun), the first rays of the morning hit the fountain where they ought to, at the sign of Aries the Ram (parentheses original).[13]

The Zodiac Fountain exemplifies the unity between stellar power and commercial power. It maintains the sacred, and often subtle, nature of the symbolism rooted in the Masonic and esoteric traditions honored by L'Enfant, Ellicott, and Washington. As fellow fraternity brothers, business leaders like Paul Revere, McMillan, and Mellon illustrate the renewal and continuity of the founding architects' commercial vision carved in stone.

The Federal Trade Commission Building

Adjacent to the Mellon "Zodiac" Fountain, at the western edge, is the Federal Trade Commission (FTC). Famously known as the "Apex Building," the FTC is deliberately situated on a triangular plot of land bordered by Constitution and Pennsylvania Avenues, and Sixth and Seventh Streets. One of the last buildings constructed during the Depression years of the 1930s, the Classical Revival style of the architecture forms the zenith of the Federal Triangle.[14]

The triangular apex points resolutely to the Goddess of Liberty on the dome of the Capitol. The corner of the Virgo constellation that extends toward the star Regulus also appears over the Capitol, reaffirming the terrestrial-celestial connection. Masonic symbolism and astral alignments are features purposefully built into the triangle's design, while the federal buildings were nominally planned to serve large clusters of the federal workforce. Their dedication to (or association with) the ancient goddess and stars is physically depicted in the architectural designs of these buildings.

Architect Edward Bennett designed the Apex Building to feature a rounded Ionic colonnade that unwinds in the direction of the Capitol from the narrow east side. The south side of the FTC doorway, facing Constitution Avenue, bears the image of a man and a woman holding a bundle of corn—a symbol of the nourishing spirit of Nature's God. A likeness of two men—an African ivory merchant and a Caucasian trader—decorates the west end, while a Virgoan illustration of a corn maiden is located on the northern side.[15] These external artistic expressions convey the involvement of the FTC with the economic life of the nation and its international trade relations.

A pair of nearly identical, allegorical figures—collectively titled "Man Controlling Trade"—is located at the east ends of the two avenues (Figure 11.4). Exercising his artistic expression, creator Michael Lantz exaggerated the freestanding depiction of two muscular men struggling to rein in two horses. The sculptures themselves are widely recognized by classical historians as symbols of the unruliness of trade and the role of government in regulating sometimes unpredictable behavior—a kindred reminder of Adam Smith's notions about self-interest and the voices of morality.

These sculptures have become informal emblems for the FTC. According to the Federal Trade Commission Act of 1914, its mission is to promote "consumer protection" and to prevent "anti-competitive" business practices.[16] Each of these symbols demonstrates the Mercurial character of trade and commerce—and modification of the nature of concentrated monopolistic power in the business transactions of a nation that strives for equality and opportunity for all.

"Man Controlling Trade"

FIGURE 11.4: The constant struggle between Hamiltonian drives for free enterprise and Jeffersonian sentiments for moral constraint is symbolized by an unruly horse and a strong man for balance and American progress.

The National Archives

In the early nineteenth century, the north side of Constitution Avenue between Seventh and Ninth Streets was home to the disgraceful, slave-auctioning Central Market. By the middle of the century, many progressive-minded legislators argued that the nearby Goddess of Liberty on the Capitol dome appeared to endorse the slave trade—an act they believed wholly inconsistent with the principles of freedom and democracy.[17] Following widespread lobbying by scholars and historians for many years, the Central Market eventually transformed into the massive neoclassical structure housing the National Archives.[18] The legacy of the Market, so closely associated with the Civil War and Emancipation, was inscribed in history when President Herbert Hoover described the location at the cornerstone ceremony in 1933, saying, "This temple of our history will appropriately be one of the most beautiful buildings in America, an expression of the American soul."[19]

The man largely responsible for designing the National Archives was a New York architect named John Russell Pope who had already made a name for himself designing other great buildings in Washington such as the National Gallery of Art, the Thomas Jefferson Memorial, and more importantly, the Masonic Temple of the Scottish Rite on Sixteenth Street. Pope envisioned a neoclassical monument suitable for a national institution, and today, the seventy-two colossal columns surrounding the Archives building produce a Corinthian-like colonnade befitting the most ornate building of the Federal Triangle. Not surprisingly, the number of columns carries symbolic meaning dating back to early Masonic, esoteric, and even Christian teachings.[20]

Two remarkably expressive pediments on the north and south sides of the National Archives building illustrate the archival process and America's esoteric history:

First, the central pediment on the Constitution Avenue side features a male sage ("Recorder of the Archives") upon a throne, holding the keys to the Archives on a large book that rests on his lap. Two male figures beside him grasp the most precious documents: the Declaration of the Independence and the U.S. Constitution. Next to them are two other male figures holding documents for cataloging, and behind them are two winged horses. These images denote the importance of documentation and cataloging; the winged horse, Pegasus in Greek mythology, represents the strength and inspiration needed for art and learning. The other figures convey less significant meaning; however, the groups of dogs at each end of the pediment symbolize guardianship of the Archives.

Second, the Pennsylvania Avenue pediment illustrates the wise, Zeus-like figure of "Destiny" enthroned in a reflective pose and flanked by twin pillars featuring eagles (Figure 11.5). The two winged figures above the eagles represent patriotic sentiments. A cavalryman and a soldier, signifying "the Arts of War," stand to the left of Destiny while to his right is a farmer on a horse, indicating "the Arts of Peace." The surrounding clusters of images represent "the Romance of History" and "the Song of Achievement."[21] This assortment of figures projects the notion that progress is determined by knowledge of history (e.g., war and peace), and knowledge gleaned from the achievements and failures documented within the Archives.

FIGURE 11.5: Zeus-like Destiny contemplates the arts of peace and the arts of war on the north side of the National Archives Building's central pediment.

In addition to the colonnades and pediments, two other sets of large sculptures sit on pedestals near the entrances to the building on Pennsylvania and Constitution Avenues. These four figures represent the past, the future, heritage, and guardianship:

- At the Pennsylvania side of the entrance, a seated male figure contemplates a book to signify preservation of the **past.** The inscription on his base that reads "Study the Past" derives from a Confucian quote: "Study the past if you would divine the future."[22]

- On the same side of the building, a young, visionary-looking female figure intently lifts her eyes from the pages of a book held in one hand, signifying anticipation of the **future** (Figure 11.6). The inscription at her base seems to have been inspired by Shakespeare's play *The Tempest*: "What is Past is Prologue."[23]

Figure 11.6: A female sculpture at the Pennsylvania Avenue side of the National Archives.

- On the south side of the National Archives, a young female sits with a child and a sheaf of wheat in her right hand (symbolizing prosperity and hope), and an urn bearing the ashes of past generations in her left, depicting **heritage.** The statue's pedestal bears the inscription, "The Heritage of the Past is the Seed That Brings Forth the Harvest of the Future"—a quote from American abolitionist Wendell Phillips.[24]

- On the Constitution Avenue side of the building, a young man wearing a helmet and sword (conveying the need to protect future generations by unleashing Martian forces) represents **guardian-ship**. The motto beneath the figure appropriately states, "Eternal Vigilance is the Price of Liberty"—another passage from Wendell Phillips.[25]

With the exception of guardianship, each of these symbols is directly associated with Virgo and expressed through Mercurial endeavors.

The Department of Justice

Like the National Archives, the architecture of the U.S. Department of Justice building exhibits a strong neoclassical influence alongside Art Deco and Greek features.[26] Carl Paul Jennewein, a German-born design-er, integrated Masonic and Virgoan themes throughout the building to conceptually unify the interior with the exterior in his architectural sculp-tures. Outside the building, twin pediments *Ars Aequi* (the rights of man) and *Ars Boni* (the good of the state), the former a semi-naked female fig-ure holding a sword and the latter a mother and child, depict the balance between individual rights and order. Collectively, they demonstrate the art of liberty; both images are symbols of Virgo.

Other themes are further evident in the fifty-seven sculptural ele-ments and sixty-eight murals Jennewein created for the building.[27] The Constitution Avenue façade above the entrance, for example, depicts a naked man on the right with a spear pinning a serpent to the ground. The inscription above the figures is a Latin axiom taken from Pliny's *Epistu-lae*: *Lege atque Ordine Omnia Fiunt*, or "Let all things be done with law and order."[28] Both Christian and Masonic traditions explain the relation-ship between man and serpent as symbolic of natural order and triumph over the dark side of human nature. It also depicts a classical disposition of Virgo, who strives to attain order—and eventually, human perfection. The same entrance bears images of a Babylonian priest, a man carrying a sheaf of corn, and a woman holding a child and another bundle of corn. These kinds of images are typical portrayals of Demeter, the corn god-dess (and Roman equivalent of Ceres) in early Greek traditions. Demeter is also a Virgoan image and an agricultural deity. The images themselves collectively reference the sanctity and sustainability of human life.

Another indication of the stellar power of Virgo is found in a second Latin phrase decorating the wall leading to the great hall of the Justice Department: *Qui Pro Domina Justitia Sequitur*, or "Who pursues (jus-

tice) on behalf of Lady Justice."[29] Further, a pair of enormous Art Deco-
era sculptures fills the great hall, radiating the Spirit of Justice in alumi-
num (a trademark of the German-born artist). The female statue of the
Lady of Justice herself, wearing a toga-style dress that completely ex-
poses one breast, raises both arms to the heavens. Noticeably absent from
this representation is a blindfold tied over the eyes of the Lady, which is
presented in the traditional portrayal of "blind justice" to denote its impartial and objective nature. The deliberate omission of the blindfold,
according to E. W. Thomas, symbolizes that justice "should be blind indeed to favor or prejudice, but clear to see which way lies the truth."[30]
The Lady's counterpart, a bare-chested man with a cloth draped around
his waist and a single arm raised high, represents the Majesty of Law.
These semi-nude sculptures reveal the authenticity of the human spirit,
the need for survival, and the strength necessary to maintain a Virgoan
order.[31]

The Internal Revenue Service Building

The Internal Revenue Service (IRS) is a bureau of the U.S. Department of the Treasury, which is in a separate building located outside the
Federal Triangle on the west side of Fifteenth Street, southeast of the
White House. Senator James McMillan first planned to construct the IRS
building within the Federal Triangle to reflect the dignity and power of
the nation. Neither his plan nor L'Enfant's original idea was ever realized due to popular opposition to the demolition of the nearby Old Post
Office, a historical landmark. Heritage preservation enthusiasts wanted to
save the traditional ambiance of the 1899 national landmark.

Designed by White House architect James Hoban, fires partially destroyed the original Treasury building several times during construction,
which began in 1801 but remained incomplete until 1842. Inside the renovated building two side-by-side murals are painted on focal points of
the ceiling. The allegorical artwork portrays the female figures of "Treasury" and "Justice," which respectively signify the "abundance" of
America's agricultural economy and socio-economic "fairness" in the
nineteenth century.[32] These two symbols depict the Mercurial balance of
a progressive nation's commercial endeavors during that era—and
beyond.

In another vein, the two figures correspond with Adam Smith's ideas
of "self-interest" in a money-driven, capitalist marketplace and "moral
choices" for greater justice. The meaning of both ideas reverberates

around the concept of balancing human desires with moral sentiments. Numerous images—including a corn goddess, zodiac signs representative of feminine character, or female archetypes of gentle and caring vitality—indicate the nation's mystical intent to establish equilibrium between the masculine and feminine in economic and monetary matters.

The relatively austere-looking IRS building has fewer overt decorations and sculptures than other federal buildings—a hopeful indication of frugality, prudence, and accountability to American taxpayers. At the central entrances to the building, four external panels featuring eagles indicate the structure's elegant, yet simple, nature. Professor Jerry Moore at California State University writes, "The IRS building represents a monumental construction, but the IRS building was never designed as a pure symbol of national identity, although more Americans deal with the IRS than any other government agency."[33] Overall, the building's classically austere and Greek Revival-style appearance effectively project the commercial republic's original purpose, significance, and personality.

The Old Post Office Building

The Romanesque Old Post Office building, located at the northwest corner of the IRS building complex on Pennsylvania Avenue and Twelfth Street, includes a distinctive clock tower. Outside, a marble statue of famous Benjamin Franklin faces Pennsylvania Avenue. Dr. Franklin—a sage literate in stars and planetary movements—was appointed in 1775 by the Continental Congress as the first postmaster general (Figure 11.7). David Ovason writes that the building's dedication to Franklin is fitting because the Italian-style campanile is "intimately linked with a setting star."[34] Across from the statue is the former Evening Star building where the venerable *Washington Evening Star* newspaper (1852-1981) was published until the *Washington Post* purchased both the tall building and the newspaper. In *The Avenue of Presidents*, Mary Cable writes that the Egyptian mystery of the tower—and its carefully measured pyramid on top—is a "graceful gesture to the past and a strong architectural marker for the Avenue."[35] The Beaux-Arts architecture is also symbolically associated with both the stars and Freemasonry.

Rarely used as a regular post office, the ten-story central atrium has been home to a variety of retail outlets, private businesses, and federal government offices. Art is an integral part of the interior, which features twenty-four murals depicting the nation's postal heritage and a ceiling mural portraying the four seasons and several zodiac signs. Figurative sculptures are found throughout the building, including a design of twisted serpents surmounted by wings—a traditional symbol of Mercury, the Roman god of communication, to signify the postal service.

FIGURE 11.7: A statue of Dr. Benjamin Franklin, first Postmaster General appointed by the Continental Congress in 1775, stands at the Pennsylvania Avenue side entrance to the Old Post Office Building.

When the District of Columbia mail depot moved to a larger building near Union Station in 1914, the original post office inherited the "old" post office title. Over the years, there have been several attempts, including one by Treasury Secretary Andrew Mellon in the 1920s, to demolish the building. Nevertheless, it has survived. The landmark was then added to the National Register of Historic Places in 1973. As the second tallest structure in the city after the Washington Monument, the Old Post Office (with the Franklin statue) marks the precise midpoint between the White House and the Capitol.

The Federal Triangle Building Complex

The mini-campus of this massive complex of buildings is a compact area of land bordering Constitution and Pennsylvania Avenues and situated between Twelfth and Fourteenth Streets. The multifaceted region houses the Departmental "Mellon" Auditorium,[36] the old Labor Department,[37] and the Interstate Commerce Commission (ICC) building—now home to the U.S. Environmental Protection Agency. San Francisco architect Arthur Brown used a classical revival design to unify the structures with a single concept consisting of squares, semi-circles, and triangles, for a common commercial purpose.[38]

The façades of each building consist of pedimental triangles typical of classical revival architecture. The Mellon Auditorium's central pediment displays a figure of the goddess Columbia, an explicitly-carved sculpture that symbolizes the country's principal identity. Our national identity originated partly from African American poet Phillis Wheatley, who wrote a poem to General George Washington in 1775 describing the goddess of Columbia as "divinely fair."[39] Wheatley penned the line, "Celestial choir, enthroned in realms of light, Columbia's scenes of glorious toils I write."[40] General Washington was impressed by her gift, creativity and courage, and thanked her for her loyalty and inspiration. By the end of the Revolution, the figure of Columbia was everywhere. Popular songs and poems celebrated her, while towns and cities became her namesake. King's College in New York became Columbia University and most importantly the new seat of the federal government, the District of Columbia, was named in her honor. The image of the goddess Columbia on the central pediment holding up a torch signifies the light of knowledge. To her left, a nude woman holding a sheaf of corn sits on a bull, representing the zodiac signs Virgo and Taurus. These and other arcane symbols of this central pediment are earthy signs of national resources, abundance, and commercial prosperity.

Masonic symbolism of the four elements is visually integrated in the original U.S. Department of Labor and the ICC buildings. The Labor Department's pediment overlooking Constitution Avenue bears a naked woman (symbolizing fire) resting her right arm on a vessel of abundance, reclining between the two Rams of Aries. A naked man leaning against the Bull of Taurus depicts the earthly matters of agriculture, manufacturing, and trade. The ICC building's pediment embodies the god Mercury, with his winged headpiece and caduceus, beside an eagle (Figure 11.8). To illustrate air, naked Mercury reclines on a horse floating through clouds. The same building's other pediment features Pisces as a naked woman, with a sea horse and a serpent's tail surrounded by leaping dolphins, to represent the water sign. In astrology, the sign's ruler is Jupiter—a planet of growth, luck, foreign expansion, and prosperity.

Like the other national buildings in the Federal City, each of these symbols points to the fact that the Federal Triangle building complex was designed to reflect more than merely the dignity and power of a nation emerging from a colonial past. It was also meant to project the connection of the spiritual world, signified by triangles and semi-circles, with the material world, represented by squares and rectangles. As highlighted earlier, these Masonic architectural designs, ancient symbols and predictable forces of influence emanated primarily from Pythagorean and esoteric traditions.[41]

FIGURE11.8: The Roman god of commerce displayed on the pediment of the original Labor Department and the Interstate Commerce Commission Buildings (the current U.S. Environmental Protection Agency Building), on the Constitution Avenue side.

The Department of Commerce

The cornerstone celebration for the U.S. Department of Commerce building was held on July 10, 1929 by President Herbert Hoover.[42] The date had been carefully chosen for when both the Moon and Mars were within the Virgo constellation.[43] In astrological and Masonic traditions, the auspicious event bespoke the aggressive nature of Mars and the emotional jubilance of the Moon over earthly matters, and marked terrestrial harmony with the Mercurial ruler of commerce. At the ceremony, President Hoover—the secretary of commerce (1921-1928) under Presidents Warren Harding and Calvin Coolidge—used George Washington's Masonic gavel. During his tenure as secretary, Hoover made the Department of Commerce one of the most dynamic and highly visible agencies in the two administrations by promoting cooperative partnerships between government and business, and advancing exports by favoring high import tariffs. His trade philosophy, known as "associationalism"—a brand of private-public cooperation—was "built on the policies of Theodore Roosevelt and Woodrow Wilson."[44] At that time, the Commerce Department was the largest office building in the world.[45]

The commerce building was also the first building constructed according to the McMillan Plan, and adhered to L'Enfant's original design. The intensity and explicit nature of the porticos in this rectangular building reveal the unity of its astronomical and astrological significance. A series of four pedimental pavilions feature a quartet of elements along the western side of Fifteenth Street between Constitution and Pennsylvania Avenues: aeronautics (air), fishery (water), mining (earth), and foreign and domestic commerce (fire).[46] More than just symbols or images, these broad concepts derive from the so-called secret knowledge of Freemasonry, other various esoteric and astrological ideas, and Greco-Roman mythology.

The eastern façade of the building consists of eight relief panels representing the purpose of the various agencies within this multifunctional department. For example, the caduceus, an ancient astrological symbol of commerce associated with the Greek god Hermes (a messenger for the gods and protector of merchants), represents the Bureau of Foreign and Domestic Commerce. In Roman mythology, Apollo gave Mercury a magic wand—similar to the staff of Asclepius, or the medical symbol—to help guide him in the underworld. The wand depicts the department first established by President Thomas Jefferson in 1807 as the Survey of the Coast. Today, the Coast and Geodetic Survey is now part of the National Oceanic and Atmospheric Administration (NOAA) within the Commerce Department. In this case, the symbolism is linked to navigation, stargazing, and guidance from Mercury. In earlier years, the Commerce Department had a stellar observatory on its roof to facilitate the testing of instruments used in geodesic surveys involving stars. The whereabouts of this observatory is no longer known.[47] Nevertheless, the National Aquarium is still located in the basement and is open to public. Overall, the complex and conglomerate department has captured the very essence of the celestial-terrestrial connections clearly expressed through zodiac symbols and stellar triangles.

The Ronald Reagan Building and International Trade Center

The Ronald Reagan Building and International Trade Center (i.e., the Reagan Trade Center), located at the northwestern corner of Pennsylvania Avenue and Fifteenth Street (next to the White House), is a new architectural triumph that connects the past with the future. The area occupied by this building complex was known in the 1890s as the "plague spot of Washington" for its brothels and saloons. The building was dedicated in May 1998, and the place was transformed into the "crown jewel" of the Federal Triangle.[48] As the "front door" to the world inside, the Reagan Trade Center veneer is an integration of crisp, modern lines with classical order.

The two styles—past and contemporary—were purposefully paired. The objective of this design was to prevent the building from being mistaken for part of the original Federal Triangle with its Greek and Roman inclinations. Yet, the Federal Triangle Development Act of 1987 mandated that the Center "reflect the symbolic importance and historic character of Pennsylvania Avenue and the nation's capital" and "represent the dignity and stability of the Federal Government" to symbolize the activities of the Roman god of Mercury.[49] Thus, the architecture of the Reagan Trade Center unifies the classical appearance and modern design of other Federal landmarks, ranging from the Mellon Zodiac Fountain to the U.S. Department of Commerce.

Occupying over three million square feet, the Reagan Trade Center is the largest building in Washington, D.C. It is a city within a city—a global marketplace with premier conference centers, exhibition spaces, executive offices, trade organizations, university programs, library and information units, government agencies (including the U.S. Agency for International Development, the Environmental Protection Agency, and the semi-governmental Woodrow Wilson International Center for Scholars), and a variety of ethnic food outlets and entertainment venues. Overall, as a unified building, the Reagan Center is considered the "American Center" for world trade relations. It is the first and only federal building dedicated to both private and public (government) ventures—reviving President Hoover's trade philosophy of associationalism. The center itself is the largest government landmark after the Pentagon, and includes offices for over 5,000 government employees on its seventy-one acre floor space.

The building's eight-story foyer, visible through glass from the Fourteenth Street entrance, gives way to the building's most dramatic interior feature: a glass skylight soaring from thirty to 125 feet over the 170-foot-diameter atrium. The skylight comprises an entire acre of glass, and serves as both a figurative and natural connection to the outer world. Fittingly, as the "gateway" to worldwide trade connections, the American Center provides links to other countries. Bringing together federal, state, and local trade groups and resources, it serves to advance commerce and freedom.

Outside the Reagan building, on Fourteenth Street between Pennsylvania and Constitution Avenues, the Oscar Straus Memorial celebrates the accomplishments of the first Jewish member in a president's cabinet. Oscar Solomon Straus was President Theodore Roosevelt's Secretary of Commerce and Labor from 1906-1909. A massive marble fountain at the center of the memorial bears the words "Statesman, Author, Diplomat." To each side of the memorial are two groups of statues commemorating Straus' Jewish background and efforts for labor and commerce: one called "Justice" to symbolize religious freedom, and the other called "Reason" to signify capitalism. These ideas—advocated by President Reagan—represent the often-debated and conflicting forces of globalization that extend beyond America's national borders.

In fact, the latest and final architectural triumph of American city planners is the "gateway" to the world. It signifies President Reagan's vision of freedom and capitalism linking America's heritage to the future of globalization through international trade and commerce. A relentless advocate for privatization, deregulation and greater economic opportunity, Reagan captured the nation's Mercurial vision of commerce and creative energy in his Farewell Address in January 1989:

> I've spoken of the shining city all my political life, but I don't know if I ever quite communicated what I saw when I said it. But in my mind it was a tall, proud city built on rocks stronger than oceans, windswept, God-blessed and teeming with people of all kinds living in harmony and peace; a city with free ports that hummed with commerce and creativity. And if there had to

be city walls, the walls had doors and the doors were open to anyone with the will and heart to get here.[50]

Although he was widely considered a conservative leader, President
Reagan's sincere words on American's founding promise and destiny
reflected his truly libertarian and independent view of the world. Essentially, Reagan described a city of Virgo—that is, a city whose character
resonates with Mercurial creativity and openness.

The Freedom Plaza between Fourteenth Street and Pennsylvania
Avenue, NW—just north of the Reagan Center and the Commerce Department—is a raised terrace of open space for the public. A bas-relief
bronze sculpture of the backside of the Great Seal of the United States
with its truncated pyramid signifies the Masonic symbolism and unfinished nature of America's continued odyssey into the future of
Americanized globalization.

A Celestial Bridge to Globalization

The architectural symbolism of this colossal office complex is subtle
and mysterious. The L'Enfant triangle—which connects the Capitol, the
White House, and the Washington Monument—essentially reflects the
stellar alignments of antiquity. Like the Pythagorean delta, the symbol of
the triangle is the primary cause for the American system and the freedom that was built on creating tensions for innovation. There exist other
important triangles apart from these celestial and terrestrial ones, such as:

- The **constitutional government** (based principally on a three-way,
  check-and-balance equilibrium among the executive, legislative,
  and judiciary branches) is meant to compete separately yet mutually monitor each other at the federal level;

- A duplication of this tripartite system to energize **interstate relations** among national, state, and local governments; and

- A host of **sovereign commercial agencies** within the Federal Triangle that competes and collaborates with the government, the
  people (in groups), and the individuals within the framework of the
  constitution.

The unity of autonomy and interdependency is common to each of these triangles, and serves both as a launching pad and as a continuum for the commercial republic to succeed from one generation to another. The farsighted Founding Fathers were interlocutors for their version of the spiritual tenets of the trinity (found in Christian and other religious traditions) for the American way of governance to preserve, protect, and promote liberty through the inherent power of commerce. Commerce transcends all religions and ethnicities beyond national boundaries to eventually establish a Jeffersonian vision of Empire of Liberty.

For the original designers, the sanctified university of commerce was a natural force to guide and drive the Americanization of globalization. In the process, the national motto of *E Pluribus Unum* is extended globally to create a New World Order of a single human race, where diversity is reborn as a unifying force by international trade relations in goods, services, and most importantly, in America's universal ideas and ideals. The European Enlightenment thinkers and American Founders envisioned such a "philosophic empire" by conviction, and employed the "commerce clause" of the U.S. Constitution to activate that universal mission. As the colonial experience illustrated, all trade relations began with the Native Indians, continued through interstate commerce, and finally through trade with foreign nations. Thus, the founding motto translates into actions with the mystery of Mercury that symbolically consecrates the Federal Triangle and those federal workers who implement constitutional provisions. Over the years, the meaning of the architectural design, the government workforce, and constitutional interpretation has also evolved; however, the primary intention keeps the genetic material intact in the overall celestial outlook and authenticity of L'Enfant's plan.

Whether associated with Egyptian, Greek, or Roman gods and goddesses, the esoteric meanings of the symbols within the commercial campus are earthly records of heavenly meaning transcribed in the constellations. Ancient philosopher Paracelsus confirmed the power of wisdom traditions this way:

> The art of astronomy enables one to understand the innate secrets of the heart and the good and evil in the nature of man. The reason is that man is made out of the Great World and has his nature therein. And because there is one human nature deriving from the earth and another from the heavens, it is necessary to discover what each one says.[51]

Indeed, the founding architects acted on this belief. This celestial bridge has taken the nation on a wildly successful commercial path, guided by a Special Providence (i.e., an extraordinary divine intervention as opposed to "general" Providence). The Federal Triangle and the modern capital city visibly exhibit the favorable influence of Virgo, not only in the political sphere but also in a plethora of economic, religious, and socio-cultural arenas. These include apartments, bars, boutiques, churches, condominiums, galleries, hotels, museums, parks, restaurants, theaters, and sports venues—a virtual orchestra of Mercurial activities in modernity. The tripartite unity, or trinity, of these highly animated clusters of power—politics, economics, and cultural life—is the soul of American Mercury itself: conceived, born, and nurtured by the hand of commercial providence.

These symbols are a testament to America's Mercurial personality. A perceptive observer may realize the totality of the grand scheme devised by the architects of our nation's capital. The symbolism of esoteric teachings and ancient philosophies—from Babylonian and Egyptian antiquity to Greco-Roman myths—was intended to reflect the era and the psyche of the Founding Fathers. The fabric of original intention has transformed the nation into a more dynamic and equitable commercial republic than ever before. The founding wisdom impressed in symbolism continues well into the fulfillment of America's secret destiny for a better world.

PART IV

JAMES MADISON'S UNIVERSAL EMPIRE

"We are the indispensable nation. We stand tall and we see further than other countries into the future."

~ Secretary of State MADELEINE ALBRIGHT
February 19, 1998

"We are a country of countries and we touch every country and every country in the world touches us."

~ Secretary of State COLIN POWELL
February 14, 2002

Twelve

Novus Ordo Seclorum and the New World Order

For more than a century, ideological extremists at either end of the political spectrum have seized upon well-publicized incidents such as my encounter with Castro to attack the Rockefeller family for the inordinate influence they claim we wield over American political and economic institutions. Some even believe we are part of a secret cabal working against the best interests of the United States, characterizing my family and me as "internationalists" and of conspiring with others around the world to build a more integrated global political and economic structure—one world, if you will. If that's the charge, I stand guilty, and I am proud of it.[1]

David Rockefeller, PhD
Chairman, Council on Foreign Relations and
the Chase Manhattan Bank

Each generation of Americans has seen the United States elevated to an even greater and more global nation. This continual progress has been punctuated by crisis situations from the nation's inception to the present generation. With the Revolutionary War, the founding generation created a new nation; President Andrew Jackson "lionized"[2] it after a tumultuous period; Abraham Lincoln preserved the Union after the tragic Civil War; Woodrow Wilson and Franklin D. Roosevelt visualized a new global order in an American image after two World Wars; Harry S. Truman designed an international architecture for a world order; Lyndon B. Johnson proclaimed "We Shall Overcome"[3] to unify the racially-divided nation; Ronald Reagan ended the Cold War; George H. W. Bush revived the founding "big idea" for a "New World Order" (NWO);[4] and Bill Clinton realized that vision through a North American Free Trade Agreement (NAFTA) and the establishment of the World Trade Organization (WTO).

In the legacy of his predecessors, President Barack Obama manifested America's ultimate destiny—not only by way of an interracial union (a Jeffersonian legacy established through his relationship with African slave Sally Hemings),[5] but also by way of a religious and national harmonization that reverberated all the way from Africa to Indonesia to eventually galvanize a more inclusive American identity. In that sense, America is reborn as God's crucible nation—a truly globalized human race in His image.

Nearly all Americans are increasingly of mixed ethnic and racial stock. Professional golfer Tiger Woods, who has declined to identify himself as black, famously chose the term *Cablinasian* (Caucasian, black, Indian, and Asian) to describe the ethnicity inherited from his African-American father and Thai mother. Woods' wife is a blonde, blue-eyed Swede and they have beautiful children. This inescapable fact is a reflection of antiquity, and the Founding Fathers expected to see the American empire become home to a common and international "human race"[6] called Americans.

Thomas Jefferson, who understood religious matters and African-American race relations more intimately than others in the early republic, once wrote that "we have no interests and passions different from those of fellow citizens. . . . Nor are we acting for ourselves alone, but for the whole human race."[7] Despite the tragic Indian Removal Act of 1830, President Andrew Jackson reiterated the Jeffersonian truth a few years later: "Providence . . . has chosen you as the guardians of freedom, to preserve it for the benefit of the human race"[8] because "all men are created free and equal."[9] These leaders knew that they were inheritors of the prior American experience with the Pilgrims and colonists and all other civilizations; yet, the Founding Fathers were a wholly new human

creation. Observing this subtle reality, John Adams wrote that the people
of America now had "the best opportunity and the greatest trust in their
hands that Providence" ever ordained "to so small a number since the
transgression of the first pair" (Adam and Eve).[10]

In a historic moment, that founding assurance matured with the politics of persistence to finally grant the providential birth of an
extraordinarily gifted and transcendent American: Barack Obama. After
swiftly emerging into national politics from the land of Lincoln, the new
president inherited two wars in Afghanistan and Iraq, an economic crisis,
global terrorism, and religiously-motivated culture wars at home and
abroad. In a divisive moment in history, President Obama has come to
epitomize the founding consciousness that "we are one people."[11]

Like Obama, our nation is genetically global. This is why the United
States, unlike any other country on earth, has engaged internationally as
a global enterprise. From the laurels of the Revolutionary War for the
cause of freedom to the current worldwide military posture, American
history attests to this fact. With the U.S. Air Force's Expeditionary
Force, B-2 Stealth bombers, U.S. Navy ships and Predators, America can
reach every corner of the globe within 24 hours to intervene in human
conflicts (from Somalia to Yugoslavia), and to assist in natural disasters
ranging from as far away as the Asian tsunami to the 2010 earthquake in
nearby Haiti.[12] In the diplomatic arena, U.S. government is committed to
supporting a host of United Nations institutions and a network of multila-
teral banks, such as the Bretton Woods Institutions (the World Bank and
the International Monetary Fund in Washington, D.C.). The United
States also supports regional development banks in Africa, Asia, and Latin America. Our government institutions—especially the U.S.
Departments of State, Energy, Commerce, and Agriculture—
continuously provide assistance for international development, new
sources of energy and technology, commercial services and trade promotion, and global food security and safety.

Aside from international trade in goods and services, the most intox-
icating American export is our ideas and ideals. American thoughts
espoused in Henry David Thoreau's *On the Duty of Civil Disobedience*
inspired Mahatma Gandhi to expel British colonial rulers from India. It
was this action that encouraged Dr. Martin Luther King Jr.'s philosophy
of non-violence, which provided the basis for the core principles of his
Civil Rights Movement. His leadership, in turn, led to the Voting Rights
Act of 1965 for African Americans.[13] The congressionally-supported National Endowment for Democracy and its family of organizations (i.e.,

the American Center for International Labor Solidarity, the Center for International Private Enterprise, the International Republican Institute, and the National Democratic Institute for International Affairs) are designed to promote pluralism, equality, and free and fair elections globally. The power of ideas is contagiously championed by American universities and colleges, which have long maintained academic partnerships and exchange programs with their counterparts in other countries. President Dwight Eisenhower's people-to-people program as well as other non-governmental and some faith-based organizations were positively engaged in international diplomacy and global development activities. These are just a few examples of the founding conviction behind America's transmittable traditions—a notion that was recaptured by President Woodrow Wilson when he said: "The world must be made safe for democracy."[14]

Born with the Great Seal

As explained in earlier chapters, the Great Seal depicts the founding vision of democracy and oneness through our national motto, *E Pluribus Unum*, "Out of many, one." At the bottom of the Seal's reverse side, the phrase *Novus Ordo Seclorum* appears. It meant, according to the U.S. Department of State, "A new order of the ages."[15] Like the dictum on the front, this axiom identifies the ultimate destiny of the United States within the world. A third idiom, "Providence (God) favors our undertakings," recognizes and blesses the passageway to achieving America's global mission. This adage is positioned over the All-seeing Eye, which itself is contained in a triangle hovering above an incomplete Egyptian Pyramid. The triangular structure mirrors the shape of the Greek letter Δ (Delta), denoting the universal symbol for perpetual "change." The stone that makes up the apex of the pyramid—a capstone—is deliberately omitted to depict the unfinished nature of the American project.

Marking a profound period of dramatic change that began with a "New American Era," the Great Seal also communicated a radical departure from the tyrannical and religious orders of Europe.[16] As explained by Charles Thompson, an illustrious Founding Father chosen by the Continental Congress to draft the final design for the Seal (after three committees spent six years deliberating intensely over it),[17] the meaning of the phrase *Novus Ordo Seclorum* was "a new order of the ages."[18] In his farewell letter to the Army on June 8, 1783, General George Washington wrote, "The foundation of our *empire* was not laid in the gloomy age of ignorance and superstition, but at an epoch when the rights of mankind were better understood and more clearly defined, than at any former period" (italics added).[19] These independent pronouncements embody the mindset of the Founding Fathers who embarked on an experiment to create a NWO—a system that is unifying, universal, and orderly. To create such global architecture, Thomson, who served as the secretary of foreign affairs and secretary to the Continental Congress (1774-89), corresponded with American representatives abroad according to his *Secret Journal of Foreign Affairs*, and supported diplomatic negotiations and "all intercourse with foreign nations."[20] Identified as the "Prime Minister of the United States,"[21] Thomson adamantly upheld his belief that the "author (God) had presented to the world a system of morals," and determined to keep His sublime order for the world.[22]

This multi-talented Thomson, who once translated the Bible, was reportedly influenced by the *Fourth Eclogue*[23] in which Virgil predicted "the birth of a child under whose reign the world is to be regenerated and the virtues of the Golden Age are to flourish anew."[24] His American vision for a new kind of empire was preserved in the concept of *Novus Ordo Seclorum*: "A mighty Order of Ages born Anew."[25] Throughout the intervening years, this iconography has offered a window into the continuity of revolutionary mindsets of the Founding Fathers, who reflected on America's struggle for independence, the unity of American people, and their role in the world.

As an official gift to departing foreign diplomats, the first U.S. Secretary of State Thomas Jefferson produced his own Diplomatic Medal in 1792, a decade after the final approval of the Seal. Augustin Dupré, the famous French engraver, had designed a gold medal displaying the motto "To Peace and Commerce" under Jefferson's meticulous instruction.[26] The parting gift symbolized Jefferson's vision of peace through commerce by portraying an Indian trader of America holding a cornucopia and welcoming Mercury, the Roman god of commerce, to the United States (Figure 12.1). The Bald Eagle decorating the reverse side of the medal was actually one of the earlier versions of the Great Seal. The meanings of Seal and the Medal exemplify the symbolic power of our national identity and the global mission of the commercial republic.

Over the course of 250 years, America has grown—from a diverse cluster of autonomous colonies and their interdependent inhabitants with various religious beliefs, political persuasions, and ethnic backgrounds— to become a politically free and economically wealthy nation with a mighty military. This was not possible by accident or luck, but by design and Providence. Sadly, Prussian chancellor Otto von Bismarck once grumbled, "God has special providence for fools, drunks, and the United States of America."[27] In spite of such misconstrued negativity, the nation continued to remain faithful to its founding principles and produced a new breed of humans: "Americans" united by conviction, cherished by freedom, and prosperous by entrepreneurship. These are the results of the concepts of autonomy and interdependence, which have germinated from the very soul of the American experience and are reflected in the universal order of creation. Such a nation is naturally self-reliant, generous, innovative, futuristic, and most importantly, global. This is quite antithetical to traditional societies and religious orthodoxies that have produced—and continued to produce—fatalistic, parochial, and fundamentalist groups. Instead, the United States has been destined to create a unique global civilization bound not by race or religion, but by its founding conviction. Thomas Paine underscored this original intention prophetically when he said, "The cause of America is in a great measure the cause of all mankind"[28]—a notion often manifested in America's global engagement by democratic and republican values.

FIGURE 12.1 First Secretary of State Thomas Jefferson's diplomatic gold medal displays the motto "To Peace and Commerce" and the Bald Eagle.

The Big Idea and Its Consequences

In his world-transforming speech to a joint session of Congress on September 11, 1990 delivered just weeks after the Iraqi invasion of Kuwait, President George H. W. Bush invoked the perennial "big idea"[29] of a NWO. He argued that a "new world order" would be "freer from the threat of terror, stronger in the pursuit of justice, and more secure in the quest for peace. An era in which nations of the world, East and West, North and South, (would) prosper and live in harmony."[30] As the United States prepared for concerted-action through the United Nations, the president added that a "new partnership of nations has begun, and we stand today at a unique and extraordinary moment."[31] Invoking the founding vision and the wisdom of antiquity, Bush said:

> A hundred generations have searched for this elusive path to peace, while a thousand wars raged across the span of human endeavor. And today that new world is struggling to be born, a world quite different from the one we've known, a world where the rule of law supplants the rule of the jungle in which nations recognize the shared responsibility for freedom and justice, a world where the strong respect the rights of the weak.[32]

When President Bush addressed the nation on January 16, 1991 to announce the beginning of the Persian Gulf War, he purposefully used the phrase "New World Order" to explain the motivations and justifications for the use of force against Iraq:

> This is an historic moment. We have in this past year made great progress in ending the long era of conflict and cold war. We have before us the opportunity to forge for ourselves and for future generations a new world order, a world where the rule of law, not the law of the jungle, governs the conduct of nations.[33]

In his emotional speech, the president resorted to quoting Paine's memorable phrase, "These are the times that try men's souls," and added:

> Those well-known words are so very true today. But even as planes of the multinational forces attack Iraq, I prefer to think of peace, not war. I am convinced not only that we will prevail, but that out of the horror of combat will come the recognition that no nation can stand against a world united.[34]

The big idea has markedly invoked a wide range of reactions and conspiracies with far reaching implications. The most heinous act of ter-

ror came from Osama bin Laden, who despised the American military
presence in the Middle East and dominant position in the world. The
murderous mastermind timed the September 11, 2001 attacks precisely
eleven years after President George H. W. Bush's speech to Congress in
order to send a vengeful and symbolic message to the United States. For
al-Qaeda, the creation of a NWO to promote Western values and universal ideals in the Muslim world is the antithesis of their misconstrued
jihadist concept of Islam. For these Muslim extremists, the American
"infidels" who built up military installations on Islam's holiest lands are
"conquerors" and Christian "crusaders." In his *Sacred Fury: Understanding Religious Violence*, Professor Charles Selengut at Drew
University in New Jersey summarizes:

> The American invaders, however, were Christians, infidels and
> nonbelievers whose religion is an affront to what bin Laden
> claimed was authentic Islamic faith. Their [Americans] belief in
> the divinity of Jesus, their culture of sexual equality and personal
> freedom, their economic capitalism, and their determination to
> spread American-style democracy to Islamic countries was ana-
> thema.[35]

A similar strain of sacred fury (in response to the founding idea articulated by President Bush) came from religious fundamentalists in the
United States.[36] The most vocal member of the "moral majority" is
represented by televangelist Pat Robertson, who gained notoriety for his
involvement in the African blood diamond scandal with Liberian dictator
Charles Taylor[37] and tyrannical President Mobutu Sese Seko of Zaire,[38]
as well as the un-Christianlike manner in which he suggested killing Ve-
nezuelan President Hugo Chavez[39] (Reverend Robertson later
apologized). More significantly, in his *New York Times* bestseller titled
The New World Order (September 1991), Robertson argued that "miscreants" (referring to President Bush, David Rockefeller, and others)
had tried to destroy America.[40] He began his volume with George H. W.
Bush's speech to Congress, writing: "Against this backdrop of history
[the collapse of the Soviet Union and the Gulf War against Iraq], from
the podium of the legislative chamber of the United States House of
Representatives, the elected president of the United States of America
has announced the beginning of a *New World Order*" (italics original).[41]
    According to his Christian ideology, Reverend Robertson character-
ized the NWO as "an Impossible Dream."[42] He also claimed that the

Founding Fathers were all Christians, and that the United States is a Christian nation. This notion stands in complete contradiction to the one articulated by America's most learned and revered evangelist, Billy Graham, who has thoroughly studied American history and the Christian Bible. Typically inconsistent and mostly dramatizing, Robertson quickly (two pages later) admitted the "Impeccable Realities" of his Impossible Dream when he concluded that "a single thread runs from the White House to the State Department to the Council on Foreign Relations to the Trilateral Commission to secret societies to extreme New Agers. There must be a new world order."[43]

The latter group referred to as secret societies and New Agers are Freemasons;[44] their influence, according to Robertson, is graphically "revealed in the great seal adopted at the founding of the United States"[45] on the back of the one dollar bill. The reverend further maintained that the Great Seal—with its Egyptian pyramid, providential eye, and the Latin motto *Novus Ordo Seclorum*—is a hidden illustration of the power of Freemasons and wealthy Jewish bankers in American economy. Conveniently translating the Latin phrase to read a "New World Order" without historical context (he often favored an apocalyptic and literal interpretation of the Bible as well), Robertson linked the axiom to a biblical prophecy of a "mystery religion designed to replace the old *Christian world order* of Europe and America" (italics added).[46] During the creation of a new nation, the Founding Fathers purposefully departed from the old European orders of Christianity and tyranny. Confused by the very basics of American history and absorbed in age-old conspiracies, Robertson then writes, "We have traced the infiltration of Continental Freemasonry by the new world philosophy of the order of the Illuminati, and its subsequent role in the French Revolution. We then were able to find clear documentation that the occultic-oriented societies . . . played a seminal role in the thinking of Marx and Lenin" and the Communist Manifesto.[47] In a *New York Times* article titled "The Crackpot Factor," Anthony Lewis uncovered that Robertson "relied heavily on a British anti-Semantic writer of the 1920s, Nesta H. Webster."[48] This partly explains his inconsistencies, historical gaps, and his hostility toward certain ethnic and even particular Christian groups.

After igniting a host of conspiracy theories, Robertson later discredited himself by admitting that there was little evidence to support such a link, saying, "All of the French membership on the Trilateral Commission were (sic) members of the French Freemasonry. This may just be a coincidence, or it may mean that prominent Frenchmen are also Masons, or it may actually be the missing link tying these sordid elements together."[49] Once again, he contradicted himself and missed the historical association between the French Revolution (1789-1799) and the Trilateral Commission (founded in 1973 by David Rockefeller with Alan Greenspan, Paul Volcker, Zbigniew Brzezinski, and others). In a passionate review of the book, Michael Lind, a protégé of conservative William F. Buckley and former executive editor of the *National Interest*, wrote that Robertson's compilation of conspiracy theories was "the Exorcism" and described the book as "All Crackpots."[50] In his own book *Up from Conservatism: Why the Right is Wrong for America*, Lind exposed the egregious points of the Republican agenda and its intellectually bankrupt hostility and hypocrisy, which have led the nation into irreconcilable divisions with religious fundamentalists.[51]

As a misguided and confused opinionator, Reverend Robertson principally blamed the first openly evangelical President Jimmy Carter for his views on a world order, and accused all U.S. Presidents from Woodrow Wilson to George H. W. Bush of being duped by the NWO. Moreover, he named institutional miscreants—the United Nations, the Public Broadcasting System, the Ford Foundation, the Rockefeller Foundation, the International Monetary Fund, the World Bank, the Brookings Institution, and other liberal Washington think tanks—as collectively having a secret mission to eliminate Christianity. Robertson believed that a NWO—first publicly articulated as a concept by President Wilson at the time of the creation of the League of Nations, and then developed through the Franklin D. Roosevelt administration—was a potent and destructive force intended to devastate America. In the final analysis, Reverend Robertson does not seem to remember that his own father (the late Democratic U.S. Senator Absalom Willis Robertson of Virginia) and the father of our nation (George Washington) were known Freemasons and members of the Society of the Cincinnati.

Is this the End of the Founding Vision?

The concept of a NWO was elevated to national consciousness when President Franklin D. Roosevelt, along with his Secretary of Agriculture Henry Wallace and Treasury Secretary Henry Morgenthau—all Freemasons—decided to invoke the phrase *Novus Ordo Seclorum* to give historical meaning to the president's New Deal, which represented a new beginning for the nation following the Great Depression.[52] The image on the reverse side of the Great Seal was revealed to the American public for the first time in 1935 when the Roosevelt administration decided to print it on the one dollar bill.[53]

The New Deal and the secular worldviews of three Freemasons prompted Methodist minister and Goodwill Industries founder Abraham Vereide in Seattle to organize "an informal association of men in positions of responsibility who are finding . . . the WAY, the TRUTH and the LIFE" through total dedication to Christ.[54] In his book *White Protestant Nation: The Rise of the Conservative Movement*, Professor Allan Lichtman at American University further indicates that this powerful white Christian group blamed early military setbacks in World War II on America's moral dereliction and "the failure at home to do right and to trust God."[55] More explicitly, they despised "godless organized labor"[56] unions and adamantly opposed President Roosevelt's New Deal. The New Deal programs, designed to provide job opportunities to the unemployed workforce and to jumpstart the economy through public work projects, also inadvertently created a powerful anti-government and anti-union business alliance. Opposing the secular nature of Freemasonry and the Roosevelt administration, these successful personalities and industrialists considered themselves the "new chosen" by God to bring U.S. government into alignment with Biblical law and morality.[57]

The network of these businessmen and fundamentalists (who formed Christian prayer groups with the Methodist minister) expanded their circles of influence and included political leaders through the International Christian Leadership, which was incorporated as the Fellowship Foundation in Chicago.[58] Since moving to the nation's capital, "the Fellowship," also simply known as "the Family," managed to access the corridors of political and economic power through a cabal of associates and friends. The pro-business, religious right group believed that their source of wealth and power is clearly a divine indication of God's blessing on the new chosen. Their focal point of male-bonding is the prayer breakfast; their primary purpose is to serve God. Women in the Family are treated as lower-grade to the powerful, predominantly white and male Christians. In his explosive book *The Family: The Secret Fundamentalism at the Heart of American Power*, former Family member Jeff Sharlet writes that the intellectual heart of their Christian doctrine is "dominionism" as the "new chosen" to replace "the rule of law and its secular contracts" with God's rule at every level of society.[59]

The Family is committed to serving as "the finest and best invisible organization"[60] behind the curtains of Christian fundamentalist groups. Their strategic assault on the First Amendment's establishment clause—

"Congress shall make no laws respecting the establishment of religion"—was the core of their primary objectives.[61] The militant approach reached a climax when Minister Vereide organized the first Presidential Prayer Breakfast on February 5, 1953 and Senator Frank Carlson, a conservative Kansas Republican and the new chairman of the Family, invited the recently sworn-in President Dwight Eisenhower to attend.[62] Citing the separation of church and state doctrine, the president resisted the invitation; however, the senator, who helped elect General Eisenhower, convinced the war hero otherwise. The audience of 400 powerful luminaries welcomed the president and expressed their major theme, "Government Under God," on a poster with Uncle Sam on his knees submitting to God.[63] It was a triumphant and historic moment for the Family, as if God's invisible hand were working its way toward a greater assignment ahead.

With powerful friends in the White House and Congress, the Family exploited prevailing sentiments of anti-communism and McCarthyism to successfully replace the original national motto, *E Pluribus Unum*, with the phrase "In God We Trust" on U.S. currency (Figure 12.2). They additionally managed to insert "under God" in the Pledge of Allegiance in 1954. Their constitutional amendment to the founding document, "This nation devoutly recognizes the authority and law of Jesus Christ," failed to pass in Congress.[64] These actions illustrate how the Family was able to galvanize an invisible movement in modern American history to establish Christianity as an official religion without fanfare and constitutional controversy.

Their stealthy mission has continued in the nation's capital. In his revealing book *Tempting Faith: An Inside Story of Political Seduction*, David Kuo, a former White House senior aide in the George W. Bush administration and a speech writer for Reverend Pat Robertson, describes his disappointment as Robertson's Christian Coalition and other fundamentalist groups "began subverting my ideas of power"[65] to advance their basic theology. The faithful Christian, who wanted to end abortion, strengthen marriage and help the poor, was disillusioned after reaching the heights of political power in the White House. He resentfully characterized the Family as "the most powerful group in Washington that nobody knows."[66]

FIGURE 12.2: The new national motto "In God We Trust" placed on U.S. currency since 1954.

The legislative authority manifested in the Family (or the Fellowship) demonstrates the enormity of factional power exercised by a nebulous network of so-called Christian elites. In a commercial republic like the United States, democratic government is required to limit the exercise of private power with the opinions of the governed. In their book *The Constitution of Good Societies*, Professors Karol Soltan and Stephen Elkin at the University of Maryland remind us of the caution expressed by James Madison, an author of *The Federalist Papers*, who believed that "factional power is a danger to individual liberty."[67] Nonetheless, the inconspicuous actions of the Family have forever altered the singularity of the most important founding vision, *E Pluribus Unum*. Constitutional Harvard Law Professor Alan Dershowitz writes:

It distorts the historical record and insults the memory of those who drafted the Declaration to believe that Jefferson, Franklin, and Adams would have anything common with the evangelical Christian fundamentalists. . . . Jefferson, Franklin, and Adams would be turning in their graves if they knew how their views were being misused by today's Religious Right.[68]

Their power doctrine of "dominionism" has had a global effect as well. The National Prayer Breakfast has been the instrument through which the Family and associates perpetuate their belief in "Biblical capitalism" and social agenda (e.g., abortion and sexual orientation) internationally. Having identified organized labor as "ungodly," the commanding "new chosen" have aided the efforts of foreign dictators ranging from Jean-Claude Duvalier in Haiti, Ferdinand Marcos in the Philippines, Jonas Savimbi in Angola, Haile Selassie in Ethiopia, Suharto in Indonesia, and others elsewhere.[69] In his inside account of the Family, dissident author Jeff Sharlet also documented American congressmen, generals, and foreign dictators meeting in "confidential cells" to pray for a "leadership led by God."[70] For these Christian fundamentalists, America was founded as a Christian nation; they are committed to the return of the Christian order of Old Europe, from which the Pilgrims escaped to America for religious freedom.

Jefferson's Warning to Posterity

The Founding Fathers created a republic (representative government) to protect the spiritual needs of the Pilgrims and to promote the material success of the economically-driven colonists. The balancing act is at the core of the American experience—not economic extremism and religious fundamentalism. For the most part, the enlightened Founders successfully established a wall of separation between church and state to prevent the infiltration of religious faction into the politics of governance; yet, they never denied religious freedom.

Thomas Jefferson, a prolific champion of religious freedom, articulated the subject matter as if warning of the Family and Reverend Robertson. In Jefferson's mind, in order to keep America's founding and the Christian spirit in the right place, the reverend should not have preached on killing a foreign leader (a clear violation of U.S. law), profited from the alleged blood diamond trade, and grossly undermined the wisdom of the Founding Fathers who were of far superior intellect and knowledge. Thomas Paine noted: "The World is my country, all mankind are my brethren, and to do good is my religion."[71] Jefferson also reminded his audience of the history of Christianity, which seems to have repeated itself in different forms since his generation, when he said, "Millions of innocent men, women, and children, since the introduction of Christianity, have been burnt, tortured, fined, and imprisoned: yet we have not advanced one inch towards uniformity. What has been the effect of coercion?"[72] In a reflective tone, Jefferson explained that coercion made "one half the world fools, and the other half hypocrites" who supported "roguery and error all over the earth."[73]

The coercive actions of the Family became self-evident, especially after two of their "new chosen"—Senator John Ensign of Nevada[74] and Governor Sanford of South Carolina[75]—publicly admitted to sexual affairs outside of marriage and dishonest conduct. This was a historic setback to the organization and its leader Doug Coe, who expected their "Christendom," according to Family defector Jeff Sharlet, to function "invisibly like the Mafia."[76] In reference to the Mafia, Coe explained that "they keep their organization invisible. Everything is transitory. Everything invisible is permanent and lasts forever. The more you can make your organization invisible, the more influence it will have."[77] Their highly esteemed "invisible" slogan has begun to depreciate after the media exposed powerful Family members entangled in the "dominionism" of women and within international affairs. The far-sighted Jefferson offered this advice: "Reason and persuasion are the only practical instruments. To make way for these, free inquiry must be indulged; and how can we wish others to indulge it while we refuse it ourselves?"[78]

Whether found within Christianity or Islam, the trickle-down nature of religious fundamentalism—both populist and elitist—has the tendency to inflict pain and suffering everywhere. Domestically, for example, the nation witnessed a Christian-motivated group, the Waco Branch of Davidians in Texas, go up in flames when the FBI engaged in confrontation.[79] The Ku Klux Klan—a racist and anti-Semitic move-ment—professes their Christian values, prides in their patriotism, and wishes to eliminate Catholics, Jews, non-whites, and immigrants. The Oklahoma City bombing was inspired by fundamentalist Christian views as well.[80] Globally, populist al-Qaeda networks in the Muslim world have added fuel to the Arab-Israel conflict and ignited anti-American sentiment and hatred.

In part, the elitist "new chosen" associates of the Family have contributed to unleashing un-American messages by supporting dictators internationally and repealing the founding conviction of America as a "secular nation."[81] The latter was clearly communicated to the Muslim world through the 1797 Barbary Treaty at the very founding of the nation. A departure from the American vision enshrined in the U.S. Constitution is essentially a denial of the founding wisdom and ancient hope for the commercial republic and Providence. As Jefferson warned, the effect of Christian coercion—or of any other extremist and religious coercion—is infinitely costly.

THIRTEEN

Madison's Grand Strategy for a Universal Empire

The empires of the future are the empires
of the mind.[1]

Sir Winston Churchill
British Prime Minister

When Sir Winston Churchill spoke the words above to a wartime audience at Harvard University on September 6, 1943, he essentially advocated an old British strategy that "English and Americans should spread their language all over the globe as a means of promoting [international] understanding and peace."[2] As head of the British Empire (for which the sun never set in the colonized lands in Australia, Canada, India, and more than fifty other countries), the prime minister was reflecting on the global conquests of Englishmen made successful through mercantilism, evangelization, and dissemination of the English language. Evidently, as the last resort, Churchill adhered to a plan for an Anglo-American world order made up of a universally-accepted system of knowledge—which itself contained a shared set of democratic institutions, republican ideas, and parliamentary procedures—to be transmitted with ease through a global *lingua franca* of commercial, scientific, and cultural affairs as well as international diplomacy.[3]

Having been influenced by his American mother, the war hero and Nobel Laureate of Literature was convinced that communication was the key to world peace; thus, this common language would inform the Anglo-American concepts of rationality, freedom, and progress for the dominant power to create a new world order. During the interwar years, Cambridge University's ground-breaking Basic English teaching project in China supported the idea of a common language through which a "mental and moral seed of the planet"[4] could be spread to advance international peace by propagating Western views, values, and virtues.

Still, historically flawed assumptions rooted in Churchill's speech prevented cross-cultural understanding due in part to the divisive role language had played in the politics of national pride and cultural identity. For example, England's war-time ally across the English Channel—France—certainly perceived Churchill's worldview as unenthusiastically as the Germans did. Despite the common language and cultural bonds that existed between the British Empire and its American colonies, both had fought wars against each other in which the French and Germans sided with the Americans. For some reasons, Churchill dismissed the distinct Anglo-American history and put forward his colonial argument for unity and peace.

Like past notions of colonialism, mercantilism, and evangelization, the power of language in dominion mindsets is hardly compelling and rarely serves as a potent force for global unity. Historical record seems to corroborate this by demonstrating instead the compelling force of the power of ideas. In the twentieth century, a new order of Enlightenment ideas and philosophies eventually triumphed over the world (as opposed to the revolutionary Marxist "ideas" of the Soviet Union, China, Cuba, and elsewhere), almost as if this were what America was created to pursue as a global strategy. As the world witnessed during the Cold War period and the post-Soviet era of hostilities in the Balkans, the Korean peninsula and in many other nation-states around the world, the power of ideas infused with language, religion, ethnicity, and domination naturally leads to conflict not only between countries but within societies. Within the empires that had existed previously, the notions of nation-states and early civilizations have either become a relic of the past, or have been replaced by internally-divided and conflict-prone societies. By contrast, when Enlightenment ideas developed into universally-accepted convictions—approved by the wise, ordained by nature, and shared by many—they seem to have endured; such was the case in the birthing of the United States.

With the collapse of the Marxist-Leninist Soviet Union, the United States has emerged as the lone and unrivaled superpower—the world's hegemonic leader. Even with the ascendance of China, India, and other emerging economic powers, America's supremacy in the military, diplomatic, economic, and cultural spheres continues to be unparalleled; however, global forces of change could certainly recalibrate and restructure the United States around its founding ideal of an empire. Unlike the Russian Empire, Chinese dynasties, and British imperialism, America is a unique empire whose fortitude is enshrined in universal laws as dictated by Special Providence. Certain of this uniquely American aspect, the Founding Fathers maintained that the United States would be an ever-ascendant, benevolent empire that would eventually expand beyond the original thirteen colonies to accommodate more people and enlarge its territory. In his book *American Empire*, Professor Bradley Thayer at Baylor University writes:

> The United States is a unique empire. It is very different from all those that have come before. The American Empire stands in marked contrast even to the British Empire, with whom it shares an ideology and economic system. It is not interested in the expansion of territorial control by conquering territory and imposing colonial rule. It is interested in the political and economic well-being of its allies. Of course, the American Empire stands in even greater contrast to the world's other empires, most of which were principally interested in exploiting their colonies as efficiently and rapidly as possible.[5]

In the evolutionary process, the American empire has forgone its imperial mission and redefined the ideas of the founding vision (which was driven in part by the dynamics of freedom within the nation's vibrant democracy). It is only with freedom and democratic transformation that the evolving American empire has the highest probability to win over the world with its philosophy of ancient hope.

A Philosophic Empire in Action

The Framers of the Constitution essentially developed the American concept of an empire of philosophy instead of a system of ideology. Toward that end, these prudent men sought guidance from the providential laws—the bedrocks of America's commercial republic—with which they needed to comply. Their deliberate actions, carried out during the last quarter of eighteenth-century America, were believed to have been sourced from a sort of providential energy. This is where the global appeal resides for the invisible attraction the United States holds for millions of people around the globe. The genesis for this spiritual birth was inspired by Sir Francis Bacon's vision of the *New Atlantis* (1627), which was based on the principles of reason, tolerance, charity, virtue, and empiricism for a utopian-type of commercial republic that connects all nations through "trade."[6]

In his utopian society, the scientific spirit reigned supreme. Sir Bacon, a religious aristocrat, wrote: "The end of our foundation is the knowledge of causes, and secret of motions of things; and the enlarging of the bounds of human empire, to the effecting of all things possible."[7] In his fabled narrative, Sir Bacon prophetically outlined an ideal empire that was explicitly inclined to associate with the munificent American project and its mission as a beacon of hope for the world.[8] The founding generation—especially John Adams, Benjamin Franklin, Alexander Hamilton, Thomas Jefferson, and James Madison—was highly influenced by the writings of the English statesman and prophet.[9] In Madison's *Notes of Debates in the Federal Convention of 1787*, the introduction to his book states:

> Through the friendship of Jefferson, Madison deliberately procured for himself a kind of five-foot shelf of books on the history of natural law, political history, economics, and science, ancient and modern confederacies, and the social philosophy of the Enlightenment, including the Baconian-inspired 37-volume set of the *Encyclopedic*, the Summa of eighteenth century knowledge.[10]

The federal system of the American empire operates using a Madisonian model; however, it derived from a variety of sources and the debates that ensued with other Founding Fathers, especially in the *Federalist Papers*. The basis of his model focused primarily on the idea that polities are comprised of individuals who make choices—through deliberative processes—to establish the political institutions that govern their own destinies. Unlike the British imperial power structure of a center-periphery colonial relationship, the American empire was modeled after a federal system of incorporated, but separate and independent, states that were linked through a web of political institutions and constitutional frameworks. This philosophic foundation has its own limitations; however, it was designed to balance the rights of individuals with centralized power at either the state or federal level.

Energized by these ideas, the Founding Fathers developed their own "imperial" ambitions for a philosophic empire through theory and practice of the constitutional commerce clause. Thus, the trade interests of the thirteen states and a system of commercial regulations were a central issue of their constitutional debates. With regards to the fundamental nature of the diverse colonies and their specific trade relations, Madison presented his basic logic to the delegates:

> The two extremes before us are, a perfect separation, and a perfect incorporation of the thirteen States. In the first case, they would be independent nations, subject to no law but the law of nations. In the last they would be mere counties of one entire republic, subject to one common law. In the first case, the smaller States would have every thing to fear from the larger. In the last they would have nothing to fear. The true policy of the small States, therefore, lies in promoting those principles, and that form of government, which will most approximate the States to the condition of counties.[11]

Once these thirteen colonies gained statehood and their inhabitants became fully-fledged American citizens, they began to enjoy basic constitutional rights, political privileges, and the participation of their citizenry in self-government. Madison's legal acumen and political framework had extended—beyond broad recognition as the father of the U.S. Constitution and American federalism—to the politics of global governance and the conduct of foreign affairs. As indicated in previous chapters, Madison, who made seemingly irreconcilable arguments in *Federalist* essays 10 and 51, was heavily influenced by the economic and ethical analysis provided by Adam Smith's *Wealth of Nations* and *Theory of Moral Sentiments*. His architectural framework was essentially a theory that the politics of governance (i.e., public policy formulation) would work like a free marketplace of competing elected representatives, government agencies, and lobbying groups. The Madisonian structure of counterpoise would produce a more effective and equitable political system than other alternatives such as military juntas, religious tyranny, or totalitarian despotism. Like Smith's invisible hand of the marketplace, the meta-principles of Madison's constitutional agenda can be universally applied. Madison himself wrote, "Such a doctrine would give just

alarm to all nations, and more than any thing would countenance the im-
putation of aspiring to a *universal empire* . . . thus every commercial
regulation in time of peace, as well as of war, would be made obligatory
on foreigners" (italics added).[12] Essentially, his concept of a universal
empire is a powerful force extending through a constitutional framework
to advance American commercial interests abroad.

The Madisonian impulse animated the vision of an American empire.
The strategy that resulted expanded territorial control not by conquering
land and imposing colonial rule, but by promoting the political freedom
and economic well-being of the inhabitants as American citizens. To
promote the benign nature of Madison's universal empire, Jefferson similarly advocated an Empire of Liberty, while Hamilton executed a
grand strategy—a commercial and industrial policy—to accomplish it.
Throughout his presidency, Jefferson supported action for an Empire for
Liberty and described the new republic as a "chosen country" and a "rising nation" that was already "advancing rapidly to destinies beyond the
reach of the mortal eye."[13] In 1809, the third president wrote to Madison
that it was the brilliance of the American mechanism that allowed "such
an empire for liberty as she never surveyed since the creation; and I am
persuaded no constitution was ever before so well calculated as ours for
extensive empire and self-government."[14] With his pioneering efforts to
establish a central banking and monetary system, Hamilton enthusiastically embraced both the visions of Jefferson and Madison—and most
importantly his own constitutional interpretation, which was often creative and expansive. Hamilton's financial ingenuity has driven America to
be an imperial nation from the very beginning of the commercial republic.

These practical philosophers have had their own disagreements and
enchantments. For example, when some Jeffersonian Republicans in the
south proposed replacing American diplomatic missions abroad with
commercial consuls to promote international trade, Hamiltonian Federalists in the north were surprised. Nevertheless, these southern
Republicans, including Madison and George Washington, maintained
that commercial relations could be sustained without political entanglements as the Jeffersonians favored disconnection from the monarchical
and religious worlds of tyranny.[15] As a result, realist Hamilton believed
that Jefferson and Madison were "utopian dreamers."[16] As if to deny this
charge, Madison wrote in 1792 that "a universal and perpetual peace . . .
will never exist but in the imaginations of visionary philosophers, or in
the breasts of benevolent enthusiasts."[17]

Though as realistic as Hamiltonian Federalists, the Jeffersonians were overly optimistic that "the progress of reason might eventually end war."[18] Of like mind, Madison finally concluded that "if anything is to be hoped, everything ought to be tried."[19] As Jeffersonian Republicans seemingly conceded to northern Federalists, the southerners upheld the view that the declaration of wars must be authorized by the people (i.e., Congress) and the costs must be covered by the generation that declared them.[20] Madison then advised that only brief "wars of necessity" for defense must remain as the last option and "all nations" must adhere to this principle.[21] This suggests that the Jeffersonians agreed to the continuous support and advocacy of an empire. In his *Empire of Liberty*, Professor Gordon Wood at Brown University summarizes that "this was an aspect of the liberal dream of a universal peace shared by the enlightened everywhere."[22] That ancient founding wisdom resonates throughout American history and beyond.

In his insightful book *Imperial Republic*, Professor James Wilson at Cleveland State University concludes that the inherent quest for an "empire" was deeply rooted in the nucleus of America's founding DNA, its national origin, and the very essence of the constitutional system.[23] With existing tensions between competing republican and imperial visions, some observers have concluded that the domineering nature of American superpower and its hypocritical actions contradict the idea of a philosophic empire; others disappointedly observe the absence of religious motivation for a Christian empire. As explained in previous chapters, the founding empire builders were sympathetically inspired by the plight of the Pilgrims and their cause for religious freedom. While preserving their spiritual needs, the constitutional architects moved away from creating a Christian nation; instead, they pursued a naturally unifying force for all peoples through a commercial empire associated more with the colonists than the Pilgrims. Nevertheless, the Founders did not deny religious faith, but embraced it as an individual right. With the colonial experience, the constitutional architects realized the need for a common thread that binds all in an empire of philosophy. For America, this thread evolved from the wisdom traditions of antiquity and the Enlightenment thinkers.

The Masonic Seeding of an Empire: "Join, or Die"

The seeds of the constitutional development of a commercial republic were planted with the ideas of Freemasonry and historic actions orchestrated by Dr. Benjamin Franklin, provincial grand master of Pennsylvania. In his proposed Albany Plan of Union in 1754, he had drawn an identical plan of confederation that derived from the American provincial grand lodges of that time. Franklin was then 48 years young; Madison was three years old; Jefferson had just celebrated his tenth birthday; and Hamilton was not yet even conceived. When they were grown up, none of these men were known to have been Freemasons. Still, they were fully informed of the ideals and ideas of the fraternity through the momentous work of Reverend Dr. James Anderson's *Constitutions of the Free-Masons* (1723), which was reprinted in 1734 by Benjamin Franklin and widely distributed in colonial America—even advertised in the *Boston Evening Post* and other newspapers.[24] In the middle of the eighteenth century, American interests and commercial contacts were imbedded with the British Empire. Franklin and his brethren desired to remain within the Empire; however, their need for independence was strong and critical.

With that Masonic state of mind and the experience of the province of Pennsylvania, which enacted the Charter of Privileges of 1702 as their fundamental law,[25] Franklin and others understood the importance of the basic framework of a provincial authority and its governance through a body of laws and the guiding principle of rule by the consent of the governed.[26] In his *Foundations of American Nationality*, Professor Evarts Greene at the University of Illinois wrote that Franklin's constitutional framework of 1754 for a "home government" was agreed in Albany, which provided a "statesmanlike plan" for "the politicians on either side of the Atlantic."[27] The federal council was proposed to provide for the common defense, to control Indian relations, and to levy taxes for these purposes; however, the president-general would always have veto power. With the understanding that Pennsylvania was a Quaker experiment in government, these constitutional planners agreed upon a scheme that guaranteed religious liberty for the other colonies. Professor Greene explained this guarantee as "freedom of worship for all law-abiding persons who acknowledged one Almighty and Eternal God to be the Creator, Upholder, and Ruler of the world."[28] This compromise was an assurance device for not only Protestant Christians but also Catholics, Jews, and others. Such religious tolerance was a fundamental tenet of the Masonic philosophy of universal brotherhood.

Needed cooperation among the colonies was not forthcoming; however, Franklin was determined to harness unity and collaboration. Accompanying an editorial column in his *Pennsylvania Gazette*, Franklin published a symbolic pictorial portraying a snake divided into eight seg-ments—each portion labeled with the initials of the existing colonial governments—and the caption: "Join, or Die" (Figure 13.1).[29] The snake or serpent in the woodcut drawing (signifying one of the three large con-stellations of Draco, Serpent, and Hydra) has a head (indicating the dragon head, Rahu, or the North Node in astrology) and a tail (representing the dragon tail, Ketu, or the South Node). In the eighteenth century, it was a popular superstition in colonial America that a serpent cut in two would come to life if the pieces were joined before sunset. The occult image captured the public imagination instantly when the cartoon-like drawing was reprinted with minor variations in the *New York Mer-cury*, the *Virginia Gazette*, the Boston *Evening Post*, and elsewhere, making it the most famous political cartoon in American history.[30] None-theless, the Albany Plan became "less popular" in the independent-minded colonial assemblies and the Franklin plan was not adopted be-cause it was too "imperial and liberal;" thus, Professor Green noted that "the war had to be fought" using the "old machinery" to secure peace and unity.[31]

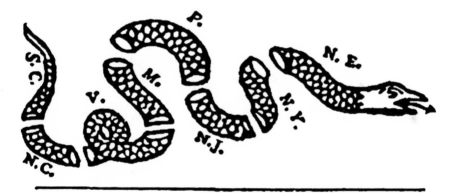

J O I N, or D I E.

FIGURE 13.1: Many historians maintain that the curves of the snake in this symbolic map is a shape of the eastern coastline and the labels portray the co-lonial governments in geographical order from **NE** (New England) of the right side of the cartoon of the snake's head being north and **SC** (South Carolina) at its tail to south. Other colonies were marked as **NY** (New York), **NJ** (New Jersey), **P** (Pennsylvania), **M** (Maryland), **V** (Virginia), and **NC** (North Carolina). At that time, the 13 colonies were divided into eight among those founded or ruled by royal charter; thus, Franklin's map has eight segments of snake.

Intellectual momentum for the Albany Plan of Union most obviously derived from Anderson's *Constitutions of the Free-Masons*, which outlined a federal system—an "orderly, balanced, and enlightened" mechanism—that would "eventually form the basis for a unified American nation."[32] This system mirrored that of the Masonic framework of governance in which the provincial grand lodge administered the broader scheme for general affairs of the community of Freemasons, while independent lodges adhered to the established order of by-laws under Anderson's *Constitutions* in the colonies.[33] The basic principles of governance employed in Freemasonry include:

- The grand lodge is supreme in the Masonic federal system

- Local lodges are self-governing and independent

- The selection of officers is carried out by secret vote using a ballot and elections

- Governance is limited by the Constitution

- The preservation of checks and balances is outlined to impeach the chief executive officer

- The popular sovereignty of representative government and majority rule are fundamental

- Fiscal responsibility is delegated to the legislative body

- A type of judicial review is conducted by the grand lodge, and

- Freedoms of speech and equal participation are hallmarks of Freemasonry.[34]

The striking similarities between the Masonic *Constitutions* and the Article of Confederation, the Constitution, and the Bill of Rights display a revealing connection that has been hardly recognized or explicitly advertised (this is one of Freemasonry's "public secrets" that has agitated Christian fundamentalists and conspiracy theorists). Referring to the Albany Plan of July 1754, Walter Isaacson (a meticulous and popular biographer of Benjamin Franklin) writes, "Franklin put forth the idea again in a proposed draft for Articles of Confederation" in July 1775. This draft "contained the seeds of the conceptual breakthrough that would eventually define America's federal system: a division of powers between a central government and those of the states."[35] Historian Thomas Burke at the New York State Commission also confirms that "Benjamin Franklin proposed a plan of confederation also based on the Albany Plan" at the Continental Congress in June 1775.[36] Burke further reveals that "some of the basic concepts of the Albany Plan of Union were attained at the Constitution Convention" at Philadelphia in 1787.[37] For example, a system of checks-and-balances, which was embodied in the Albany Plan of Union, remained an integral part of the federal Constitution.[38]

Though Freemasonry—an elite, but subtle and powerful, gentlemen's organization—had grown in popularity throughout the thirteen colonies, it was not the right time for the nation to form a union to solidify this brotherhood-type government. Yet Franklin was confident that a network of lodges practicing the same principles and Masonic-educated brethren at the community level were prepared to act in unison. At the end of his life, Franklin was still convinced that the approval of his Albany Plan would have prevented the Revolutionary War and created "a harmonious empire."[39] The eternal optimist reflected on the past by saying:

> The different and contrary reasons of dislike to my plan makes me suspect that it was really the true medium; and I am still of opinion it would have been happy for both sides the water [Atlantic] if it had been adopted. The colonies, so united, would have been sufficiently strong to have defended themselves; there would then have been no need of troops from England; of course, the subsequent pretence for taxing America, and the bloody contest it occasioned, would have been avoided. But such mistakes are not new; history is full of errors of states and princes.[40]

The politics of reality in the mid-eighteenth century were not as dangerous and eminently volatile as they were a quarter century later. The highly perceptive and farsighted Franklin was ahead of his time and determined to devise a gamut of diplomatic and political measures against the hostile French in Canada (and Ohio Country), the Dutch in New Amsterdam (New York), and even the Spanish in Florida. With the lessons learned from prior failures to unite the colonies, Franklin kept acting on good faith to safeguard their own interests. As he participated in the Albany Congress summoned by the Board of Trade in 1753 to plan for defending the colonies against European powers and to promote trade with the antagonistic Six Iroquois Nations (Cayuga, Mohawk, Oneida, Onondaga, Seneca, and Tuscarora), Franklin was convinced that a political union could finally be established a year later when the Albany Congress convened in 1754. Still, his plan was not adopted.

His unyielding determination to create a union had certainly been influenced by the ideas of Anderson's *Constitutions* and the influence of Enlightenment thinkers, especially Sir Francis Bacon's *New Atlantis*. The entrepreneurial and missionary zeal of Franklin was also proven by his dedication to Masonic tradecraft and devotion to liberal education for a more equitable and democratic society. He was once accused of advancing Masonic-inspired activities in 1755, saying, "The people who are the promoters of the *free* schools, are *Grand Masters* and *Wardens* among the Freemasons, their very pillars" (italics original).[41] Similar incidents confirmed that prevailing sentiments had contributed slightly and negatively to the realization of Franklin's vision for a united empire, which would have expanded the American territory once occupied by the Dutch, the French, and the Spanish.

The Hidden Hand of Manifest Destiny

The colonial history of the British, Dutch, French, Spanish, and others has generally been one in which imperial masters were portrayed as brutal exploiters who expeditiously destroyed other lands, cultures, and people for their own indulgence and wealth accumulation. Nevertheless, the intention of Franklin's Albany Plan illustrates that the aspiration behind an American empire was different. Furthermore, the shared conviction for establishing an empire of philosophy endured. Even before the nation was founded, for example, the American colonies unsuccessfully attempted to conquer Canada in 1775. After 1800, the nation's young democracy mutually reinforced its thrust for empire as settlers began to move toward western frontiers. This clever and founding mission was the primary vector in which major events in American history were influenced.

Territorial expansion first began with the Louisiana Purchase in 1803, which came about through exchange instead of conquest. The new territory and other annexations were divided into new states instead of remaining as colonies. In some situations, like the annexation of Florida and the war with Mexico, the United States expanded its territory by force; however, these territories never became permanent colonies. Subsequent political leaders preserved the founding intention in public consciousness by continuing to expand the American territory. For instance, in arguing for California's statehood on the senate floor on March 11, 1850, Senator William Seward captured the Madisonian vision, saying, "Four years ago, California, a Mexican Province, scarcely inhabited and quite unexplored, was unknown even to our usually immoderate desires, except by a harbor, capacious and tranquil, which only statesmen then foresaw would be useful in the oriental commerce of a far distant, if not merely chimerical, future."[42] Like the trio of Jefferson, Hamilton and Madison, Senator Seward (a diehard believer in the "Manifest Destiny"[43] introduced by John O' Sullivan in 1845) reaffirmed the original conviction for an empire and favored westward expansion:

> The Atlantic States, through their commercial, social, and political affinities and sympathies, are steadily renovating the Governments and the social constitutions of Europe and of Africa. The Pacific States must necessarily perform the same sublime and beneficent functions in Asia. If, then, the American people shall remain an undivided nation, the ripening civilization of the West, after a separation growing wider and wider for four thousand years, will, in its circuit of the world, meet again and mingle with the declining civilization of the East on our own free soil, and a new and more perfect civilization will arise to bless the earth, under the sway of our own cherished and beneficent democratic institutions.[44]

Long before the concept of Manifest Destiny was introduced as a divinely ordained force, a desire for "the continent of North America to be our proper dominion"[45] was made clear when Secretary of State John Quincy Adams informed President James Monroe in 1819 that:

> From the time we became an independent people, it was as much a *law of nature* that this should become our pretension, as that the Mississippi should flow to the sea. Spain had pretensions on

our southern, Great Britain on our northern borders. It was impossible that centuries should elapse without finding them
annexed to the United States (italics added).[46]

Florida was acquired by 1819; the Republic of Texas and the entire
Western frontier joined the United States in 1845. When Secretary of
State William Seward (former senator) purchased Alaska from Russia in
1867, the nation had almost doubled its territory in less than one hundred
years since the founding. After defeating the Spanish Empire during the
Spanish-American War of 1898, the United States served as the protector
of Cuba, Guam, the Philippines and Puerto Rico, followed by the annexation of Hawaii in the same year.

The Westward expansion toward Asia and the Pacific caused tragic calamities for the rightful inhabitants of those countries and native Indian
tribes as well as their long-cherished cultures and traditions. Some historians argued that America's underlying motive was the expansion of
industrial and financial power, while others described it as "the imperialism of free trade" ruled by the American empire with "informal control if
possible; trade with rule when necessary."[47] The latter was explained by
the occupation of Hawaii, the Philippines, and other American protecto-
rates in the Pacific and the Caribbean. This was clearly Hamiltonian
action inspired by Jeffersonian idealism to promote America's commercial values—and to build a Madisonian empire.

The old notion of Manifest Destiny has long since become globalized; today, it is practiced not by acquiring more land and property
overseas, but through a Madisonian scheme of harmonious agreements
and constitutional modifications at regional and global levels. The 1991
North American Free Trade Agreement (NAFTA) was used to bring
Canada and Mexico closer to the United States, and the World Trade Organization (WTO) followed in 1995 as a global mechanism to unite
nations. After years of American-led globalization, these two historic
agreements marked the initiation of a Madisonian vision for a universal
empire. Thomas Paine, who believed that "trade will always be a protection,"[48] was a prophet of sorts when he penned these words, "From a
small spark, kindled in America, flame has arisen not be extinguished.
Without consuming . . . it winds its progress from nation to nation and
conquers by a silent operation."[49] The apostle of freedom believed America to be on a "silent operation" to destroy despots and religious
extremists around the globe. This action itself has created unintended

consequences for the United States from anti-globalists and anti-Americans alike.

Why Do They Hate Us?

America raised this profound question in the aftermath of the 9/11 attacks, when for the first time a foreign enemy assaulted the continental United States (the only other assault on the country being the 1941 attack on Pearl Harbor in Hawaii by the Japanese). Some observers pointed to American foreign policies in the Middle East and the Persian Gulf as the cause for these attacks. Both China and Russia opposed the American invasion of Iraq in March 2003, and even European allies like France and Germany chose not to support the military action. Global sympathies that arose in the wake of 9/11 quickly turned against the United States; later revelations of intelligence failures and misleading testimony before the UN Security Council further galvanized anti-Bush sentiment not only around the world, but within the United States and his own administration.

President George W. Bush maintained that radical Islamic groups hate our freedom. One month after September 11, 2001, President Bush revealed America's Mercurial "trade" response when he outlined the long-term U.S. strategy: "Terrorists attacked the World Trade Center, and we will defeat them by expanding and encouraging world trade."[50] In his foreword to the 2002 *National Security Strategy of the United States*,[51] President Bush also summarized the American preference for democracy and economic openness, calling them "the best foundations for domestic stability and international order."[52] In keeping with the Bush doctrine—"the growth of democratic movements and institutions in every nation and culture"[53]—post-9/11 American foreign policy elevated trade to an even higher priority than before. The president commented, "Free trade and free markets have proven their ability to lift whole societies out of poverty—so the United States will work with individual nations, entire regions, and the entire global trading community to build a world that trades in freedom and therefore grows in prosperity."[54] The administration's National Security Strategy articulated this belief, stating:

The concept of 'free trade' arose as a moral principle even before it became a pillar of economics. If you can make something that others value, you should be able to sell it to them. If others make

something that you value, you should be able to buy it. This is
real freedom, the freedom for a person—or a nation—to make a
living.[55]

The simple premise of this concept dates back to early European Enlightenment thinkers. Like Adam Smith and other philosophers, National
Security Council officials reasoned that domestic peace and international
order derive from commercial freedom. Hence, trade would bring prosperity and democracy to the Middle East region, subsequently reducing
the likelihood of another terrorist attack on the United States. In this regard, Jefferson concurred that "war is not the best engine for us to resort
to," and then he elaborated, "Nature has given us one *in our commerce*,
which, if properly managed, will be a better instrument for obliging the
interested nations . . . to treat us with justice" (italics by Jefferson).[56]
Madison agreed that diplomatic persuasion through the instruments of
America's commercial power was "the most likely means of obtaining
our objects without war."[57]

Al-Qaeda operatives, anti-globalists, and other religious fundamentalists have opposed this very same logic. For them, the United States has
been promoting a gamut of controlling devices through geopolitical ma-
neuverings and the economics of empire building. American
manipulation has been extended through the dominion of big business on
Wall Street and corporate interests in oil-rich regions, particularly the
Persian Gulf. Besides these issues, however, religious fundamentalists
have always opposed the self-reliance of market forces and democratic
governance. Nevertheless, market forces safeguard religious freedoms,
propel international trade, and secularize the effects of globalization. The
ideas of freedom and democracy are antithetical to the philosophies of
extremists and religious fanatics, which are more likely to reject the spirit
of humanity, the sanctity of human life, and commercial prosperity—all
fundamental elements of the American way of life.

In his provocative book *The Roman Predicament*, Professor Harold
James at Princeton University argues that widespread mistrust of American supremacy has led to the perception that America is imposing its will
on the rest of the world.[58] James further observes that peaceful commerce
can help build a stable, prosperous, and integrated international society.
However, that peaceful liberal economic order will also lead to domestic
clashes (like anti-globalization demonstrations in Seattle, Washington
D.C., and elsewhere) and international rivalries (such as those with China, Russia, and Iran). According to Professor James, low-intensity

conflicts will eventually destroy the commercial system that is the very basis of prosperity and global integration. By exploring the rise and fall of the Roman Empire with the help of two famous classics—Smith's *Wealth of Nations* and *The Decline and Fall of the Roman Empire* by Edward Gibbon—the professor concludes, "The liberal commercial world order subverts and destroys itself."[59] Although there remain some parallels between the eighteenth century commentaries offered by Smith and Gibbon on the Roman Empire and James' comparative analysis on the American dilemma, the former two authors differ from James in that they construct their prognostic analysis based on mercantilism and imperial interests, which do not prevail in the contemporary global rule-based trading system under the World Trade Organization (WTO).

But progress in global trade under the WTO's Doha Development Agenda has been slow. The international trading system under the organization has emerged from the heart of American foreign policy tradition and its founding vision. This integral vision has been animated through the Constitution's commerce clause, the Great Seal of the United States, and its depiction on the dollar bill. The latter symbolizes the commercial instrumentality of currency in realizing America's global dominance; our currency is at once a visible hand, a source of power, and our destiny ordained with "In God We Trust."

American Mercury's Invisible Attraction

In a sort of Karmic reaction, the effect of American superpower flows from a philosophic vision of the Founding Fathers followed by a range of historic actions. Long before Sir Francis Bacon, the idea of an empire of philosophy influenced ancient kingdom builders; none held universal appeal as much as the ideas of freedom championed by the founding generation. The first serious plan of action for a confederation of colonies—masterminded by Benjamin Franklin in the Albany Plan of Union—formed this kind of subtle and ancient philosophy, which also contained the powerful ideas and parliamentary procedures included in Anderson's *Constitutions of the Free-Masons*. The perennial philosophy of universal brotherhood and natural laws ordained by Providence, which clearly derived from Freemasonry ideas and ideals endorsed by Washington, Franklin, and other Masonic founding architects, were delicately enshrined in America's founding documents without fanfare. For these enlightened Founding Fathers, the universal nature of the American project was self-evident, prophetic, and as natural as the sunrise. Indeed, this inconvenient truth is a disappointment to some Christian fundamentalists, Islamic extremists, and conspiracy theorists.

The Supreme Court of the United States—the ultimate venue for resolving vital national issues like slavery, abortion, child labor, monopolies, war powers, or prayer in public schools—is a prism through which American society is ultimately defined as one nation of Christians, Muslims, Hindus, Buddhists, and others. In affirmation of religious pluralism and appreciation of global diversity, a trio of ancient lawgivers—Moses, flanked by Confucius to his right and Solon on his left—occupies the monument to "Justice, the Guardian of Liberty" displayed on the eastern pediment of the Supreme Court Building (Figure 13.2). Although Moses is a well-known Judeo-Christian personality for his Ten Commandments, renowned Greek lawmaker Solon and great Chinese philosopher Confucius are less familiar. A pantheon of other figures is also engraved in the chamber; the eighteen prominent historical lawgivers on the courtroom's north and south walls include Muslim prophet Muhammad, Jewish King Solomon, Roman Emperors Augustus and Charlemagne, and a larger-than-life frieze of French General Napoleon. Explaining his artistic work, sculptor Hermon MacNeil, who worked with the famous architect Cass Gilbert on the Supreme Court's construction in the 1930s, wrote: "Law as an element of civilization was normally and naturally derived or inherited in this country from former civilizations. The 'Eastern Pediment' of the Supreme Court Building suggests therefore the treatment of such fundamental laws and precepts [is] derived from the East."[60]

The underlying principle is justifiable reassurance that the founding vision continues to be a global one, and American laws will remain universally accepted and honored. The Uniform Commercial Code (UCC or the Code) adopted in the United States is an example of the evolution of an international commercial code and harmonization, as it is increasingly being adopted by other countries as well. The most fundamentally transformative vector has always been the Constitution's commerce clause, which served to geographically expand the American empire and was later used as the meta-principle for WTO to modify both the laws and practices of member countries.

The commonly shared, psychic impulse of the Founding Fathers unconsciously established a global strategy for territorial and commercial expansion of the new nation in the American mindset. The same strategy was literarily expressed in the founding papers and other correspondences. It is why America has always welcomed immigrants and foreign visitors as multipliers of wealth and power; demand for education, transportation, and other commercial services created a range of opportunities for self-improvement in the arts, music, literature, and science. An intellectual mecca of universities and cultural centers with global outreach developed as a result. For example, the serendipitous encounter of President Barack Obama's parents at the University of Hawaii's East-West Center validated the founding conviction *E Pluribus Unum*, "Out of many, one." The United States has indeed been a place of global vision and local action—which led to the popular phrase "think globally, act locally"—for uniting people as one "human race" called Americans. This adventure has been the American odyssey, indeed.

FIGURE 13.2: A sculptural display of ancient lawgivers—Moses at the center with Confucius (left) and Solon—on the eastern pediment of the U.S. Supreme Court Building.

The founding philosophers' reasoning and logical thinking—especially that of America's first scientist, Dr. Benjamin Franklin—got Americans interested in science and engineering and diffused knowledge beyond racial, religious, and national boundaries. The force of science and technology in our deeply religious nation (as compared to Europe) propels economic dynamism in all communities, enhances social relations in formerly restricted groups, and promotes commercial relations with other countries. Navigational commerce and technology have improved international trade and maritime relations from the very beginning; scientific investigation still continues to explore new energy sources and other resources. As space technology and Internet communication have developed (through military and university research programs), the nation has been ever-energized for greater understanding of the mysteries of the universe. People are increasingly connected to hardly-known friends of friends through social networks (like Facebook, LinkedIn, and Twitter) that are made possible by the Internet and other technological innovations. The beneficiaries of these innovations are not only the wealthy but also the middle-class. As the nation of innovators, America is constantly being reborn, recycled, and renovated. These are the dynamics of America's transformative power both individually and globally—and the source of national entrepreneurship and the American dream.

The American dream has always been linked to American political economy, which has a special quality within the world. Politics is an art of compromise, innovation, and perfection for a "more perfect" Union. The same concept is applied to wealth creation. But the greatest of all creations was the U.S. Constitution—the result of a long and arduous journey that began with the Pilgrims and colonists, carried on with the Albany Plan of Union and culminated with the Constitutional Convention. Just as Adam Smith's invisible hand in the marketplace drives underlying economic forces to satisfy human greed, James Madison's meta-principles in the Constitution compel ethical human behavior to achieve a philosophic empire. These competing forces, defined and refined by Enlightenment thinkers and founding architects alike, constitute self-interested actors and institutions trying to achieve a balance by creating imaginative tensions (deriving from greed and morality) for greater innovation and improved solutions. Though the fundamentals have not changed much, political artists (like Abraham Lincoln and Franklin Roosevelt) and economists (such as British John Maynard Keynes and American Milton Friedman) from all walks of life have improved America's outlook and progress over the passage of time. The vessel that carries these marketplace and Constitutional forces is manifested in global networks of trade—trade in goods, services, and most importantly, trade in the ideas of freedom. The mutually reinforcing and evolving mechanism may have modified the republican institutions, but the founding conviction has preserved the engine of the American empire and statesmanship.

Whenever America has failed to maintain the balance between markets and governments, progress in the nation and the world has been endangered. In all this, the concept of political autonomy (or national sovereignty) and economic interdependence (in international trade) prevails at the center of America's founding vision, as reflected in the universal order (the notions of autonomy and interdependence found in the cosmos). In his perceptive book *Freefall: America, Free Markets, and the Sinking of the World Economy*, Nobel Laureate Professor Joseph Stiglitz at Columbia University explains the causes of the current global financial crisis and illustrates how America's bad leadership, economic policies, and behavior dramatized the nation and the world.[61] He concludes by resorting to the founding wisdom: "Will we seize the opportunity to restore our sense of balance between the market and the state, between individualism and the community, between man and nature, between means and ends?"[62] The Founding Fathers expounded on these perennial questions and devised the machinery of political economy for succeeding generations to reflect on governing their individual actions and political decisions. In addition to the usual suspects outlined by Adam Smith and James Madison, Professor Stiglitz also identifies "moral deficit" and the "unrelenting pursuit of profit" as responsible for the national and global economic crisis.[63]

In such "times that try men's souls,"[64] as Thomas Paine once observed, doubts naturally arise: America's founding constitutional mechanism has been questioned and the validity of Providence has been tested. Here, the Chindian challenge (from China and India) involving over two billion people provides insight into the American experience. China has essentially employed a Hamiltonian economic model with a centralized government in Beijing helmed by Communist leadership. After independence from Great Britain in 1947, India began as a Gandhian democracy of village republics (Gham Rajas) that resonated with Jeffersonian ideas of small republics in agricultural hamlets. Soon after, however, India turned toward Hamiltonian-like manufacturing and the idea of an industrial nation under Sri Nehru. Using the Indian-style Hindu equilibrium of the caste system, the world's largest democracy began to pursue free market economic policies in the early 1990s and generated unprecedented growth rates. The Chinese doctrine of a Mandate from Heaven (like Washington, D.C., the Forbidden City in Beijing was also designed according to astrological significance) severed its connection from feudal Chinese heritage when the Jeffersonian-like Dr. Sun Yat-Sen, father of modern China, tried to transform the dynastic regimes into a unified democratic republic in the early twentieth century. (Educated in Hawaii, Japan and Hong Kong, Dr Sun Yat-Sen was a great admirer of

Abraham Lincoln). Following new economic reform policies in the early 1980s, a Hamiltonian-like Deng Xiaoping made China a rising global power. His most famous maxim—"It doesn't matter whether a cat is white or black, so long as it catches mice"[65]—dangerously underestimated the power of the Jeffersonian ideals (e.g., the Tiananmen Square protests of 1989) that underpinned the Chinese people's desire for freedom, democracy and livelihood, all of which were adamantly advocated by the father of modern China.[66] Deng's economic pragmatism will sooner or later demand for a Jeffersonian-like China to find peaceful equilibrium between self-interest and moral sentiments in order to address corruption, environmental degradation, limited religious freedoms and minority rights, and eventually lead to political stability and peace.

Despite their opposite political orientations, Chindia was certainly inspired by America's philosophic empire; therefore, there is no time and space for pessimism—America will endure as a master builder for a better nation and a more secure world. This has always been a source of invisible attraction to the commercial republic, which is governed by democratic ideals and republican virtues. As highly cognitive revolutionaries, the Founding Fathers fully understood the fundamental nature of human behavior, which innately self-calibrates between self-interest and morality to seek normalcy and stability (as opposed to military force or despotism). They accordingly devised a system of self-governance that could be universally adopted in various cultures, whether in China, India, or elsewhere.

In a democratic republic like ours, representatives debating in congressional halls over the nature and direction of the nation deserve sympathy and more understanding, because Congress has always faced challenges in balancing market forces with government regulation (this, among other things, accounts for economic imbalances). Often, the private minds and entrepreneurial spirit of the American public are an unrecognized and underappreciated "Congress" at large. As a result, elected leaders must listen to the meritocracy beyond the elections, as some enduring contributions—like the American flag, national anthem, continental railroads, and Internet search engines like Google—derived from outside of government. The wondrous nature of American democracy and its people is that it has the agility to correct itself in both political and economic realms because, as Alexander Hamilton declared, "Your people, sir—your people is a great beast."[67]

The nation's optimistic outlook, along with the long-lasting federal institutions incorporated into the machinery of American Providence and commerce, is self-assured if Congress acts accordingly. This action requires constant reflection on the short-term stewardship of their states and congressional districts (not the longevity contest in Congress) in pursuit of the Founders' original mission to usher the great nation into an even greater future. The practical wisdom of antiquity comes from no other than President George Washington, who knew when to fight, govern, and gracefully retire to Mount Vernon when his tasks were accomplished. The first president knew the difference between the statesmanship as a dynamic guardian of the nation and the status quo of aging in the seat of political power as a self-serving gerontologist.

As a vivid and constant reminder, the enduring founding ideas symbolically impressed in the nation's capital—along the sanctified Constitution Avenue starting from the Mellon Zodiac Water Fountain to the U.S. Institute of Peace by the Potomac River—communicate America's destiny not only to political and economic leaders, but also to everyone who understands the universal language of symbols in wisdom traditions (Figure 13.3). Figuratively, the Zodiac Fountain signifies the universality of America's international "human race" and the Institute of Peace affirms the enlightened intelligence of founding conviction for a more peaceful world. America's brilliance in universal symbolism and philosophic empire is neither the language nor the strategy advocated by Prime Minister Winston Churchill; a global empire requires a global language that can extend far beyond the English-speaking world. This is the very essence of James Madison's universal and philosophic empire, which was explicitly endorsed by Jefferson, Hamilton, and Washington.

FIGURE 13.3: Symbolic connection to James Madison's universal and philosophic empire.

In that respect, the former colonial leader was right: "The empires of the future are the empires of the mind."[68] Such is the empire that will bring unity and peace to all nations through the symbols of American Mercury, which has indeed produced impressive results in areas like communication technologies, biotechnological innovations, and the international architecture for the global trading (WTO), financial (IMF), and governance (UN) systems for human progress everywhere. Commercial providence—undergirded by America's "In God We Trust" currency—is then the heart and soul of America's invisible attraction; it is a marvel of the "public secret" and our eventual destiny, for which "God bless America" is often invoked in gratitude and reverence.

EPILOGUE

President Barack Obama's State of the Union address in January, 2010

"America is . . . the land of the future, where, in the ages that lie before us, the burden of the World's History shall reveal itself."

~ German Philosopher GEORG WILHELM FRIEDRICH HEGEL, 1832

God's Crucible Nation: Predestiny or Free Will?

When our Founders declared a new order of the ages; when soldiers died in wave upon wave for a union based on liberty; when citizens marched in peaceful outrage under the banner 'Freedom Now'—they were acting on an ancient hope that is meant to be fulfilled. History has an ebb and flow of justice, but history also has a visible direction, set by liberty and the Author of Liberty.[1]

President George W. Bush, Second Inaugural Address, 2005

For more than three thousand years, secret societies have labored to create the background of knowledge necessary to the establishment of an enlightened democracy among the nations of the world . . . Men bound by a secret oath to labor in the cause of world democracy decided that in the American colonies they would plant the roots of a new way of life. Brotherhoods were established to meet secretly, and they quietly and industriously conditioned America to its destiny for leadership in a free world.[2]

Manly P. Hall, Author of *The Secret Destiny of America*, 1944

As a global nation, America has always acted in world affairs within the framework of its founding conviction, Manifest Destiny, and exceptionalism. Thus, the American odyssey is inherently associated with the perennial debate between predestiny and free will. Our Founding Fathers delved into these paradigms not only because the first English colonists (acting on their own free will) and the Pilgrims (acting out the doctrine of Christian predestination) settled in Virginia and Massachusetts respectively, but also because of the natural and moral works of ancient philosophers and Enlightenment thinkers. As the great interlocutors, the learned founding generation understood the history and geography of the world and America's place in the grand scheme of cosmology and philosophy.

Unlike any other nation on earth, America's philosophic empire was born with purpose on an auspicious birthday—not created in the interests of one group or another. The specific purpose and date for the creation of our empire remains the cause of freedom for which our forefathers sacrificed their lives to guarantee the inalienable rights of life, liberty, and the pursuit of happiness for all. As a "shining city on a hill"[3] with global aspirations, the proposed vehicle to achieve this lofty goal comes by way of a commercial republic within a constitutional structure that is universally applicable, often envied, and admired by many.

In this epilogue, I would like to propose a timely question for the new generation of globalized Americans—from Alaska to Texas—to reflect on the nation's rendezvous with destiny and the mechanics at work as I understand them. This book presents very brief introductory remarks on predestination and free will, as the founding men of faith attempted to conceptualize each, for continued dialogue. Since our history is prologue, I study the past through the prism of the Founding Fathers' writings and actions in order to visualize future possibilities. Thus, this book is not necessarily all about history; it is about impregnation of the past to better understand the future of history and to creatively engage in a post 9/11 conversation within the current status of international relations:

> Does predestination or free will require or inspire the United States to borrow money from China (a Hamiltonian means) to invade Mesopotamia and promote democracy (a Jeffersonian end) in order to establish a Madisonian empire of liberty in the Muslim world, where Americanization and globalization have had the least visible influence to date?

America: Then and Now

For an imperialist-minded Founding Father like Alexander Hamilton, British-like corporate expansion (as practiced in his time by the East India Company) in the Arabian Peninsula would have most certainly been a welcome decision for commercial purposes and oil imports. Thomas Jefferson, who doubled the size of the country with the Louisiana Purchase, may have endorsed the idea as one of his preferred mottos, "Resistance to tyrants is obedience to God,"[4] seems well-suited to the region of fundamentalists, theocrats, and despots. George Washington, John Adams, and James Madison (having experienced provocation on issues of freedom, trade, and navigation by the British and Barbary States) may have been reluctant to wage a pre-emptive war against a nonaggressive nation over faulty intelligence, as President George W. Bush did in Iraq.

President Bush undoubtedly acted on the founding conviction of "a new order of the ages" and the promise of "an ancient hope that is meant to be fulfilled" as he declared in his second Inaugural Address on January 20, 2005.[5] Following the president's prophetic remarks, perpetual concerns (like those raised under his father just prior to the first Gulf War in 1991) were revived once again: Was this action predestined or of free will? For President Bush, Iraq was a "war of choice rather than necessity."[6] The president rationalized his action: "We are led, by events and common sense, to one conclusion: The survival of liberty in our land increasingly depends on the success of liberty in other lands. The best hope for peace in our world is the expansion of freedom in all the world."[7] In the same speech, he proclaimed that "history has an ebb and flow of justice, but history also has a visible direction, set by liberty and the Author of Liberty."[8] His moral philosophy, like the Founding Fathers' notion of destiny, was valid and genuinely American; however, his actions were vividly counterproductive and tragic. Moreover, his policies undermined the founding vision, have failed so far to establish democracy in the greater Middle East, spent over one trillion dollars, killed over 4,000 Americans, injured (both physically and psychologically) more than 40,000 brave service members, and caused agony for thousands of families all over the world, including American ones. Still, the president defiantly declared, "We have no desire to dominate, no ambitions of empire."[9] As far as America's Manifest Destiny and exceptionalism are concerned, such denial is historically disingenuous. The Bush calculus (of not knowing the history and geography of Mesopotamia) proved strategically dangerous and exacted incalculable losses to humanity.

America has always endured through dreadful situations. As long as freedom reigns, the nation can and will reinvent itself. This galactic episode (i.e., a "war of choice") in American history requires reflection because America is no longer confined to merely domestic justice and security alone. We are globally intertwined with shared norms and human values. Complexity in international relations has evolved as we borrow money from China to pay for wars in Iraq, Afghanistan, and elsewhere. It is quite remarkable that President Bush offered insight into American history as it certainly has an "ebb and flow of justice" as well as "a visible direction, set by liberty and the Author of Liberty."[10] This may be broadly interpreted in both a national and international context as follows:

> **National**: American experience with the flow of justice began with the founding generation in a complex and paradoxical socio-economic structure and religio-cultural environment during their time. Philosophically enlightened, politically savvy, and often personally challenged, the Founding Fathers experienced a prisoners' dilemma in a series of human flaws related to the moral issues of property rights, women's rights, the slave trade, and respect for Native Indian culture. Their notion of universal brotherhood differed distinctly when it came to their actions on the citizenship and humanity of women, slaves, and native tribes. As the nation progressed through continual struggle for more than a century, the "ebb and flow of justice" started to manifest itself with the women's suffrage and Civil Rights movements, and the institution of sovereign rights for tribal governance on Indian reservations. As history is always written by winners, hagiographic views of our Founding Fathers must be understood within a framework of human fragility, personal contradiction, and political paradox in a historical context.

> **International**: China, whose relationship with America is symbiotic, mirrors human flaws in cultural and religious affairs. As once in the United States, the extraordinary success of China's Hamiltonian-like economic, financial, and industrial strategies have overshadowed Jeffersonian inspirations in religious matters and minority rights (i.e., in Tibet and Xinjiang). As Hamiltonian China pursues trade and development strategies for human progress, the unintended consequences of U.S. foreign policy compels America to engage more in war and peace issues (e.g., the Middle East) than in its commercial mission. In this global vacuum, secular China and its centralized political structure successfully founded inroads for their Hamiltonian pathways in Asia, Africa, Latin America, and elsewhere in the world.

With a history of civil wars and foreign invasions, China has had its own challenges and trepidations. The new generation of Chinese, however, is increasingly and subtly inspired by unfolding economic opportunity and greater freedom (e.g., the introduction of intraparty democracy and the election of relatively young, reform-minded Xi Jinping as party leader), which may in turn open up more gateways for a Jeffersonian world through Hamiltonian means. The question is, given America's long march for equal opportunity for women and civil rights for African-Americans, does the enlightened Chinese leadership need a hundred years to become a "more" perfect Confucian union? As history has accelerated our understanding of human nature and innovation in an endearing formula, China has pursued their revered strategist Sun Tzu's advice: "Know the enemy and know yourself; in a hundred battles you will never be in peril. When you are ignorant of the enemy but know yourself, your chances of winning or losing are equal. If ignorant both of your enemy and of yourself, you are certain in every battle to be in peril."[11] It appears that the Founding Fathers' understanding of human nature and the design of the commercial republic is universal and admired (and applied) by the Chinese and others. Unlike the communism practiced by the former Soviet Union, Chinese communism self-destructs creatively and profitably in a stable and innately forced Confucian-like environment.

In these perspectives, America's global vision of a philosophic empire has been advanced—not necessarily by America alone but alongside other nations like China. After WWII, Japan and Germany, for example, became instruments of America's global mission. Furthermore, the United States created the United Nations (UN) in America's image. With America's guidance and pursuance, China became a member of the World Trade Organization (WTO), which is a contemporary and global extension of the U.S. Constitution's commerce clause.[12] With its peaceful rise as a responsible stakeholder in the global community, does China undergird for an American-style Madisonian commercial empire with Confucian characteristics? In support of such a vision, President George W. Bush said, "Free trade and free markets have proven their ability to lift whole societies out of poverty—so the United States will work with individual nations, entire regions, and the entire global trading community to build a world that trades in freedom and therefore grows in prosperity" (Figure E1).[13] Did this prophetic statement shepherd China through its own free will to become an American surrogate for the president to achieve his democracy promotion agenda (with Chinese financing) in the Middle East and elsewhere?

FIGURE E1: America's grand strategy is embedded in free trade and global commerce, and sanctified by Providence for its Mercurial destiny.

Like Japan and Germany, China is a triumph for America's philosophic vision; the leading roles of Chimerica (China and America) in the UN and WTO mutually aid each nation in realizing their global aspirations. President Harry S. Truman said, "It will be just as easy for nations to get along in a republic of the world as it is for us to get along in a republic of the United States."[14] The Masonic grand master of Missouri understood the meaning of universal brotherhood and the ideals of Freemasonry. So did the founding brethren, who expounded on the natural and moral philosophies of predestination and free will that lie at the heart of America's global mission and its eventual destiny or fate. This odyssey continues by its very nature, but the judicious application of free will is the only choice for American (and Chinese) leadership to create a more peaceful world.

The Founders and the Paradox

Our history attests that either predestiny or free will made America the most powerful nation in the world. As counterparts of idealistic realism (heavenly ideals and earthly realities), both predestiny and free will contributed to the organic process of metaphysical selection for the invention and formation of America's philosophic empire. The doctrine of predestination largely relates to the past, as free will continues from the present moment to the future (like a constant Karmic modifier of predestiny). Thus, each exists in the same continuum of complicated metaphysical dynamics. Free will operates selectively and imperfectly in that occultic (unseen) environment of time and space, while predestiny governs unconditionally and preciously as immutable natural law. The fluid nature of these forces and their organic interactions in a metaphysical sphere is difficult to comprehend through human reasoning and the rational mind.

Different mystic traditions and religious philosophies (including Buddhism and Hinduism) offered a variety of interpretations into the working dynamics of these unforeseen powers. As generally understood, this mystical yet validating mechanism interacts and counterbalances a gamut of forces through an immutable process of natural selection in which punishment (i.e., tragic earthquakes, hurricanes, and floods) and reward (e.g., salubrious seasonal weather for crop harvests) at the hand of Nature's God work toward maintaining equilibrium and exacting justice. The Founding Fathers, especially those initiated into Freemasonry and other esoteric orders, evidently understood the general workings of these matters of Nature's God as they applied to the American project and personal affairs (such as Benjamin Franklin's astrology and George Washington's celestial observation). Their faith in Providence was ordained as part of American destiny, but they could not escape the issue of free will. This was the only choice for the learned men, who often wrestled with cognitive dissonance; they acted decisively in founding the new nation.

To dislodge such cognitive dissonance somewhat, two Biblical passages within the context of the founding generation provide a glimpse into the philosophical entanglements and the dichotomy that exists between free will and predestiny. Endorsing the Christian belief in predestination, Jeremiah in the Bible cites, "Before I formed you in the womb I knew you, and before you were born I consecrated you; I appointed you as a prophet to the nations."[15] John Jay, an author of the *Federalist Papers* and a Founding Father, adhered to this worldview in favor of "Christians" when he said:

> Almost all nations have peace and war at the will and pleasure of rulers whom they do not elect, and who are not always wise or virtuous. Providence has given to our people the choice of their rulers, and it is the duty, as well as the privilege and interest, of our Christian nation to select and prefer Christians for their rulers.[16]

Nevertheless, in a private letter to Samuel Miller on February 18, 1822, the federalist author questioned the "orthodoxy" of the Christian Trinity as "incomprehensible and consequently inexplicable by human Ingenuity."[17] It was utterly hopeless for the Founding Fathers to act rationally and independently if the Christian doctrine of predestation were to govern every matter of personal affairs and of national importance.

In support of free will, Deuteronomy states, "I call heaven and earth to witness against you today that I have set before you life and death, the blessings and the curses. Choose life so that you and your descendants may live."[18] The canon of Christian love in Jesus Christ (i.e., universal love or "brotherly love" in Freemasonry) appears to have served as the interlocutor between predestiny and free will, as divine and mundane matters calibrated accordingly in the continuum of metaphysics. John Adams wrote, "One great advantage of the Christian religion is, that it brings the great principle of the law of nature and nations—Love your neighbor as yourself, and do to others as you would that others should do to you—to the knowledge, belief, and veneration of the whole people."[19] As a Unitarian and deist, the second president rejected the idea of eternal damnation in Christianity and remarked in a letter to Thomas Jefferson, "What calamities that engine of grief has produced!"[20]

As described in preceding chapters, the Founding Fathers abandoned the notion of a Christian nation embraced by the Pilgrims (who escaped from precisely such a religious environment in England where they were persecuted) and endorsed by their Calvinistic theology. Other Protestant principles—drawn from the Christian doctrines of Jacob Arminius[21] and Emanuel Swedenborg[22]—rejected the doctrine of Calvinist predestination and supported the idea of free will, which had a profound influence on Wesleyan and Methodist theology in the United States. While keeping church and state in separate domains for mutual enrichment and the exercise of freedom, the founding generation chose guidance for such governance through Enlightenment rationalism. Promoting the Virginia Statute of Religious Freedom authored by Thomas Jefferson, James Madison wrote in *Memorial and Remonstrance*: "During almost fifteen centuries has the legal establishment of Christianity been on trial. What have been its fruits? More or less, in all places, pride and indolence in the clergy; ignorance and servility in the laity; in both, superstition, bigotry, and persecution."[23] In admiration of the morality of Jesus but troubled by the divinity in Christ and mysteries in the Bible, Jefferson said, "My fundamental principle would be the reverse of Calvin's, that we are saved by our good works which are within our power, and not by our faith which is not within our power."[24] Benjamin Franklin similarly wrote, "I received from my infancy a pious education in the principles of Calvinism [but] after having doubted in turn of different tenets . . . as I found them combated in the different books that I read, I began to doubt of revelation itself."[25]

Nonetheless, their founding conviction and action illustrated that they believed in free will and predestination as well as autonomy and interdependence without being imprisoned by any particular natural or moral philosophy or religious orthodoxy. Although the Founding Fathers disagreed on specific theological persuasions, independent-minded men like Adams, Franklin, Jefferson, and Madison concurred on general Christian principles and America's Special Providence. The relationship between human nature and freedom within the governance of Nature's God or the Great Architect of the Universe was more important to these men as the U.S. Declaration of Independence dictated that the "Laws of Nature" entitled them to "self-evident truth" and "unalienable rights" for all.[26] Jefferson maintained that "those general principles of Christianity are as eternal and immutable as the existence and attributes of God; and that those principles of liberty are as unalterable as human nature, and our terrestrial mundane system."[27]

The ideas embedded in the Declaration of Independence, the Constitution, and the governing mechanism of the republic confirmed the integrative rationalism drawn from various theological and political philosophies. The subtle but pervasive debate between free will and predestination was captured correctly when Madison wrote these famous words:

> It may be a reflection on human nature, that such devices should be necessary to control the abuses of government. But what is government itself, but the greatest of all reflections on human nature? If men were angels, no government would be necessary. If angels were to govern men, neither external nor internal controls on government would be necessary.[28]

The empirical worldview of human nature further suggests that these men of faith were influenced by rationality for common good while adhering to their general belief in Providence. Solidifying this view, Madison concluded:

> No people ought to feel greater obligations to celebrate the goodness of the Great Disposer of Events and the Destiny of Nations than the people of the United States. His kind providence originally conducted them to one of the best portions of the dwelling place allotted to the great family of the human race. . . . And to the same Divine Author of every good and perfect gift we are indebted for all those privileges and advantages, religious as well as civil, which are so richly enjoyed in this favored land.[29]

The Grand Experiment

In the end, these philosophical musings from assorted writings and perspectives provide little justice to the complexity of such perennial issues, which definitely require further study. The debate should not, however, be limited to the dichotomy between predestiny and free will. Instead, it should expand on the continuing American experiment with various hybrids, and demand our nation of innovators to think free from ideology like the *integrative* Founding Fathers did for the commercial republic to act as the catalysts and transformers of human progress, unity, and freedom.

Authentic freedom takes root first when ideology and prejudice dissipate from the human mind and are then replaced by genuine security and peace. The essence of the American empire is the empire of mind;

commercial providence was instrumental in fostering a single human race as America's globalizing human stock based on its founding conviction, *E Pluribus Unum*, "Out of many, one," manifested with President Barack Hussein Obama. In his most well-known speech delivered before the Lincoln Memorial on August 28, 1963, Reverend Dr. Martin Luther King, Jr., prophesied such eventual manifestation when he said, "I have a dream that one day this nation will rise up and live out the true meaning of its creed: 'We hold these truths to be self-evident, that all men are created equal.'"[30] Two score and seven years later, America's original purpose of equality, unity, and freedom has proved nationally achievable, globally desirable, and universally acceptable to the wise—though they are in short supply.

The United States is a crucible nation by design, where all the races of the world meet and are reborn within America's expanding "melting pot." God's children seemingly blend together as "inter-beings" in the union of *E Pluribus Unum*, which connects them to the world. The Jefferson-Hemings affair was a testament to the natural fusion of all races in the new democratic republic. Today, the affair's legacy is not limited to a "united states" of black and white America, but literally proclaims the union of all races as ethnic minorities will soon become the majority, while interracial (and inter-faith) marriages gain greater momentum and wider acceptance. (The American education system, international exchange programs, and U.S. military personnel stationed around the world are the force multipliers of God's crucible nation). This unique American *experiment* began with the founding vision for commercial providence, and the *science* of liberty has produced the last and best hope for the world in which Nature's God resides. With this manifest Providence, the idea of an America guided by the secular high priest of Freemasonry can never be destroyed—as long as freedom reigns.

Consequently, serendipitous innovations in science, technology, and policy—such as the pacemaker, the predator drone, Twitter, and e-commerce—will accelerate the best of America yet to come. Ahead of us awaits a rendezvous with destiny for the new generation of Americans— a rendezvous to herald the arrival of a better world that is presently unimaginable. Though today's better world of magical communication and amazing technology was inconceivable to the founding generation, their wisdom and understanding of human nature—constituted and constrained in our check-and-balance system of institutions—will keep on expanding globally to make the world safer for commerce and democracy. This was the founding purpose of the exceptional American project, and it will always be our ancient hope for a more peaceful world.

NOTES

Preface: *Providence and Empire*

1. Alexis de Tocqueville, Henry Reeve, ed., *Democracy in America*, Part I (Cambridge, MA: Sever and Francis, 1863), 13.

2. Benjamin Franklin, William Temple Franklin, ed., *Memoirs of Benjamin Franklin* (New York: Derby and Jackson, 1859), 183.

3. Artur Weiser, *The Psalms: A Commentary* (Louisville, KY: Westminster John Knox Press, 2000), 198.

4. See the concluding remarks of theology and ethics in Deuteronomy in J. Gary Millar, *Now Choose Life: Theology and Ethics in Deuteronomy* (Downers Grove, IL: Intervarsity Press, 2001), 181-183.

5. See the essays found in Robert John Russell, Nancey Murphy, et al., eds., *Chaos and Complexity: Scientific Perspectives on Divine Action* (Notre Dame, IN: University of Notre Dame Press, 1996).

6. Walter Mead Russell, Walter Russell Mead, *Special Providence: American Foreign Policy and How It Changed the World* (New York: Alfred A. Knopf, 2004), 310.

7. Walter Mead Russell, 310-334.

8. John Micklethwait and Adrian Wooldridge, *The Right Nation: Conservative Power in America* (New York: Penguin Press, 2004), 186.

9. Samuel Eliot Morison, ed., *The Oxford History of the United States 1783-1917* (New York: Oxford University Press, 1927), 413. See also Walter Russell Mead, vii.

10. Alexis de Tocqueville, Democracy in America, Part I, 310.

11. Alexis de Tocqueville, Democracy in America, Part I., xxxiii.

12. Alexis de Tocqueville, Democracy in America, Part II., 194.

13. Alexis de Tocqueville, Democracy in America, Part II., 166.

14. David Hume, *An Enquiry Concerning Human Understanding* (Oxford, England: Clarendon Press, 1902).

15. David Hume, 140.

16. Alexis de Tocqueville, Henry Reeve, ed., *The Republic of the United of States of America*, (New York: A. S. Barnes and Company, 1856), 453.

17. Alexis de Tocqueville, *The Republic of the United of States of America*, 3.

18. Alexis de Tocqueville, *The Republic of the United of States of America*, 27-28.

19. William Shakespeare, *The Tempest* (San Francisco, CA: Grabhorn Press, 1951), 64.

20. Frank Freidel, *Franklin D. Roosevelt: A Rendezvous with Destiny* (Newtown, CT: American Political Biography Press, 2005), 578.

Chapter 1: A Rendezvous with Destiny

1. President Barack Hussein Obama's historic speech at Cairo University in Egypt on June 4, 2009. The entire text of President Obama's prepared remarks to the Muslim world was published in *The New York Times* on June 4, 2009. See the White House press release at http://www.whitehouse.gov/the_press_office/Remarks-by-the-President-at-Cairo-University-6-04-09.

2. President Roosevelt delivered one of his most inspiring speeches, "A Rendezvous with Destiny," before the 1936 Democratic National Convention in Philadelphia on June 27, 1936. See Frank Freidel, *Franklin D. Roosevelt: A Rendezvous with Destiny* (Newtown, CT: American Political Biography Press, 2005), 578.

3. Ibid.

4. Thomas Paine, Isaac Kramnick, ed., *Common Sense* (New York: Penguin Books, 1982), 120.

5. Charles H. Callahan, *Washington: The Man and the Mason* (Washington, D.C.: Press of Gibson Brothers, 1913), 159. See also Marvin Kitman, *The Making of the President 1789: The Unauthorized Campaign Biography* (New York: Grove Press, 2000), 302; and Paul Gutjahr, *An American Bible: A History of the Good Book in the United States, 1777-1880* (Palo Alto, CA: Stanford University Press, 1999), 39. Note: The Masonic Bible was taken from St. John's Lodge No. 1 in New York, where Chancellor Robert Livingston was grand master of Freemasons. At least five presidents have taken the oath of office on the St. John's Bible: Washington, Warren Harding, Dwight Eisenhower, Jimmy Carter, and George H. W. Bush. Of the five, only Washington and Harding were Freemasons. George W. Bush requested the Masonic Bible in 2001 but was prevented from using the fragile, ten-pound book by pouring rain on inauguration day.

6. New evidence suggests that President George Washington never said, "I swear—so help me God," according to Forrest Church. He questions Washington Irving, who wrote sixty-seven years after the event and attributed these words to the president for the first time in his *George Washington: A Biography*. Like the story of young Washington cutting down the cherry tree, these words have fallen into question. See the chapter on "Did George Washington Say 'So Help Me God'" in Forrest Church, *So Help Me God: The Founding Fathers and First Great Battle Over Church and State* (Orlando, FL: Houghton Mifflin Harcourt, 2007), 445-449. Beth Hahn, history editor for the U.S. Senate Historical Office, revised her earlier comment that Washington said 'So help me God' in a video posted on the website of the Joint Congressional Committee on Inaugural Ceremonies. She correctly stated that President Theodore Roosevelt (a Freemason) neither used a Bible nor recited the codicil. Presidents Herbert Hover (a Quaker) and Franklin Pierce chose to affirm rather than swear. Hahn admitted that the first eyewitness documentation of a president saying 'So help me God' is an account of President Chester Arthur in 1881. Moreover, George Washington's Mount Vernon Estate and Gardens announced, "Scholars debate whether Washington added these final four words to the oath as set forth by the Constitution." See Cathy Lynn Grossman, "No Proof Washington Said 'So Help Me God'—Will Obama?" *USA Today*, January 9, 2009. See the entire article online at http://www.usatoday.com/news/religion/2009-01-07-washington-oath_N.htm. In the final analysis, it is difficult to prove that all presidents have followed Washington's example, which is itself contested.

7. United States Presidents, *Inaugural Addresses of the Presidents of the United States: From George Washington to Bill Clinton* (Charleston, SC: Biblio Life Press, 2007), 8.

8. See Frank E. Grizzard, Jr., *The Ways of Providence: Religion and George Washington* (Buena Vista, VA: Mariner Companies, Inc., 2005), 4-5. Also, see George Washington, Julius Friedrich Sachse, ed., *Washington's Masonic Correspondence as Found among the Washington Papers in the Library of Congress* (Lancaster, PA: Press of the New Era Printing Company, 1915), 22, 26, passim.

9. Steven Waldman, *Founding Faith: Providence, Politics, and the Birth of Religious Freedom in America* (New York: Random House, 2008), 58.

10. Manly P. Hall, *The Secret Destiny of America* (Los Angeles, CA: Philosophical Research Society, 1944), 77.

11. James H. Billington, *Fire in the Minds of Men: Origins of the Revolutionary Faith* (Edison, NJ: Transaction Publishers 1999), 92.

12. Ibid.

13. Ibid.

14. David Holmes, *The Faiths of the Founding Fathers* (New York: Oxford University Press, 2006), 106.

15. Barbara Feinberg, *The Articles of Confederation: the First Constitution of the United States* (Brookfield, CT: The Millbrook Press, 2002), 87.

16. Ron Chernow, *Alexander Hamilton* (New York: Penguin Press, 2004), 235.

17. Thomas Jefferson, *The Writings of Thomas Jefferson* (New York: Riker, Thorne and Company, 1854), 113.

18. See the drafts of "religion clauses" proposed in the 1789 debates of the First Congress in Barbara McGraw, *Rediscovering America's Sacred Ground: Public Religion and Pursuit of the Good in a Pluralistic America* (Albany, NY: SUNY Press, 2003), 199-202.

19. See Catherine L. Albanese, *A Republic of Mind and Spirit: A Cultural History of American Metaphysical Religion* (New Haven: CT: Yale University Press, 2007), 124-127.

20. Gordon S. Wood, *The Americanization of Benjamin Franklin* (New York: Penguin Press, 2004), 44.

21. Various sources indicate different numbers. In his historical account of various fraternities, for example, George Toll cited "approximately 150 lodges" in George S. Toll, *Alpha Epsilon Pi: The First Sixty-Five Years, 1913-1978* (Indianapolis, IN: Alpha Epsilon Pi Foundation, 1980), 5. Other sources present over one hundred. See Charles Whitlock Moore, *The Freemasons' Monthly Magazine* (Boston: Hugh H. Tuttle, 1864), Volume 23, 361-264 and James Wasserman, *The Secrets of Masonic Washington* (Rochester, VT: Destiny Books, 2008), 26-29. See also Steven C. Bullock, *Revolutionary Brotherhood: Freemasonry and the Transformation of the American Social Order, 1730-1840* (Chapel Hill: The University of North Carolina Press, 1996) and Sidney Morse, *Freemasonry in the American Revolution* (Whitefish, MT: Kessinger Publishing, 1992). These sources generally report over one hundred lodges.

22. James Wasserman, 37.

23. Brooke Allen, *Moral Minority: Our Skeptical Founding Fathers* (Chicago, IL: Ivan R. Dee Publisher, 2007).

24. Ibid.

25. Two excellent books explore the Founding Fathers and the collective fraternity through which they gained scientific and philosophical knowledge: see I. Bernard Cohen, *Science and the Founding Fathers: Science in the Political Thought of Thomas Jefferson, Benjamin Franklin, John Adams, and James Madison* (New York: W. W. Norton Books,

1997) and Steven Waldman, *Founding Faith: How Our Founding Fathers Forged a Radical New Approach to Religious Liberty* (New York: Random House, 2009).

26. Nancy Gibbs and Michael Duffy, *The Preacher and the Presidents: Billy Graham in the White House* (New York: Center Street, 2007), 316. See also Lisa Miller, "God and the Oath of Office," *The Newsweek*, January 10, 2009. See the entire article at http://www.newsweek.com/id/178871

27. See Sir David Frost, *Billy Graham in Conversation* (Oxford, England: Lion Publishing, 1998).

28. See Article II in William Addison Blakely, ed., *American State Papers Bearing on Religious Legislation* (New York: National Religious Liberty Association, 1891), 54-55.

29. Karen Armstrong, *The Case for God* (New York: Random House, 2009), 278.

30. Karen Armstrong, *A History of God: From Abraham to the Present, the 4000-year Quest for God* (New York: Random House, 1993), 28.

31. See a consultative correspondence between Professor Charles Norton and the U.S. State Department to revise the Great Seal of the United States in Gaillard Hunt, *The History of the Seal of the United States* (Washington, D.C.: United States Department of State, 1909), 54-55.

32. When drafting the Declaration of Independence in Philadelphia in 1776, Franklin, Jefferson, and Adams spoke of a "Creator," "Nature's God," "the supreme judge of the world," and "divine providence"—the God of America's public religion. See Jon Meacham, *American Gospel: God, the Founding Fathers, and the Making of a Nation* (New York: Random House, 2007), 20, 71, passim.

33. Jon Meacham (see above) is a Pulitzer prize-winning author and editor of *Newsweek* magazine.

34. Francis Fukuyama, "L'Enfant's Washington," *The American Interest*, Vol. 2, No 5, May - June 2007. See the article online at http://www.the-american-interest.com/article.cfm?piece=282

35. Ian Axford, "The Masonic City: By George! What a Show," *Freemasonry Today*, Issue 16, Spring 2001. See the entire article at http://www.freemasonrytoday.com/16/p05.php

36. Albert Pike, *Morals and Dogma of the Ancient and Accepted Scottish Rite of Freemasonry* (New York: Masonic Publishing Company, 1874), 631-32.

37. David Ovason, *The Secret Zodiacs of Washington DC: Was the City of Stars Planned by Masons?* (New York: Random House, 2006).

38. James Madison, *The Writings of James Madison* (New York: G. P. Putnam's Sons, 1908), 92.

39. Barry W. Lynn, *Piety & Politics: The Right-Wing Assault on Religious Freedom* (New York: Random House, 2007), 111.

40. See the U.S. Department of the Treasury's webpage on History of the Motto "In God We Trust" in http://www.ustreas.gov/education/fact-sheets/currency/in-god-we-trust.shtml

41. Ibid.

42. Secretary Chase had power of authorization under the Act of Congress dated January 18, 1837. See the U.S. Department of the Treasury's webpage above.

43. Francis Scott Key, *Poems of the Late Francis S. Key* (New York: Robert Carter and Brothers, 1857), 33.

44. Moreover, in a letter to William Boldly on November 11, 1907, Theodore Roosevelt wrote, "It seems to me eminently unwise to cheapen such a motto by use on coins, just as it would be to cheapen it by use on postage stamps, or in advertisements." See

Theodore Roosevelt, Joseph Bucklin Bishop ed., *Theodore Roosevelt and His Time Shown in His Own Letters* (New York: Charles Scribner's Sons, 1920), 72.

45. Theodore Roosevelt, 72.

46. William Joseph Brennan, Stephen Sepinuck and Mary Treuthart, eds., *The Conscience of the Court: Selected Opinions of Justice William J. Brennan JR. on Freedom and Equality* (Carbondale, IL: Southern Illinois University Press, 1999), 83.

47. Karen Armstrong, *The Case for God*, 278.

48. This widely used English translation is drawn from Pierre Teilhard de Chardin, *The Phenomenon of Man* (New York: Harper Perennial, 2008), 71. See further development of this idea in Christopher Mooney, *Teilhard de Chardin and the Mystery of Christ* (New York: Harper and Row, 1966), 46-55; and Anne Hunt Overzee *The Body Divine: The Symbol of the Body in the Works of Teilhard de Chardin and Ramanuja* (New York: Cambridge University Press, 1992), 51-52.

49. Pierre Teilhard de Chardin, *The Phenomenon of Man* (New York: Harper Perennial, 2008), 71-72.

Chapter 2: *E Pluribus Unum:* Out of Many, One

1. President Harry S. Truman spoke these words in a speech in Chicago on March 17, 1945. See Seymour Kurtz, *The New York Times Encyclopedic Almanac* (New York: The New York Times, 1972), 144.

2. See an excellent historical account of *E Pluribus Unum* in Neil Baldwin, *The American Revelation: Ten Ideals That Shaped Our Country from the Puritans to the Cold War* (New York: St. Martin's Press, 2006), 43-60.

3. Walter Isaacson, *American Sketches: Good Leaders, Creative Thinkers, and Heroes of a Hurricane* (New York: Simon and Schuster, 2009), 23.

4. See his autobiography in Barack Obama, *Dreams from My Father: A Story of Race and Inheritance* (New York: Three Rivers Press, 2004).

5. Gary Scott Smith, *Faith and the Presidency: From George Washington to George W. Bush* (New York: Oxford University Press, 2006).

6. Frank E. Grizzard, Jr., *The Ways of Providence: Religion and George Washington* (Buena Vista, VA: Mariner Companies, Inc., 2005), 4-5. Also, see George Washington, Julius Friedrich Sachse, ed., *Washington's Masonic Correspondence as Found among the Washington Papers in the Library of Congress* (Lancaster, PA: Press of the New Era Printing Company, 1915), 22, 26, passim.

7. George Washington, *Writings of George Washington* (New York: G. P Putnam's Sons, 1908), 322.

8. John Adams, *The works of John Adams: Second President of the United States* (Boston: Charles C. Little and James Brown, 1851), 452

9. See George W. Bush's second Inaugural Address in *U.S. Presidential Inaugural Addresses* (Charleston, NC: BiblioLife, 2008), 353.

10. William Conley Harris, *E Pluribus Unum: Nineteenth-Century American Literature and the Constitutional Paradox* (Iowa City: University of Iowa Press, 2005), 192-205.

11. Barack Obama, *Words on a Journey: The Great Speeches of Barack Obama* (Rockville, MD: Arc Manor Classics, 2008), 28.

12. Benjamin Franklin, Albert Henry Smyth, ed., *The Writings of Benjamin Franklin* (New York: The MacMillan Company, 1906), 601.

13. Lisa Miller and Richard Wolffe, "Campaign 2008: Finding His Faith," *Newsweek*, July 12, 2008. See the entire article at http://www.newsweek.com/id/145971

14. Presidential Candidate Barack Obama spoke on "A Politics of Conscience" on June 23, 2007 in Hartford, CT. See his campaign website Organizing for America for the entire speech, http://www.barackobama.com/2007/06/23/a_politics_of_conscience_1.php

15. George W. Bush's second Inaugural Address in 2005.

16. For a critical analysis of this reference, which I drew directly from Jill Lepore, "Prior Convictions: Did the Founders Want Us to be Faithful to Their Faith?" *The New Yorker*, April 14, 2008, read the entire article at http://www.newyorker.com/arts/critics/atlarge/2008/04/14/080414crat_atlarge_lepore?currentPage=all

17. Frank Lambert, *The Founding Fathers and the Place of Religion in America* (Princeton, NJ: Princeton University Press, 2003).

18. Alexander Hamilton, James Madison, John Jay, *The Federalist Papers* (Stilwell, KS: The Digireads.com Publishing, 2004). See *Federalist No. 6* by Alexander Hamilton, 19.

19. See Eugene Davidson, *The Making of Adolf Hitler: The Birth and Rise of Nazism* (Columbia, MO: University of Missouri Press. 1997), 5.

20. Walter Truett Anderson, *All Connected Now: Life in the First Global Civilization* (Boulder, CO: Westview Press, 2001).

21. Henry Leonard Stillson, ed., *History of the Ancient and Honorable Fraternity of Free and Accepted Masons and Concordant Orders* (Boston: The Fraternity publishing company, 1890), 39.

22. See Robert Lomas, *Turning the Solomon Key: George Washington, the Bright Morning Star, and the Secrets of Masonic Astrology* (Beverly, MA: Fair Winds Press, 2007) and Jessica Harland-Jacobs, *Builders of Empire: Freemasons and British Imperialism, 1717-1927* (Chapel Hill, NC: The University of North Carolina Press, 2007).

23. For a brief history of the Great Seal, see U.S. Department of States, *The Seal of the United States: How It Was Developed and Adopted* (Washington, D.C.: Department of State, 1892).

24. H. Paul Jeffers, *The Freemasons in America: Inside the Secret Society* (New York: Citadel Press, 2006), 100.

25. Benjamin Franklin, 135.

26. Just as the two Latin phrases, *Annuit Coeptis* and *E Pluribus Unum*, contain 13 letters to represent 13 original colonies on the Great Seal of the United States, both 1776 (four digits) and its Roman numeral MDCCLXXVI (nine letters) have a combined 13 digits/letters. The number 13 symbolizes the steps on the pyramid (the Eye of Providence), the stars above the eagle, the vertical bars on the shield, and the leaves on the olive branch. Some conspiracy theorists try to connect this to Masonic symbolism, numerology, and occult science. For a deeper understanding of this symbolism and the Founding Fathers' Masonic connection, read David Ovason, *The Secret Symbols of the Dollar Bill: A Closer Look at the Hidden Magic and Meaning of the Money You Use Every Day* (New York: HarperCollins Publishers , 2004).

27. Mitch Horowitz, *Occult America: The Secret History of How Mysticism Shaped Our Nation* (New York: Random House, 2009), 173.

28. Benson Bobrick, *The Fated Sky: Astrology in History* (New York: Simon and Schuster, 2006), 251. See also Dane Rudhyar, *The Astrology of America's Destiny* (New York: Random House, 1974).

29. See some examples of astrological calculations by Benjamin Franklin in Joyce Chaplin, *The First Scientific American: Benjamin Franklin and the Pursuit of Genius* (New York: Basic Books, 2007), 57-63 and Benjamin Franklin, Walter Isaacson, ed., *A Benjamin Franklin Reader* (New York: Simon and Schuster, 2003), 117.

30. Gahl Sasson and Steve Weinstein, *A Wish Can Change Your Life: How to Use the Ancient Wisdom of Kabbalah to Make Your Dreams Come True* (New York: Simon and Schuster, 2003), 134.

31. Ebenezer Sibly, *A New and Complete Illustration of the Celestial Science of Astrology; or, the Art of Foretelling Future Events and Contingencies, by the Aspects, Positions, and Influences, of the Heavenly Bodies Founded on Natural Philosophy, Scripture, Reason, and the Mathematics* (London: The Proprietor, 1826), 1054.

32. Ebenezer Sibly, 1056.

33. Ebenezer Sibly, 1052-1054.

34. Only two other nations established after 1776 can claim an exact birth date: Israel and the Russian Federation. The first Prime Minister, David Ben-Gurion, publicly proclaimed the state of Israel on May 14, 1948 at a Jewish Council meeting in the Tel Aviv Museum, which ended British mandatory rule. With the collapse of the former Soviet Union (formally the Union of Soviet Socialist Republics, USSR), the Russian Federation was born on December 12, 1993 with the adoption of the Russian Constitution by national referendum.

35. See David Ovason, *The Secret Zodiacs of Washington DC: Was the City of Stars Planned by Masons?* (New York: Random House, 2009).

36. Robert Kagan, *Of Paradise and Power: America and Europe in the New World Order* (New York: Knopf, 2003), 3.

37. David Ovason.

38. Thomas Paine published his famous *Common Sense* anonymously on January 10, 1776. It became an immediate bestseller with 56 editions printed in that year alone. See Thomas Paine, Isaac Kramnick, ed., *Common Sense* (New York: Penguin Books, 1982), p. 86.

39. Mark Tabbert, *American Freemasons: Three Centuries of Building Communities* (New York: New York University Press, 2005), 16.

40. President Harry S. Truman spoke upon receiving an honorary law degree from the University of Kansas City on June 28, 1945. See the American Presidency Project at the University of California at Santa Barbara website http://www.presidency.ucsb.edu/ws/index.php?pid=12190

41. See the entire Farewell Address by President George Washington at the Yale University's Avalon Project: http://www.yale.edu/lawweb/avalon/washing.htm

42. Jefferson, who was not a known Freemason, wrote to Thomas Lomax on March 12, 1799. See Thomas Jefferson Randolph, ed., *Memoir, Correspondence, and Miscellanies from the Papers of Thomas Jefferson* (Charlottesville, VA: F. Carr and Company, 1829), 425.

43. President Barack Obama's Inaugural Address on January 20, 2009. See the White House webpage: http://www.whitehouse.gov/blog/inaugural-address.

44. A recent DNA study confirmed that Jefferson and his liaison with an African slave named Hemings produced children. See the 2000 *Report of the Research Committee on Thomas Jefferson and Sally Hemings* at the official Monticello webpage at http://www.monticello.org/plantation/hemingscontro/hemings_report.html. Also see Annette Gordon-Reed, *Thomas Jefferson and Sally Hemings: An American Controversy* (Charlottesville, VA: University of Virginia Press 1998).

Chapter 3: Freemasonry as a Catalyst and High Priest

1. Dan Brown, *The Lost Symbol: A Novel* (New York: Doubleday, 2009), 31.

2. Henry W. Coil, *Freemasonry through Six Centuries* (Fulton, MO: Ovid Bell Press, 1967).

3. See John J. Robinson, *Born in Blood: The Lost Secrets of Freemasonry* (New York: Dorset Press, 1989) and Richard Leigh, Henry Lincoln, and Michael Baigent, *The Holy Blood And The Holy Grail* (New York: Random House, 2004).

4. Albert Gallatin Mackey, *The History of Freemasonry: Its Legendary Origins* (Minneola, NY: Dover Publications, 2008).

5. See a history of the Knights Templar in Simon Brighton, *In Search of the Knights Templar: A Guide to the Sites in Britain* (London: Sterling Publishing Company, 2006).

6. Dudley Wright, *Roman Catholicism and Freemasonry* (Whitefish, MT: Kessinger Publishing, 2003).

7. H. Paul Jeffers, *Dark Mysteries of the Vatican* (New York: Citadel Press, 2010), 56.

8. H. Paul Jeffers, 55.

9. H. Paul Jeffers, 56. See the original edict in Dudley Wright, 213-215.

10. H. Paul Jeffers, 56.

11. William Joseph Whalen, *Christianity and American Freemasonry* (San Francisco, CA: Ignatius Press, 1998), 137.

12. William Joseph Whalen, 138.

13. This was confirmed by the Curia of the Catholic Archdiocese in St. Paul, Minnesota through a personal phone interview on May 13, 2009.

14. There exist documents that date Freemasonry back to the sixteenth century. See David Stevenson, *The Origins of Freemasonry: Scotland's Century, 1590-1710* (Cambridge: Cambridge University Press, 1990).

15. For a history of national intelligence, see Nathan Miller, *Spying for America: The Hidden History of U.S. Intelligence* (New York: Dell, 1989); G.J.A O'Toole, *Encyclopedia of American Intelligence and Espionage* (New York: Facts on File, 1988); and Allan Dulles, *Great True Spy Stories (*New York: Harper and Row, 1968).

16. Jay Tolson, "Inside the Masons," *U.S. News and World Report,* Vo. 139, No. 8, September 5, 2005, 32.

17. See Art De Hoyos and S. Brent Morris, eds., *Freemasonry in Context: History, Ritual, Controversy* (Lanham, MD: Lexington Books, 2004).

18. James Barron, "A Secret Society Opens Its Doors: To Find New Members, New York Freemasons Go Public," *The International Herald Tribune,* October 4, 2006, 1.

19. Mark Tabbert, *American Freemasons: Three Centuries of Building Communities* (Lexington, MA: National Heritage Museum, 2005), 11.

20. Merle Miller, *Plain Speaking: An Oral Biography of Harry S. Truman* (New York: Berkley Publishing Corporation, 1974), 26.

21. Washingtonpost.com online with Peter Carlson, "Fezzes, Sphinxes and Secret Handshakes," *The Washington Post*, November. 19, 2001.

22. Mark A. Tabbert, *American Freemasons: Three centuries of Building Communities* (New York: The New York University Press, 2005). Tabbert, curator of the National Heritage Museum and master of a Masonic lodge in Massachusetts, writes an

inside story that offers an interesting overview of the history of Freemasonry and its attributes.

23. See David Stevenson, *The First Freemasons: Scotland's Early Lodges and Their Members* (Aberdeen, U.K.: Aberdeen University Press, 1988).

24. Dan Brown, 30-31.

25. Ibid.

26. York and Scottish Rites maintain different sets of rites, rituals and costumes, and they have their own degrees that build upon the first three degrees. Technically, the three degrees in the Scottish Rite are the first three degrees in the York Rite Masonry. Several Masons are members of both rites.

27. See a "myth-busting introduction to the history and practice of Freemasonry" in S. Brent Morris, *The Complete Idiot's Guide to Freemasonry* (New York: The Penguin Group, 2006). See also Christopher Hodapp, *Freemasons for Dummies* (New York, Wiley Press, 2005).

28. See Arturo de Hoyos, "A Brief Overview of the Scottish Rite's Origins and Rituals," *The Scottish Rite Journal,* September-October 2007 Issue:
http://www.scottishrite.org/ee.php?/journal/pastarticles/a_brief_overview_of_the_scottish _rites_origins_and_rituals.

29. The York Rite has three ranks and the Scottish Rite has thirty-three degrees in its hierarchy of advancement. The number thirty-three referred to the age of Jesus Christ.

30. Jay Tolson, 34.

31. See Jay Tolson, 34 and see also Mark Tabbert.

32. Prince Hall and fourteen other African-American "brothers" underwent initiation in a British military lodge in 1775 in Boston. After Hall's death in 1807, the popular Prince Hall Freemasonry spread to "Rhode Island, Pennsylvania, and elsewhere to become a powerful crucible of African-American leadership" by "providing charity and other support to the black community." African-Americans may join any lodge but Prince Hall Freemasonry remains a separate part of the American Masonic tradition. See Jay Tolson, 34.

33. Harry Paul Jeffers, *Freemasons: A History and Exploration of the World's Oldest Secret Society* (New York: Citadel Press, 2005), 237.

34. Albert Gallatin Mackey, *An Encyclopedia of Freemasonry and Its Kindred Sciences* (Philadelphia: Moss and Company, 1879), 667.

35. Edith J. Steblecki, *Paul Revere and Freemasonry* (Boston: Paul Revere Memorial Association, 1985), 52-53.

36. The first official history by James Anderson, *The Constitutions of the Free-Masons (London: William Hunter 1723),* was later revised and published as *The New Book of the Constitutions of the Ancient and Honorable Fraternity of Free and Accepted Masons (London: J. Butler, 1751).*

37. Harry Paul Jeffers, *The Freemasons in America: Inside the Secret Society* (New York: Citadel Press, 2006).

38. Bernard Fay, *Revolution and Freemasonry, 1600-1800* (Boston: Little and Brown Company, 1935), 310.

39. Bernard Fay, 230.

40. Barbara J. Bird, "The Roman God Mercury: An Entrepreneurial Archetype," *Journal of Management Inquiry,* September 1, 1992, Vol. 1, No. 3, 205-212.

41. *See the nomenclature in David Hackett Fischer,* Paul Revere's Ride *(New York: Oxford University Press, 1995), 27.*

42. See Arthur Versluis, *The Esoteric Origins of the American Renaissance* (New York: Oxford University Press, 2001).

43. See a copy of *Poor Richard's Almanac* with illustrations in Walter Isaacson, *Benjamin Franklin: An American Life* (New York: Simon and Schuster, 2003). See the inside pages of the covers.

44. See Bernard Fay.

45. Caroline Matilda Kirkland, *Memoirs of Washington* (New York: D. Appleton and Company, 1857), 2-3.

46. Caroline Matilda Kirkland, 3.

47. See J. Hugo Tatsch, *Facts about George Washington as a Freemason* (Kila, MT: Kessinger Publishing, 1942) and Michael J. Bednar, *L'Enfant's Legacy: Public Open Spaces in Washington, D.C.* (Baltimore: The Johns Hopkins University Press, 2006).

48. Esther Forbes, *Paul Revere and the World He Lived In* (New York: Houghton Mifflin company, 1942), 383.

49. See President George Washington's address to the Common Council of the City of Philadelphia on April 20, 1789. George Washington, *Writings of George Washington: Being His Correspondence, Addresses, Messages, and Other Papers, Official and Private, Selected and Published from the Original Manuscripts with a Life of the Author, Notes, and Illustrations*, Jared Sparks, ed., (Boston: Little, Brown and Company, 1855), 145.

50. Wayne Whipple, *The Story-Life of Washington. A Life History in Five Hundred True Stories Selected from Original Sources and Fitted Together in Order* (Philadelphia: The John C. Winston Company, 1911), 709.

Chapter 4: Worldviews of Pilgrims and Colonists

1. Reverend John Higginson, Puritan minister of the First Church, delivered his famous sermon on "The Cause of God and His People in New England" in Cambridge, Massachusetts on May 27, 1663. See Thomas Wentworth Higginson, *Makers of America: Life of Francis Higginson, First Minister on the Massachusetts Bay Colony, and Author of New England's Plantation, 1630* (New York: Dodd, Mead and Company, 1891), 134.

2. Perez Zagorin, *Francis Bacon* (Princeton, NJ: Princeton University Press, 1999), 123-24.

3. Perez Zagorin, 174.

4. Francis Bacon, Clark Sutherland Northup ed., *The Essays of Francis Bacon* (New York: Houghton Mifflin Company, 1908), xxvi.

5. Historian Goldwin Smith, however, claimed that Massachusetts is the "cradle of American democracy" as Rhode Island may claim to be the "cradle of liberty of conscience." See Goldwin Smith, *The United States: An Outline of Political History, 1492-1871* (New York: McMillan and Company, 1893), 20

6. Felix Gilbert, *To the Farewell Address: Ideas of Early American Foreign Policy* (Princeton, NJ: Princeton University Press, 1970).

7. Adrienne Koch, *Jefferson and Madison: The Great Collaboration* (New York: Alfred Knopf, 1950).

8. Ibid.

9. Felix Gilbert, 136.

10. Manly P. Hall, *The Secret Destiny of America* (Los Angeles, CA: Philosophical Research Society, 1944). Read the entire book online at http://yamaguchy.netfirms.com/7897401/hall/dest_01.html

11. Ibid.

12. Ibid.

13. See additional information on Hamilton's birthplace at the Museum of Nevis History in the Caribbean island of Nevis available at http://www.nevis-nhcs.org/nevishistory.html

14. See a detailed account of the first settlement by the president of the College of William and Mary, Lyon Gardiner Tyler, *The Cradle of the Republic: Jamestown and James River* (Richmond, VA: Whittet and Shepperson Printers, 1900).

15. William T. Davis. ed., *Bradford's History of Plymouth Plantation, 1606-1646* (New York: Barnes and Noble, 1908), 107.

16. Thomas Wentworth Higginson, 134.

17. Felix Gilbert, 6.

18. Ibid.

19. Quoted Sir Francis Bacon in Lyon Gardiner Tyler, 21.

20. Thomas Paine, Isaac Kramnick, ed., *Common Sense*, (New York: Penguin Books, 1982), 86.

21. Paul Jeffers, p.29.

22. Washington wrote to the Master Wardens of King David's Lodge in Newport, Rhode Island, on August 16, 1790. See George Washington, *The Writings of George Washington: Being His Correspondence, Addresses, Messages, and Other Papers, Official and Private* (Boston: Little, Brown, and Company, 1855), 190.

23. Adolophus Frederick A. Woodford, *A Defense of Freemasonry* (London: George Kenning, 1874), 64.

24. See the entire Farewell Address by President George Washington at the Yale University's Avalon Project at http://www.yale.edu/lawweb/avalon/washing.htm

25. Ibid.

26. James Madison also helped Washington in the Farewell Address; however, he never delivered it orally. The *Philadelphia Daily American Advertiser* and other newspapers throughout the country published the final Address on September 19, 1796. See the Farewell Address in the collection of the New York Public Library: http://www.nysl.nysed.gov/library/features/gw

27. Alexis de Tocqueville, Translated by Henry Reeve, *Democracy in America* (Cambridge, MA: Sever and Francis, 1863).

Chapter 5: *Adam Smith on Founding America*

1. Adam Smith, Germain Garnier, ed., *An Inquiry into the Nature and Causes of the Wealth of Nations* (London: T. Nelson and Sons, 1852), 6-7.

2. Frank Lambert, *The Founding Fathers and the Place of Religion in America* (Princeton, NJ: Princeton University Press, 2003), 3.

3. John Winthrop (1587-1649), *The Journal of John Winthrop* (Boston, MA: Belknap Press of Harvard University Press, 1996), xi and 10.

4. See a historical analysis of the concept and its multiple meanings in Deborah L. Madsen, *American Exceptionalism* (Edinburgh, U.K.: Edinburgh University Press, 1998).

5. Washington Paschal, *The Constitution of the United States Defined and Care-fully Annotated* (Washington, D.C.: W. H. & O. H. Morrison, 1868), 254.

6. Roy C. Smith, *Adam Smith and the Origins of American Enterprise: How America's Industrial Success was Forged by the Timely Ideas of a Brilliant Scots Economist* (New York: St. Martin's Press, 2004), xiii.

7. Adam Smith, 334.

8. Adam Smith, 332.

9. Adam Smith, *The Wealth of Nations* (1776) and his *The Theory of Moral Sentiments* (London: A. Millar, 1759), passim.

10. Adam Smith, *The Wealth of Nations,* 184.

11. Adam Smith, *The Wealth of Nations,* passim.

12. Thomas Paine, Collected Writings: Common Sense, The Crisis, Rights of Man, The Age of Reason, Pamphlets, Articles, & Letters (New York: Library of America, 1995), 52, 52-53, and 91.

13. A number of researchers provided evidence that Adam Smith got advice and commentary on the draft of writings from his "friend" Benjamin Franklin when he was in Scotland and England. See Thomas D. Eliot, "The Relations between Adam Smith and Benjamin Franklin before 1776," *Political Science Quarterly*, Vol. 39, No. 1, March 1924, pp. 67-96; Ronald W. Clark, *Benjamin Franklin: A Biography* (London: Phoenix Press, 1983), 54-55; and James Bennett Nolan, *Benjamin Franklin in Scotland and Ireland* (Philadelphia: University of Pennsylvania Press, 1956).

14. Adam Smith, *The Wealth of Nations,* passim.

15. Adam Smith, *The Theory of Moral Sentiments.*

16. Emma Rothschild, *Economic Sentiments: Adam Smith, Condorcet, and the Enlightenment* (Cambridge, MA: Harvard University Press, 2001), 223. Professor Rothschild's husband, Nobel Prize winning economist Amartya Sen, also makes a similar argument on freedom in his book, *Development as Freedom* (New York: Oxford University Press, 1999).

17. Adam Smith, *The Theory of Moral Sentiments,* passim.

18. See George Washington, Jared Sparks, ed., *Writings of George Washington: Being His Correspondence, Addresses, Messages, and Other Papers, Official and Private, Selected and Published from the Original Manuscripts with a Life of the Author, Notes, and Illustrations* (Boston: Little, Brown, and Company, 1855), 2.

19. George Washington, *Washington's Farewell Address to the People of the United States* (Baltimore, MD: John L. Cook, 1810), 16.

20. Adam Smith, *The Theory of Moral Sentiments,* passim.

21. Robert D. Kaplan, "A Sense of the Tragic: Developmental Dangers in the Twenty-First Century," in *Jerome E. Levy Occasional Paper Economic Geography and World Order*, August 2001 (Newport, RI: United States Naval War College), 15-16.

22. Ibid.

23. Ibid.

24. James Madison, "The Federalist Paper No. 51," in *The Federalist* (New York: Modern Library, 1788), 337.

25. Alexander Hamilton, James Madison, and John Jay, *The Federalist on the New Constitution, Written in the Year 1788* (Washington, D.C.: Glazier and Company, 1831), 47.

26. Alexander Hamilton, James Madison, and John Jay, *The Federalist on the New Constitution, Written in the Year 1788* (Washington, D.C.: Glazier and Company, 1831), 219-220.

27. Christian G. Fritz, *American Sovereigns: The People and America's Constitutional Tradition Before the Civil War* (New York: Cambridge University Press, 2008), 1.

28. Abraham Lincoln, *The Gettysburg Address* (New York: Houghton Mifflin Company, 1998), p. 6.

29. Thomas Jefferson, Albert Ellery Bergh, ed., *The Writings of Thomas Jefferson,* (Washington, D.C.: The Thomas Jefferson Memorial Association, 1907), 31.

30. Thomas Jefferson, Paul Leicester Ford, ed., *The works of Thomas Jefferson* (New York: G. P. Putnam's Sons, 1905), 64.

31. Adam Smith, *The Wealth of Nations*, 365, 121, 170, passim.

32. Thomas Paine, *Common Sense: Addressed to the Inhabitants of America on the Following Interesting Subjects* (Philadelphia, PA: John Mycall, 1776).

33. Thomas Jefferson, Andrew A. Lipscomb, ed., *The Writings of Thomas Jefferson: Containing His Autobiography, Notes on Virginia, Parliamentary Manual, Official Papers, Messages and Addresses, and Other Writings, Official and Private*, (Washington, D.C.: The Thomas Jefferson Memorial Foundation, 1904), 273.

34. Thomas Jefferson, Julian P. Boyd, ed., *The Papers of Thomas Jefferson, March 1789 to November 1789* (Princeton, NJ: Princeton University Press, 1958), 405.

Chapter 6: *Hamiltonian Means to Jeffersonian Ends*

1. Adlai E. Stevenson, II, Governor of Illinois (1949-53) and UN Ambassador (1961-65), gave a speech to Unitarians, "Liberalism Versus Competitive Indoctrination," at the ninetieth anniversary service of the Unitarian Church of Bloomington in Illinois on October 30, 1949. This speech is preserved in pamphlet form. See Richard Gilbert, *Building Your Own Theology: Exploring* (Boston, MA: Unitarian Universalist Association of Congregations, 2005), 9. As the Democratic nominee, Stevenson twice ran unsuccessfully for the presidency against President Dwight Eisenhower in 1952 and 1956. He later served as the U.S. Ambassador to the United Nations under President John F. Kennedy. For an excellent narrative of this great American, see Alvin Liebling, ed., *Adlai Stevenson's Lasting Legacy* (New York: Palgrave Macmillan, 2007).

2. Thomas Jefferson, Andrew A. Lipscomb, ed., *The Writings of Thomas Jefferson: Containing His Autobiography, Notes on Virginia, Parliamentary Manual, Official Papers, Messages and Addresses, and Other Writings, Official and Private*, (Washington, D.C.: The Thomas Jefferson Memorial Foundation, 1904), 45.

3. See the Federalist Papers No. 6 by Alexander Hamilton in Henry Cabot Lodge, ed., *The Federalist: A Commentary on the Constitution of the United States*, (New York: G. P. Putnam's Sons, 1888), 29.

4. Richard Gilbert, 9.

5. Thomas Jefferson's concept of an Empire of Liberty was initially meant to describe territorial expansion (i.e., the Louisiana Purchase), but it has broader meaning that includes freedom and justice around the world. See an excellent analysis of Jefferson's views in Robert Tucker and David Hendrickson, *Empire of Liberty: The Statecraft of Thomas Jefferson*, (New York: Oxford University Press, 1990).

6. Darren Staloff, *Hamilton, Adams, Jefferson: The Politics of Enlightenment and the American Founding* (New York: Hill and Wang, 2005), 63.

7. Patrick Henry gave his last public speech on 4 March 1799. See Edward Channing, *A History of the United States: Federalists and Republicans 1789-1815* (New York: The Macmillan Company, 1917), 231

8. John Adams, Charles Francis Adams, ed., *The Works of John Adams, Second President of the United States: With a Life of the Author, Notes, and Illustrations* (Boston: Little, Brown and Company, 1854), 511.

9. Thomas Jefferson, Albert Ellery Bergh, ed., *The Writings of Thomas Jefferson* (Washington, D.C.: The Thomas Jefferson Memorial Association, 1907), 300

10. See James Madison, Federalist Paper No. 37. Alexander Hamilton, James Madison, John Jay, in Henry Cabot Lodge, ed., *The Federalist: A Commentary on the Constitution of the United States* (New York: G. P. Putnam's sons, 1888), 222.

11. Robert Kocis, *Machiavelli Redeemed: Retrieving His Humanist Perspectives on Equality, Power, and Glory* (Bethlehem, PA: Lehigh University Press, 1998).

12. Niccolo Machiavelli, *Machiavelli: The Prince* in Quentin Skinner Russell Price, eds., *Cambridge Texts in the History of Political Thought* (New York: Cambridge University Press, 1998), 31.

13. John Lamberton Harper, *American Machiavelli: Alexander Hamilton and the Origins of U.S. Foreign Policy* (New York: Cambridge University Press, 2004).

14. Ron Chernow, *Alexander Hamilton* (New York: The Penguin Press, 2004).

15. Brian Cavanaugh, *Fresh Packet of Sower's Seeds: Third Planting* (Mahwah, NJ: Paulist Press, 1994), 42.

16. Richard G. Capen, Jr., *Empowered by Faith: Experiencing God's Love Every Day* (Grand Rapids, MI: Zondervan Press, 2006), 125.

17. Adam Smith, *An Inquiry into the Nature and Causes of the Wealth of Nations* (London: A. Strahan and T. Cadell, 1776). Read the entire book: http://www.adamsmith.org/smith/won-index.htm, p. passim.

18. Adam Smith, *The Theory of Moral Sentiments* (London: A. Millar, 1759). Read the entire book online at http://www.adamsmith.org/smith/tms/tms-index.htm, p. passim.

19. John Adams, Charles Francis Adams, ed., *The Works of John Adams, Second President of the United States: With a Life of the Author, Notes, and Illustrations* (Boston: Little, Brown and Company, 1854), 511.

20. See Doris Kearns Goodwin, *Team of Rivals: The Political Genius of Abraham Lincoln* (New York: Simon and Schuster, 2006).

21. Quoting Paul M. Bessel, a 32-degree Freemason, in H. Paul Jeffers, *The Freemasons in America: Inside the Secret Society* (New York: Citadel Press, 2006), 74.

22. See a historical background of President Lincoln's Gettysburg Address, for which he drew on various knowledge and spiritual traditions documented in Gabor Boritt, *The Gettysburg Gospel: The Lincoln Speech That Nobody Knows* (New York: Simon and Schuster, 2008). The author never mentioned the influence of Freemasonry but the 272-word Address bears strong resemblance to many Masonic themes, including the idea of protecting unity and saving the Union.

Chapter 7: The Commerce Clause as the Force for Unity

1. Charles de Montesquieu, "Of the Spirit of Commerce" in *The Spirit of Laws*, Book 20, Chapter 2, First published in 1748 (New York: Cosimo Classic, 2007), 316-17.

2. David Hume, "Of Commerce" in *Essays, Moral, Political, and Literary*, Political Discourses, Vol. II, First in published 1752 (London: Longmans, Green and Company, 1898), 115.

3. Thomas Hobbes, *Leviathan: Or, The Matter, Forme and Power or a Commonwealth, Ecclesiastical and Civill,* A. R. Waller, ed., First published in 1651 (London: C. J. Clay and Sons, 1904), 86.

4. Immanuel Kant, *Project for a Perpetual Peace: A Philosophical Essay* (London: S. Couchman for Vernor and Hood, 1796), 42.

5. Immanuel Kant, Carl J. Friedrich, ed., *The Philosophy of Kant: Immanuel Kant's Moral and Political Writings* (New York: Modern Library, 1949), 430-476.

6. Charles de Montesquieu.

7. Charles de Montesquieu, 317.

8. Charles de Montesquieu, 316.

9. Charles de Montesquieu, 317.

10. Adam Smith, Joseph Shield Nicholson, ed., *An Inquiry into the Nature and Causes of the Wealth of Nations,* First Published in 1776 (London: T. Nelson and Sons, 1895), 4.

11. Adam Smith, *The Theory of Moral Sentiments* (London: A. Millar, 1759), 265.

12. Charles de Montesquieu, 316.

13. John P. Foley, ed., *The Jeffersonian Cyclopedia: A Comprehensive Collection of the Views of Thomas Jefferson* (New York: Funk and Wagnalls Company, 1900), 362.

14. John Foley, 361.

15. Ralph L. Andreano, ed., *New Views on American Economic Development: A Selective Anthology of Recent Work* (Cambridge, MA: Schenkman Publishing, 1965), 112.

16. Ellen H. Brown, *The Web of Debt: The Shocking Truth about Our Money System* (London: Third Millennium Press 2007), 41.

17. Ellen Brown, 42.

18. Ibid.

19. Albert Henry Symth, ed., *The Writings of Benjamin Franklin* (New York: The McMillan Company, 1906), 332.

20. Gaillard Hunt, ed., *The Writings of James Madison: Comprising His Public Papers and His Private Correspondence, Including Numerous Letters and Documents Now for the First Time Printed* (New York: G. P. Putnam's Sons, 1901), 156.

21. John Adams, Charles Francis Adams, ed., *Letters of John Adams* (Boston: Charles Little and J. Brown, 1841), 276.

22. James D. Richardson, *A Compilation of the Messages and Papers of the Presidents, 1789-1897* (Washington, D.C.: Government Printing Office, 1896), 16.

23. George Washington wrote to Major-General Armstrong on May 26, 1781. See Worthington Chauncey Ford, ed., *The Writings of George Washington* (New York: G. P. Putnam's Sons, 1891), 192.

24. See the United States Senate webpage at http://www.senate.gov/civics/constitution_item/constitution.htm#a1_sec8

25. Ezra Prentice and John Egan, *The Commerce Clause of the Federal Constitution* (Chicago: Callaghan and Company, 1898), 1.

26. Prentice and Egan, 6.

27. Ibid.

28. Conservative and liberal scholars offer different legal interpretations of the Commerce Clause. Yale Law Professor Akhil Reed Amar maintains that the word "commerce" referred to all forms of human interactions in 1787 when the Framers drafted the Constitution. Professor Amar notes that the "free and easy commerce of social life" and "our Lord's commerce with his disciples" were part of common prose in the late

1780s. See Akhil Reed Amar, *America's Constitution: A Biography* (New York: Random House, 2005). Interpretations by conservative legal scholars suggest that the clause limits its power to "trade" relations, or the "exchange" of one thing for another. See Robert H. Bork and Daniel E. Troy, "Locating the Boundaries: The Scope of Congress's Power to Regulate Commerce," *Harvard Journal of Law and Public Policy*, Vol. 25, Summer 2002, 849-93. See the online version of the article at http://www.constitution.org/lrev/bork-troy.htm

29. With the Trade Act of 1974, Congress granted the president Trade Promotion Authority (TPA) for the first time in U.S. history. This allowed the president to negotiate trade agreements with foreign nations. In such agreements, Congress can only disapprove or approve without amendment or filibuster. Presidential candidate George W. Bush, who campaigned for TPA as an integral part of his political platform in 2000, restored the second executive authority by signing the Trade Act of 2002. It expired in July 2007.

30. During the second period of Trade Promotion Authority (TPA) under President George W. Bush, Congress enacted "implementing legislation" for the U.S. Free Trade Agreement with Chile (2003), Singapore (2003), Australia (2004), Morocco (2004), the Dominican Republic (2005), Bahrain (2006), and Oman (2006). Several other trade agreements have come to Congress under TPA: Peru, Columbia, and South Korea. As of September 2008, there was no legislative action. Other potential bilateral trade negotiations with Malaysia and Thailand have also been initiated.

31. Akhil Reed Amar, *America's Constitution: A Biography* (New York: Random House, 2005), 107.

Chapter 8: The Pythagorean Potomac Delta

1. Charles Dickens, *The Works of Charles Dickens* (London: Chapman and Hall, 1898), 138.

2. The Pythagoreans understood 3 as the first odd (the male number), 4 as the square of 2 (the female number), and 5 as the offspring of the two (3 + 2). In Freemasonry, the number 3 is also prominent (e.g., 3 degrees for a Master Mason and 3 principal officers, etc.). The squares and triangles (3, 4, and 5) produced in the Pythagorean Theorem also signify a celestial and terrestrial relationship.

3. President Washington took his inaugural oath in New York City in 1789. After that, Philadelphia served as the nation's capital from 1790 until it was moved to the current location in 1800.

4. Christiane Joost-Gaugier, *Measuring Heaven: Pythagoras and His Influence on Thought and Art in Antiquity and the Middle Ages* (Ithaca, NY: Cornell University Press, 2006), 56.

5. The Tiber was very important to Roman trade and commerce, and L'Enfant initially planned to widen Tiber Creek for commercial purposes. See Frederick Albert Gutheim and Antoinette J. Lee, eds., *Worthy of the Nation: Washington, DC, from L'Enfant to the National Capital Planning Commission* (Baltimore, MD: The Johns Hopkins University Press, 2006), 14-18.

6. Don Higginbotham, *George Washington: Uniting a Nation* (Lanham, MD: Rowman and Littlefield Publishers, 2002), 25.

7. The phrase "Potomac solution" was developed by this author after reviewing a number of original writings. See Henry Cabot Lodge, *George Washington* (Boston, MA: Houghton Mifflin, 1917), 109.

8. The letter was dated April 10, 1783. See William Pitt Palmer, ed., *Virginia State Papers and Other Manuscripts* (Richmond: James E. Goode Printer, 1883), 467.

9. The Residence Act of 1790 was officially titled "An Act for Establishing the Temporary and Permanent Seat of the Government of the United States." For more on the history of moving the nation's capital from its temporary location in New York in 1789 and the capital *pro tem* of Philadelphia from 1790 to 1799, see the Library of Congress webpage: http://www.loc.gov/rr/program/bib/ourdocs/Residence.html

10. The Congressional Act specified that the District of Columbia (D.C.) should not exceed 100 square miles on the Potomac delta valley (see Article 1 of the U.S. Constitution). The State of Maryland provided 69¼ square miles and the Commonwealth of Virginia contributed 30¾ square miles to the new Federal District. In 1846, Congress returned Arlington County, which was originally part of the District of Columbia, back to Virginia. The District now covers about 67 square miles.

11. Cisco Wheeler, *Behold, A White House* (Longwood, FL: Xulon Press, 2009), 140. Wheeler has drawn this language from David Ovason, *The Secret Architecture of Our Nation's Capital: The Masons and the Building of Washington, D.C.* (New York: HarperCollins Publishers, 1999), 49.

12. David Ovason, 49.

13. Under the Residence Act of July 16, 1790, President Washington appointed Thomas Johnson and two illustrious Freemasons—Dr. David Steward and Daniel Carroll, brother of Catholic Bishop John Carroll—as commissioners. See Wesley Pippenger, *District of Columbia Original Land Owners, 1791-1800* (Westminster, MD: Heritage Books, 2007), 5.

14. On the same day, George Washington wrote in his diary that he "appointed L'Enfant to design a Federal City to be built within the district." See George Washington, *The Diaries of George Washington*, Volume 6 (Charlottesville: University Press of Virginia, 1979), 104.

15. For a compressive biography, see Silvio A. Bedini, *The Life of Benjamin Banneker: The First African-American Man of Science* (Baltimore, MD: Maryland Historical Society, 1999).

16. The measurements were irregular according to some reports. See Columbia Historical Society, *Records of the Columbia Historical Society* (Washington, D.C.: Columbia Historical Society, 1907), 64 and S. Brent Morris and John W. Boettjer, *Cornerstones of Freedom: A Masonic Tradition* (Washington, D.C.: Scottish Rite Supreme Council, 1993).

17. According to the U.S. National Park Service's webpage, Banneker laid forty boundary stones at one-mile intervals to demarcate boundaries. See the U.S. National Park Service homepage: http://www.nps.gov/nr/travel/wash/lenfant.htm

18. Charles Cerami, *Benjamin Banneker: Surveyor, Astronomer, Publisher, Patriot* (New York: Wiley Press, 2002).

19. George Washington, Jared Sparks, ed., *The Writings of George Washington* (Boston: MA: Ferdinand Andrews Publisher, 1839), 148.

20. See the original plan of the city intended to be the permanent seat of the government by Pierre Charles L'Enfant (1754-1825) in the Library of Congress webpage: http://www.loc.gov/exhibits/treasures/tri001.html

21. Pierre L'Enfant's father worked for the architect Andre Lenotre at Versailles in Paris. L'Enfant was familiar with Lenotre's works and was influenced by other capital designs in Rome, St. Petersburg (Russia), and London. See a detailed account of his life

in Hans Paul Caemmerer, *The Life of Pierre Charles L'Enfant: Planner of the City Beautiful, the City of Washington* (Washington, D.C.: National Republic, 1950).

22. Stewart Alsop, *The Center: People and Power in Political Washington* (New York: Harper and Row, 1968), 83.

23. On November 20, 1791, George Washington wrote to David Stuart of L'Enfant's qualifications as a planner. See George Washington, John C. Fitzpatrick, ed., *The Writings of George Washington from the Original Manuscript Sources, 1745-1799* (Washington, D.C.: U.S. Government Printing Office, 1939), Vol. 31, 419-24.

24. Jean Jules Jusserand, *With Americans of Past and Present Days* (New York: Charles Scribner's Sons, 1916), 170. Also, see Hans Paul Caemmerer, 152.

25. For an extensive personal background on Major Pierre L'Enfant, first president of the Society of the Cincinnati, read the chapter on "Major L'Enfant and the Federal City" by French ambassador to U.S., Jean Jules Jusserand, *With Americans of Past and Present Days* (New York: Charles Scribner's Sons, 1916), 135-198.

26. See a detailed list of correspondences between Thomas Jefferson and Pierre L'Enfant in Elizabeth Sarah Kite, *L'Enfant and Washington 1791-1792: Published and Unpublished Documents Now Brought Together for the First Time* (Baltimore, MD: The Johns Hopkins Press, 1929). Also see Henry Hope Reed, *The United States Capitol: Its Architecture and Decoration* (New York: W. S. Norton & Company, 2005).

27. Edward Savage produced the 1796 oil painting of the Washington family housed in the National Gallery of Art's Andrew Mellon Collection. See a detailed description of this portrait in David Ovason, *The Secret Architecture of Our Nation's Capital: The Masons and the Building of Washington, D.C.* (New York: HarperCollins Publishers, 1999), 40-43 and 333-335.

28. Charles Dickens, *The Works of Charles Dickens* (London: Chapman and Hall, 1898), 138.

29. James Dabney McCabe, *Behind the Scenes in Washington* (Manchester, NH: Ayer Publishing, 1974),139

30. For a fascinating story of Capitol architect Thomas U. Walter and Statue of Freedom sculptor Thomas Crawford, see Kathryn Allamong Jacob, *Testament to Union: Civil War Monuments in Washington, D.C.* (Baltimore, MD: The Johns Hopkins University Press, 1998), 29-33.

31. See the U.S. Government's Architecture of the Capitol webpage: http://www.aoc.gov/cc/art/freedom.cfm

32. Alfred Russell Wallace, *The Bookman: An Illustrated Magazine of Literature and Life* (New York: Dodd, Mean and Company), 200.

33. For a comprehensive description, see Randolph Keim, *Washington and Its Environs: A Descriptive and Historical Handbook to the Capital of the United States of America* (Washington City: For the Compiler, 1879), 15-197.

34. The *Apotheosis of Washington* depicts George Washington ascending to the heavens and becoming a god (apotheosis). See Barbara A. Wolanin, *Constantino Brumidi: Artist of the Capitol* (Washington, D.C.: U.S. Government Printing Office, 1998), 125-46. See Chapter 9: http://www.access.gpo.gov/congress/senate/brumidi/Brumidi_9.pdf

35. Francis V. O'Connor, "Symbolism in the Rotunda" (Chapter 10) in Barbara A. Wolanin, *Constantino Brumidi: Artist of the Capitol* (Washington, D.C.: U.S. Government Printing Office, 1998), 148. See the Chapter: http://www.access.gpo.gov/congress/senate/brumidi/Brumidi_10.pdf

36. Barbara Wolanin, *Constantino Brumidi: Artist of the Capitol* (Washington, D.C.: U.S. Government Printing Office, 1998), 136. See the signature: http://www.access.gpo.gov/congress/senate/brumidi/index.html

37. See a photo of *The Car of History* in Henry Hope Reed, *The United States Capitol: Its Architecture and Decoration* (New York: W. S. Norton and Company, 2005), 97.

38. Clio and her Chariot of Time appeared on a stamp issued in 1989 on the 200th anniversary of the first session of the House in New York City, the first capital.

39. Henry Hope Reed, *The United States Capitol: Its Architecture and Decoration* (New York: W. S. Norton and Company, 2005), 92-93. These three zodiac signs are Sagittarius, Capricorn, and Aquarius.

40. Robert Hieronimus and Laura Cortner, *The United Symbolism of America: Deciphering Hidden Meanings in America's Most Familiar Art, Architecture, and Logos* (Franklin Lake, NJ: Career Press, 2008).

41. Jeffrey F. Meyer, *Myths in Stone: Religious Dimensions in Washington, D.C.* (Berkeley, CA: University of California Press. 2001), 7.

42. Luke 8:17.

Chapter 9: *The Anatomy of Commercial Providence*

1. Ralph Waldo Emerson, *The Conduct of Life and Society and Solitude* (London: McMillan and Company, 1883), 230.

2. Francis Bacon, *Advancement of Learning: And Novum Organum* (New York: The Colonial Press, 1900), 24, 50 and 216.

3. Francis Bacon, 86. See the historic conversation about the "trinity" between Jefferson and Alexander Hamilton in Richard B. Bernstein, *Thomas Jefferson: The Revolution of Ideas* (New York: Oxford University Press, 2004), 116-117.

4. On December 10, 1692, Sir Isaac Newton wrote to the Reverend Dr. Richard Bentley at the Bishop of Worcester's House in Park Street, Westminster, London From Cambridge University. See Isaac Newton, *Four letters from Sir Isaac Newton to Doctor Bentley Containing Some Arguments in Proof of a Deity* (London: R. and J. Dodsley, 1756), 5.

5. Albert Einstein and Maurice Solovine, *Albert Einstein, Letters to Maurice Solovine* (Paris: Gauthier-Villars, 1956), 114-115. Note: The Latin words *a priori* alluded, since their first used in 1710, to the saying "from cause to effect" found in the English Dictionary. This was a logical term for reasoning without reference to particular facts or experience.

6. See his lecture in Max Planck, *Scientific Autobiography and Other Papers* (New York: Philosophical Library, 1949), 151-187.

7. Walter Isaacson, *Einstein: His Life and Universe* (New York: Simon and Shuster, 2007), 551.

8. M. M. Doreal (Translated), *The Emerald Tablets of Thoth-The-Atlantean* (Indianapolis, IN: Dog Ear Publishing, 2002), 81-82.

9. The wisdom of the ancient philosopher offers the perception of human life that seems to have been understood by Freemasons. There are seven principles of Hermetic philosophy, which include: 1) Mentalism—Everything is mental, and the Universe is a mental creation; 2) Correspondence—"As above, so below;" 3) Rhythm—Everything moves in cycles; 4) Vibration—Everything moves with a unique frequency; 5) Polarity—

Everything is dual in nature, and has an opposite; 6) Causation—Every cause has its effect; 7) Gender—Everything has both masculine and feminine aspects. This philosophy has been the core of many spiritual and religious traditions. See Gregory Calise, *Perceptions of Reality: An Exploration of Consciousness* (Victoria, Canada: Trafford Publishing, 2003), 56-57. In his book, David Schwerin applied the seven principles of Hermes to the world of commerce and corporate boardrooms. See *Conscious Capitalism: Principles for Prosperity*, (Woburn, MA: Butterworth-Heinemann, 1998), 188.

10. Francis Bacon, *The Two Books of Francis Bacon: Of the Proficience and Advancement of Learning, Divine and Human* (London: Parker and Bourn, 1863), 161.

11. Ralph Waldo Emerson, 230.

12. See a copy of *Poor Richard's Almanac* with illustrations of the anatomy of the human body as governed by the twelve constellations in Walter Isaacson, *Benjamin Franklin: An American Life* (New York: Simon and Schuster, 2003), see insides of the cover pages.

13. Bernard Fay, *Franklin: The Apostle of Modern Times* (Boston: Little Brown and Company, 1929), 157.

14. Ibid.

15. Ibid.

16. Christopher Knight and Robert Lomas, *The Book of Hiram: Freemasonry, Venus, and the Secret Key to the Life of Jesus* (New York: Sterling Publishing Company, 2005), 289.

17. Benjamin Franklin, Albert Henry Smyth, ed., *The Writings of Benjamin Franklin* (New York: Macmillan Company, 1907), 9-10.

18. Jessica Harland-Jacobs, *Builders of Empire: Freemasons and British Imperialism, 1717-1927* (Chapel Hill: The University of North Carolina Press, 2007).

19. Robert Lomas, *Turning the Solomon Key: George Washington, the Bright Morning Star, and the Secrets of Masonic Astrology* (Gloucester, MA: Fair Winds Press, 2006).

20. See George Washington, *The Diaries of George Washington*, Volume 6 (Charlottesville: University Press of Virginia, 1979), 105.

21. See Albert Pike, *Morals and Dogma of the Ancient and Accepted Scottish Rite of Freemasonry* (New York: Masonic Publishing Company, 1874).

22. Alfred John Pearce, *The Science of the Stars* (London: Simpkin, Marshall and Company, 1881).

23. Sarah Luria, *Capital Speculations: Writing and Building Washington, D.C.* (Hanover, NH: University of New Hampshire Press, 2006), 6-16.

24. Thomas Jefferson catalogued the French translation of Ptolemy's original, as well as other ancient works. It is therefore believed that Jefferson was very familiar with the esoteric knowledge of those of Freemasons. There is no evidence, however, to prove that Jefferson was a member of any Masonic lodge. See James Gilreath and Douglas Wilson, eds., *Thomas Jefferson's Library: A Catalog with the Entries in His Own Order* (Washington, D.C.: Library of Congress, 1989). See also footnote 17 in Chapter Ten.

25. Claudius Ptolemy, Translated by Frank E. Robbins, *Ptolemy: Tetrabiblos* (Cambridge: Harvard University Press, 1980).

26. David Ovason, *The Secret Architecture of Our Nation's Capital: The Masons and the Building of Washington, D.C.* (New York: HarperCollins, 2002), 350.

27. Wilhelmus Bogart Bryan, *A History of the National Capital: From Its Foundation through the Period of the Adoption of the Organic Act* (New York: The Macmillan Company, 1914), 151.

28. David Ovason, p. 254.

29. John K. Young, *Sacred Sites of the Knights Templar: Ancient Astronomers and Freemasons at Stonehenge, Rennes-Le-Chateau, and Santiago De Compostela* (Gloucester, MA: Fair Winds, 2003), 199-205.

30. David Ovason, 253-263.

31. David Ovason, 134-135; footnote 33, 419.

32. See Benjamin Franklin, *Poor Richard: The Almanacks for the Years 1733-1758* (New York: Limited Editions Club, 1964).

33. See an illustration of the Dragon's Head and Tail inside the cover pages of Walter Isaacson, *Benjamin Franklin: An American Life* (New York: Simon and Schuster, 2003).

34. See the complete conversation in astrological language between Benjamin Franklin and his fellow student and friend Titan Leeds in Benjamin Franklin, Albert Henry Smyth, ed., *The Writings of Benjamin Franklin,* (New York: Macmillan Company Limited, 1905), 196-197 and 201-202. Franklin also associated this astrological conjunction with diagnosing bodily ailments. See inside cover pages of Walter Isaacson.

35. George H. W. Bush reinvigorated historic sentiments that the United States "acted on the *ancient knowledge* that strength and clarity lead to peace" (italics added). See the entire speech on the University of California at Santa Barbara webpage: http://www.presidency.ucsb.edu/ws/index.php?pid=25955

36. Robert Lomas.

37. David Ovason, 349.

38. David Ovason, 355.

39. David Lynn Holmes, *The Faiths of the Founding Fathers* (New York: Oxford University Press, 2006).

40. Ibid.

41. See William Stevens Perry, *Episcopate in America: Sketches Biographical & Bibliographical of the Bishops of the American Church* (New York: The Christian Literature Company, 1895), lv-lvi.

42. See the National Shrine webpage at http://www.nationalshrine.com.

43. Maria Luisa Ambrosini and Mary Willis, *The Secret Archives of the Vatican* (New York: Barnes and Noble, 1996), 222.

44. Marcus Aurelius, *The Meditations of Marcus Aurelius* (London: Elibron Classics, 1887), 86.

45. Donald Regan, *For the Record: From Wall Street to Washington* (New York: Harcourt Brace Jovanovich, 1988).

46. Caspar Weinberger and Gretchen Roberts, *In the Arena: A Memoir of the 20th Century* (Washington, D.C.: Regnery Publishing, 2001), 148.

47. See the foreword by C. Fred Kleinknecht, the thirty-third degree Sovereign Grand Commander of the Supreme Council of Southern Jurisdiction in Washington, D.C., in David Ovason, vii.

48. The phrase "ancient hope" was used by President George W. Bush in his second Inaugural Address on January 20, 2005.

Chapter 10: The Mercurial Ruler and Sacred Constitution Avenue

1. In 1775, Hamilton wrote these mighty lines in his first Revolutionary pamphlet, "The Farmer Refuted." See Alexander Hamilton, John Hamilton ed., *The Works of Alexander Hamilton* (New York: John F. Throw Printer, 1850), 80.

2. See an in-depth analysis on the subject matter in Michael D. Chan, *Hamilton on Commerce and Statesmanship* (Columbia: University of Missouri Press, 2006).

3. Gerard Martin Moeller, *AIA: Guide to the Architecture of Washington, D.C.* (Baltimore, MD: The Johns Hopkins University Press, 2006), 160.

4. David Ovason, *The Secret Architecture of Our Nation's Capital: The Masons and the Building of Washington, D.C.* (New York: HarperCollins, 2002).

5. On the map, the location of the Washington Monument is not perfectly aligned with the White House and the Capitol as originally drawn by L'Enfant. Andrew Ellicott wanted to have a reliable foundation for the Monument and moved it slightly to a secure and solid location on the marshland. The minor change was necessary for a geological and practical reason. See Ovason, 261-62.

6. George Washington, Julius Friedrich Sachse, ed., *Washington's Masonic Correspondence as Found among the Washington Papers in the Library of Congress* (Lancaster, PA: Press of the New Era Printing Company, 1915), 22, 26, passim.

7. Paracelsus, Translated by Nicholas Goodrick-Clarke, *Paracelsus: Essential Readings* (Berkeley, CA: North Atlantic Books, 1999), 110.

8. Manly P. Hall, *The Secret Teachings of All Ages* (Baltimore, MD: Forgotten Books, 1928).

9. Franz Hartmann, *The Life of Philippus Theophrastus Bombast of Hohenheim, Known by the Name of Paracelsus and the Substance of His Teachings* (London: Kegan Paul, Trench, Trubner and Company, 1896), 241-242.

10. Franz Hartmann, 242.

11. Susan Miller, *Planets and Possibilities: Explore the World of the Zodiac Beyond Just Your Sign* (New York: Grand Central Publishing, 2001).

12. See Albert G. Mackey, *Encyclopedia of Freemasonry and Its Kindred Sciences* (Philadelphia, McClure Publishing Company, 1917), 173 and 627-28. The Supreme Council, 33°, in Washington, D.C., is the governing body of Scottish Rite Freemasonry in the Southern Jurisdiction of the United States.

13. Lynne Withey, *Dearest Friend: A Life of Abigail Adams* (New York: Simon and Schuster, 2002), 81.

14. Cokie Roberts, *Founding Mothers: The Women Who Raised Our Nation* (New York: William Morrow, 2004).

15. See Carol Berkin, *Revolutionary Mothers: Women in the Struggle for America's Independence* (New York: Vintage Books, 2006) and Linda Grant De Pauw, *Founding Mothers: Women of America in the Revolutionary Era* (New York: Houghton Mifflin Company, 1994).

16. David Ovason, *The Secret Architecture of Our Nation's Capital: The Masons and the Building of Washington, D.C.* (New York: HarperCollins, 2002).

17. Some literature suggests that Thomas Jefferson was most likely initiated to the Masonic fraternity while he was in France. Most records were destroyed with the French Revolution, but his writings convinced this author that Jefferson was a Freemason like George Washington and Benjamin Franklin. See also footnote 24 in Chapter Nine.

18. Jefferson, who was not a known Freemason, wrote to Thomas Lomax on March 12, 1799. See Thomas Jefferson Randolph, ed., *Memoir, Correspondence, and Miscellanies from the Papers of Thomas Jefferson* (Charlottesville, VA: F. Carr and Company, 1829), 425.

19. William Short was a member of the Virginia Council of State and served as Jefferson's secretary in France. George Green Shackelford describes Short as one of the most successful diplomats after Franklin, Adams, and Jefferson. See George Green

Shackelford, *Jefferson's Adoptive Son: The Life of William Short, 1759-1848* (Lexington, KY: University Press of Kentucky, 1993).

20. Jefferson wrote to William Short in New York on April 1790. See Thomas Jefferson Randolph, ed., *Memoir, Correspondence, and Miscellanies from the Papers of Thomas Jefferson* (Charlottesville: F. Carr and company, 1829), 57.

21. For an excellent historical account of L'Enfant's plan, see Scott W. Berg, *Grand Avenues: The Story of the French Visionary Who Designed Washington, D.C.* (New York: Pantheon Books, 2007).

22. Anthony T. Browder, *Egypt on The Potomac: A Guide to Decoding Egyptian Architecture and Symbolism* (Washington D.C.: Institute of Karmic Guidance, 2004).

23. The national headquarters of the Supreme Council the Scottish Rite has been located at 1733 Sixteenth Street, NW since 1915. See http://www.scottishrite.org/where/hq.html

24. R. C. Lodge, *Plato's Theory of Ethics: The Moral Criterion and the Highest Good* (London: Routledge and Kegan Paul, 1928), 17.

25. During my University of Maryland's teaching tour in Turkey, I visited the tourist city of Bodrum, located just south of Ephesus facing the Aegean Sea. See Sarah Pomeroy, Stanley Burstein, Walter Donlan, and Jennifer Roberts, *Ancient Greece: A Political, Social, and Cultural History* (New York: Oxford University Press, 1999), 342. See also a historical account of the building on the House of Masonic Temple's webpage: http://www.scottishrite.org/where/hq.html.

26. In 1791, Pierre L'Enfant outlined this Grand Avenue between the Capitol and the Washington Monument on his map as a garden-like promenade, like those within European cities—especially Paris. Ihna Thayer Frary described the Grand Avenue as "400-feet in breath, and a mile in length, bordered with gardens, ending in a slope from the houses on each side." See Ihna Thayer Frary, *They Built the Capitol* (Freeport: Books for Libraries Press, 1969), 11.

27. David Ovason, *The Secret Architecture of Our Nation's Capital: The Masons and the Building of Washington, D.C.* (New York: HarperCollins, 2002), 267.

28. See Ihna Thayer Frary, 11.

29. See Scott W. Berg.

30. Elizabeth Sarah Kite, *L'Enfant and Washington, 1791-1792* (Baltimore: The Johns Hopkins University Press, 1929), 19.

31. On his drive to the Inaugural Address on January 20, 1960, President John F. Kennedy noticed the dilapidated nature of Pennsylvania Avenue and appointed Daniel Patrick Moynihan to devise a plan to revitalize the ceremonial route. See a detailed account of this story in Godfrey Hodgson, *The Gentleman from New York: Daniel Patrick Moynihan* (New York: Houghton Mifflin Books, 2000), 78-82.

32. David Ovason, 351.

33. James Ferguson, *Astronomy Explained upon Sir Isaac Newton's Principles* (Philadelphia: Matthew Carey, 1809), 447-51.

34. David Ovason, 207-216.

35. Read his memoir in Everett McKinley Dirksen, *The Education of a Senator* (Urbana, IL: University of Illinois Press, 1998).

36. David Ovason, 270.

37. A memorandum dated May 14, 1974, from Mary C. Long of the Art and Research Staff in the Capitol, in file: *Frescoes—Corridors, Senate—Signs of Zodiac.* Quoting Ovason, 269 and 447.

38. Eleanor Roosevelt, *My Days* (New York: Dodge Publishing Company, 1938), 226.

39. A reference to the Liberal Arts and Sciences can also be found in Freemasonry's oldest extant document, the Halliwall Manuscript. See: http://freemasonry.bcy.ca/texts/regius.html#liberal

40. National Academies, *The Academy Building: A History and Descriptive Guide* (Washington, D.C.: National Academies, 1974), 11.

41. National Academies, 13.

42. Drawn from the National Academy of Sciences' brochure, *The Celestial Map at the Einstein Memorial*; this is available for public distribution.

43. Astronomers from the U.S. Naval Observatory in Washington, D.C., produced the stellar map.

44. American architect Robert Berks made this sculpture of Albert Einstein in 1979. See Gerard Martin Moeller, *AIA Guide to the Architecture of Washington, D.C.* (Baltimore, MD: The Johns Hopkins University Press, 2006), 183.

45. George Washington, Jared Sparks, ed., *The Writings of George Washington* (Boston: Ferdinand Andrews Publisher, 1839), 25.

46. Benjamin Rush, Dagobert Runes, ed., *The Selected Writings of Benjamin Rush* (New York: Philosophical Library, 2008), 18-19.

47. Harold Edward Stassen, Marshall Houts, ed., *Eisenhower: Turning the World Toward Peace* (St. Paul, MN: Merrill Publishing Corporation, 990), 286. See also Patrick Mendis, "United Nations at 50: Reflections of Former Minnesota Governor Stassen," *Asian Pages* (November 15, 1995), 2.

48. Thomas R. Hietala, *Manifest Design: American Exceptionalism and Empire* (Ithaca, NY: Cornell University Press, 2003), 2.

49. Charles Dickens, *American Notes and Pictures from Italy* (Alcester, U.K.: Read Books Press, 2007), 101.

Chapter 11: Altar of Empire: The Virgoan Federal Triangle

1. See President Ronald Reagan's entire Farewell Address to the nation on January 11, 1989 at the presidential library archives: http://www.reagan.utexas.edu/archives/speeches/1989/011189i.htm

2. Paul Dickson, *War Slang: American Fighting Words and Phrases since the Civil War* (Dulles, VA: Brasseys Inc. 2004), 12.

3. David Ovason, *The Secret Architecture of Our Nation's Capital: The Masons and the Building of Washington, D.C.* (New York: HarperCollins Publishers, 1999), 350.

4. David Cannadine, *Mellon: An American Life* (New York: The Random House, 2008), 375.

5. Ihna Thayer Frary, *They Built the Capitol* (Manchester, NH: Ayer Publishing, 1969), 11.

6. Senator James McMillan represented Michigan from 1889 to his death in 1902. Senator McMillan, a retired railroad mogul with an engineering and architectural background, was initiated as a Mason.

7. George Gurney, *Sculpture and the Federal Triangle* (Washington, D.C.: Smithsonian Institution Press, 1985).

8. Isabelle Gournay, "Washington: The DC's History of Unresolved Planning Conflicts," in David L. A. Gordon, ed., *Planning Twentieth Century Capital Cities* (New York: Routledge, 2006), 115.

9. As chair of the Senate Committee for the District of Columbia, Senator McMillan established a behind-the-scenes alliance with the American Institute of Architects, national park advocates, and more importantly the Washington Board of Trade, a powerful organization in the absence of an elected city council. See Isabelle Gournay, 117.

10. James Wasserman, *The Secrets of Masonic Washington* (Rochester, VT: Destiny Books, 2008), 115-130 and David Ovason, 281-310.

11. Edward Savage engraved this oil-painted portrait of "The Washington Family" in 1796, representing the president, his wife Martha, and his two adopted children. See Justin Winsor, ed., *Narrative and Critical History of America* (New York: Houghton, Mifflin and Company, 1888), 574

12. Paul Richard, "From the Collection: Washington's Prize Possessions," *The Washington Post*, September 24, 2006, N7.

13. Ibid.

14. George Gurney, 376.

15. Albert Pike, grand commander of Freemasonry in Washington, D.C., wrote about such symbolism: "Isis, the same as Ceres, was, as we learn from Eratosthenes, Constellation Virgo, represented by a woman holding an ear of wheat" (corn). See Albert Pike, *Morals and Dogma of the Ancient and Accepted Scottish Rite of Freemasonry* (New York: Masonic Publishing Company, 1874), 506.

16. President Woodrow Wilson signed the Federal Trade Commission (FTC) Act of 1914 to regulate monopolies and unlawful trade practices, and the Clayton Antitrust Act, which tightened some of the loopholes in the Sherman Act. The FTC Act prohibited pricing agreements, outlawed interlocking directorates in large corporations, and made it illegal for a company to purchase stock from a competitor. William Stull Holt, *The Federal Trade Commission: Its History, Activities and Organization* (Washington, D.C.: The Institute for Government Research, 1922). See the Federal Trade Commission Act of 1914 [15 USC 41 et seq.] in http://uscode.house.gov/download/pls/15C48.txt

17. Constance McLaughlin Green, *The Secret City: A History of Race Relations in the Nation's Capital* (Princeton, NJ: Princeton University Press, 1967).

18. Timothy Walch, ed., *Guardian of Heritage: Essays on the History of the National Archives* (Washington D.C.: National Archives and Records Administration, 1985).

19. President Hoover spoke at the laying of the cornerstone of the National Archives Building on February 20, 1933. See Herbert Hoover, *The State Papers and Other Public Writings of Herbert Hoover* (New York: Doubleday, Doran and Company, 1934), 596.

20. To understand the significance of the number 72, see Jostein Ådna, Hans Kvalbein, eds., *The Mission of the Early Church to Jews and Gentiles* (Tubingen, Germany: Mohr Siebeck, 2000) and Guenther Wachsmuth, *Reincarnation as a Phenomenon of Metamorphosis* (London: Rudolf Steiner Press, 1937).

21. See the National Archives' two pediments:
http://www.archives.gov/about/history/building-an-archives/pediments.html

22. United States Congress, *The 1980 Midyear Review of the Economy: The Recession and The Recovery* (Washington, D.C.: U.S. Congress Joint Economic Committee, 1980), 1. See also the National Archives homepage for additional information:
http://www.archives.gov

23. William Shakespeare, *The Tempest* (San Francisco, CA: Grabhorn Press, 1951), 64.

24. Timothy Walch, *Guardian of Heritage: Essays on the History of the National Archives* (Washington, D.C.: National Archives & Records Administration, 1985), 24.

25. This popular axiom is often attributed to Thomas Jefferson; however, it is not found anywhere in his biographies or writings. The first recorded use of that phrase was during a 1790 speech by Irish statesman John Philpot Curran: "The condition upon which God hath given liberty to man is eternal vigilance." American abolitionist Wendell Phillips said in 1852 that, "Eternal vigilance is the price of liberty." See Ralph Keyes, *The Quote Verifier: Who Said What, Where, and When* (New York: Macmillan Press, 2006), 237.

26. In 2001, the Department of Justice Building was renamed the Robert F. Kennedy Department of Justice Building to honor Robert F. Kennedy, who was Attorney General (1961-1964) under his brother, President John F. Kennedy.

27. Carl Paul Jennewein, *C. Paul Jennewein* (Atlanta: University of Georgia Press, 1950), 40-47.

28. James M. Goode, *The Outdoor Sculpture of Washington, D.C.: A Comprehensive Historical Guide* (Washington, D.C.: Smithsonian Institution Press, 1974), 159.

29. The Latin motto on the seal of the Justice Department has been enigmatic and puzzling to some. It simply means, "Who pursues justice for the lady" or the Lady Justice. The curious motto, *Qui pro Domina Justitia Sequitur*, was first used by Lord Treasurer Burleigh when he told Queen Elizabeth, "Madam, here is your attorney-general, *Qui Pro Domina Regina Sequitur*." The Queen then replied: "It should be, '*attornatus generalis qui pro Domina verttate sequitur*." Attorney General Black changed it to "*Qui pro Domina Justitia Sequitur*." See the Youth Companion Series, *The Ship of State* (Boston: Ginn and Company, 1903), 239. Also see the U.S. Department of Justice's explanatory note for a lengthy discussion on this Latin motto and its history: http://www.usdoj.gov/jmd/ls/dojseal.htm.

30. E. W. Thomas *The Judicial Process: Realism, Pragmatism, Practical Reasoning and Principles* (New York: Cambridge University Press, 2005), 358.

31. Unaware of their significance and judicial history, Attorney General John Ashcroft ordered the two statues covered with drapes in 2002. The controversial and conservative Attorney General's decision to install $8,000 drapes seemed a symbolic foreshadowing of the alleged cover-ups and secrecy that would plague the Department in the years to follow. Paul Corts, Assistant Attorney General for Administration, removed the drapes in 2005. The act seemed to allow a newly unveiled and clear-eyed Lady of Justice to seek the truth. See Dan Eggen "Sculpted Bodies and a Strip Act at Justice Dept.," *The Washington Post*, June 25, 2005, A2.

32. These mural paintings are on the ceiling of the restored private office used by former Secretary of the Treasury Solomon Chase, Lincoln's first Treasury Secretary, during 1861-64.

33. Jerry D. Moore, *Architecture and Power in the Ancient Andes: The Archaeology of Public Buildings* (New York: Cambridge University Press, 1996), 95.

34. Ovason, 311.

35. Mary Cable, *The Avenue of the Presidents* (Boston: Houghton Mifflin, 1969), 208.

36. Following an initiative led by Senator Daniel Patrick Moynihan and philanthropist Paul Mellon, Jr. (son of the former secretary of the U.S. Treasury Department), the Departmental Auditorium was renamed the Andrew W. Mellon Auditorium in 1995.

37. The building was constructed for the Department of Labor, but the tenancy changed to the U.S. Customs Service in 1979. The Customs Service is now part of the Department of Homeland Security.

38. Arthur Brown also designed the Opera House and the City Hall in San Francisco. See Pamela Scott and Antoinette Lee, *Buildings of the District of Columbia* (New York: Oxford University Press, 1995).

39. Thomas J. Steele, "The Figure of Columbia: Phillis Wheatley Plus George Washington," *The New England Quarterly*, Vol. 54, No. 2, June 1981, 264-266.

40. On October 26, 1775, Phillis Wheatley wrote to George Washington from Providence, RI, to which he replied on February 2, 1776 from Cambridge, MA. See John Wesley Cromwell, *The Negro in American History: Men and Women Eminent in the Evolution of the American of African Descent* (Washington, D.C.: The American Negro Academy, 1914), 83-85.

41. See a description and meaning of these symbols in Manly Palmer Hall, *The Secret Teachings of All Ages: An Encyclopedic Outline of Masonic, Hermetic, Qabbalistic and Rosicrucian Symbolical Philosophy*, 1928. Read the entire text online: http://www.sacred-texts.com/eso/sta/

42. J. Hugo Tatsch, *Facts about George Washington as a Freemason* (Whitefish, MT: Kessinger Publishing, 1998), 26. Unlike his successor President Franklin D. Roosevelt, President Herbert Hoover was not a known Freemason.

43. See David Ovason, 303-305 and footnote 83 in Chapter 10, 450-451.

44. Michael J. Hogan, *The Marshall Plan: America, Britain, and the Reconstruction of Western Europe, 1947-1952* (New York: Cambridge University Press, 1989), 4.

45. This unique distinction now goes to the headquarters of the Department of Defense, the Pentagon, with over 3.7 million square feet of space for its 23,000 employees in Arlington, Virginia.

46. These were designed and sculpted by James Fraser in 1934.

47. For a more detailed account, see David Ovason, 306.

48. See the homepage of the Ronald Reagan building and international trade center: http://www.itcdc.com/

49. Congress passed the Federal Triangle Development Act in 1987. See the Act in the House webpage: http://uscode.house.gov/download/pls/40C67.txt

50. See Ronald Reagan above.

51. Paracelsus, 109.

Chapter 12: *Novus Ordo Seclorum and the New World Order*

1. David Rockefeller, *Memoirs* (New York: Random House, 2002), 405. In addition to leading the Council on Foreign Relations, Dr. Rockefeller has been actively involved in a wide range of leadership positions at Rockefeller University, the University of Chicago, the Carnegie Endowment for International Peace, the Trilateral Commission, the Bilderberg Group, the Peterson Institute for International Economics, the Council of the Americas, Harvard University, and the Chase Manhattan Bank, among others.

2. See an account of these difficult years in Jon Meacham, *American Lion: Andrew Jackson in the White House* (New York: Random House, 2008).

3. Robert Dallek, *Lyndon B. Johnson: Portrait of a President* (New York: Oxford University Press, 2004), 205.

4. On September 11, 1990 (a year before the 9/11 tragedies), the president's famous speech titled *Toward a New World Order*, was delivered to a joint session of Congress. See George H. W. Bush, "Toward a New World Order," September 11, 1990, *Public Papers of the Presidents of the United States, George H. W. Bush, 1990* (Washington, D.C.: Government Printing Office, 1991).

5. The late Reverend Jerry Falwell, leader of the Moral Majority and a Christian fundamentalist preacher, defended segregation and railed against integration in a sermon in 1958, warning that it would lead to miscegenation, which would "destroy our [white] race eventually." See Walt Harrington, *American Profiles: Somebodies and Nobodies Who Matter* (Columbia, MO: University of Missouri Press 1992), 119.   Anti-miscegenation laws existed in the U.S. states until the Supreme Court made them unconstitutional in 1967. See an assessment of interracial sexual relationships in the early republic in Jan Ellen Lewis and Peter S. Onuf, eds., *Sally Hemings and Thomas Jefferson: History, Memory, and Civic Culture* (Charlottesville, VA: University of Virginia Press, 1999).

6. See an analysis of religion and race in Brenda Salter McNeil, *A Credible Witness: Reflections on Power, Evangelism and Race* (Downers Grove, IL: InterVarsity Press, 2008).

7. Thomas Jefferson, Paul Leicester Ford, ed., *The Works of Thomas Jefferson* (New York: G. P. Putnam's Sons, 1905), 378.

8. Cyrus Townsend Brady, *The True Andrew Jackson* (Philadelphia, PA: J. B. Lippincott Company, 1906), 490.

9. This famous phrase is drawn from the U.S. Declaration of Independence. See Frederic Jesup Stimson, *The Law of the Federal and State Constitutions of the United States* (Clark, NJ: The Lawbook Exchange, 2004), 76.

10. John Adams, Charles Francis Adams, ed., *The Works of John Adams: Second President of the United States* (Boston: Charles C. Little and James Brown, 1851), 290.

11. See Martin Dupuis, Keith Boeckelman, *Barack Obama: The New Face of American Politics* (Santa Barbara, CA: Greenwood Publishing 2008), 130.

12. See a case study of the American military involvement in the Asian tsunami in Patrick Mendis and Jaime Alvarado, "New Multilateralism in Action for Peace: A Case Study of the US-led Operation Unified Assistance (OUA) in the Asian Tsunami Disaster," *Global Economic Review*, Volume 36, Issue 2, June 2007, 183-192.

13. Patrick Mendis, *Human Side of Globalization* (Deer Park, NY: Linus Publications, 2009), 244.

14. Woodrow Wilson, Donald Day, ed., *Woodrow Wilson's Own Story* (Boston, MA: Little, Brown and Company 1952), 247.

15. For an official history of the Great Seal of the United States, see the U. S. Department of State, *The Great Seal of the United States* (Washington, D.C.: State Department's Bureau of Public Affairs, 2003). See also the State Department's webpage at http://www.state.gov/documents/organization/27807.pdf. *Seclorum* comes from the original Latin in Virgil's *Eclogue IV* (line 5) "*Magnus ab integro seclorum nascitur ordo.*" (Translation: A great series or mighty order of ages is born anew).

16. See the U. S. Department of State, 5.

17. See Lewis Reifsneider Harley, *The Life of Charles Thomson: Secretary of the Continental Congress and Translator of the Bible from the Greek* (Philadelphia, MD: George W. Jacobs and Company, 1900).

18. Ibid.

19. John Kingston, *The Life of General George Washington* (Baltimore: A. Miltenberger, 1813), 111.

20. Lewis Reifsneider Harley, 108.

21. Historian Fred S. Rolater identified Secretary Charles Thomson of the Continental Congress (1774-89) as the "Prime Minister of the United States" in *The Pennsylvania Magazine of History and Biography*, Vol. 101, No. 3, July 1977, 322-348.

22. Lewis Reifsneider Harley, 180.

23. Boyd Stanley Schlenther, *Charles Thomson: A Patriot's Pursuit* (Newark, DE: University of Delaware Press, 1990).

24. Virgil, Charles Knapp, ed., *The Aeneid of Vergil, Book VII* (Chicago: Scott, Foresman and Company, 1900), 44.

25. This phrase was described a century later by Yale University military Professor Charles Totten. See Charles A. L. Totten, *The Great Seal of "Manasseh," The United States of America* (New Haven, CT: The Our Race Publishing Company, 1897), 343.

26. William S. Appleton, *Augustin Dupre and His Work for America* (Cambridge, MA: Massachusetts Historical Society, 1890), 4-6.

27. Samuel Eliot Morison, ed., *The Oxford History of the United States 1783-1917* (New York: Oxford University Press, 1927), 413. See also Walter Russell Mead, *Special Providence: American Foreign Policy and How It Changed the World* (New York: Alfred A. Knopf, 2004), vii.

28. Thomas Paine, Isaac Kramnick, ed., *Common Sense* (New York: Penguin Books, 1982), 63.

29. George H. W. Bush.

30. Ibid.

31. Ibid.

32. Ibid.

33. See the speech "George H. W. Bush Announces U.S. Attack on Iraq, 1991" on the U.S. State Department's webpage at http://usinfo.state.gov/infousa/government/overview/bush_iraq.html

34. Ibid.

35. Charles Selengut, *Sacred Fury: Understanding Religious Violence* (Lanham, MD: Rowman and Littlefield Publishers, 2008), 33.

36. Even before President Bush's historic speech, many Christian fundamentalists advocated Biblical perspectives and promoted popular conspiracy theories. See William T. Still, *New World Order: The Ancient Plan of Secret Societies* (Lafayette, LS: Huntington House Publishing, 1990). Also see Michael Benson, *Inside Secret Societies: What They Don't Want You to Know* (New York: Citadel Press, 2005).

37. Colbert I. King, "Pat Robertson's Gold," *The Washington Post*, September 22, 2001, A29.

38. Philip H. Melling, *Fundamentalism in America: Millennialism, Identity and Militant Religion* (Edinburgh, U.K.: Edinburgh University Press, 1999), 54.

39. Gene Puskar, "Pat Robertson Calls for Assassination of Hugo Chavez," *The USA Today*, August 22, 2005. See the article at http://www.usatoday.com/news/nation/2005-08-22-robertson-_x.htm

40. Pat Robertson, *The New World Order* (Dallas, TX: Word Publishing, 1991).

41. Pat Robertson, 3.

42. Pat Robertson, 4.

43. Pat Robertson, 6.

44. Arturo de Hoyos and S. Brent Morris, eds., *Freemasonry in Context: History, Ritual, Controversy* (Lanham, MD: Lexington Books, 2004), 287-288. See also Daniel

Pipes, *Conspiracy: How the Paranoid Style Flourishes and Where It Comes From* (New York: Simon and Schuster, 199), 9-11.

45. Pat Robertson, 36.

46. Pat Robertson, 36. See also a critical analysis in Chip Berlet and Matthew N. Lyons, Right-Wing Populism in America: Too Close for Comfort (New York, NY: Guilford Press, 2000), 258.

47. Pat Robertson, 68.

48. Anthony Lewis, "Abroad at Home; The Crackpot Factor," *The New York Times*, April 14, 1995, A15.

49. Pat Robertson, 68.

50. Michael Lind, *Up from Conservatism: Why the Right is Wrong for America*, (New York: Simon and Schuster, 1997), 99-100.

51. See Michael Lind.

52. Jason Goodwin, *Greenback: The Almighty Dollar and the Invention of America*, (New York: Macmillan, 2003), 64-65.

53. David Ovason, *The Secret Symbols of the Dollar Bill: A Closer Look at the Hidden Magic and Meaning of the Money You Use Every Day* (New York: HarperCollins, 2004), 14-15.

54. Allan J. Lichtman, *White Protestant Nation: The Rise of the Conservative Movement* (New York: Atlantic Monthly Press, 2008), 199.

55. Ibid.

56. Jeff Sharlet, *The Family: The Secret Fundamentalism at the Heart of American Power* (New York, Harper's, 2008), 111.

57. For an in-depth analysis of the Family, read Wayne Madsen, *Expose: The "Christian" Mafia*, January 22nd, 2006 in RINF Forum at http://www.rinf.com/columnists/news/expose-the-christian-mafia-parts-1-2

58. Norman Grubb, *Modern Viking: The Story of Abraham Vereide, Pioneer in Christian Leadership*, (Grand Rapids, MI: Zondervan Publishing House, 1961).

59. Jeff Sharlet, 44.

60. Jeff Sharlet, 46.

61. Jeff Sharlet, 226-227.

62. Ibid. The Presidential Prayer Breakfast has been called the National Prayer Breakfast since 1953.

63. Jeff Sharlet, 197.

64. See a critical historical analysis in Alan M. Dershowitz, *Blasphemy: How the Religious Right is Hijacking Our Declaration of Independence* (Hoboken, NJ: John Wiley and Sons, 2007), 68-69.

65. J. David Kuo, *Tempting Faith: An Inside Story of Political Seduction* (New York: Simon and Schuster, 2006), 95.

66. J. David Kuo, 21.

67. Karol Edward Soltan and Stephen L. Elkin, *The Constitution of Good Societies* (University Park, PA: Penn State University Press), 120.

68. Alan M. Dershowitz, 69.

69. Jeff Sharlet, passim.

70. Jeff Sharlet, 19.

71. Calvin Blanchard, *The Life of Thomas Paine: Mover of the Declaration of Independence* (New York: D. M. Bennett, 1877), 46.

72. Thomas Jefferson, Albert Ellery Bergh, ed., The Writings of Thomas Jefferson (Washington, D.C.: The Thomas Jefferson Memorial Association, 1907), 223.

73. Ibid.

74. Manuel Roig-Franzia, "The Political Enclave That Dare Not Speak Its Name: The Sanford and Ensign Scandals Open a Door on Previously Secretive 'C Street' Spiritual Haven," *The Washington Post*, June 26, 2009, A1.

75. Robbie Brown and Shaila Dewan, "Mysteries Remain after Governor Admits an Affair," *The New York Times*, June 24, 2009, A1.

76. Jeff Sharlet, 21.

77. Ibid.

78. Thomas Jefferson, 223.

79. Joel Dyer, *Harvest of Rage: Why Oklahoma City is Only the Beginning* (Boulder, CO: Westview Press, 1998).

80. Ibid.

81. See Article II in William Addison Blakely, ed., *American State Papers Bearing on Religious Legislation* (New York: National Religious Liberty Association, 1891), 54-55.

Chapter 13: Madison's Grand Strategy for a Universal Empire

1. Richard Bradley, *Harvard Rules: The Struggle for the Soul of the World's Most Powerful University* (New York: HaperCollins Publisher, 2005), xiv.

2. Ibid.

3. French was the *lingua franca* of international diplomacy until around World War I, after which it was gradually supplanted by English. English has gained in global dominance since the early part of the twentieth century, and today it is estimated that approximately two-thirds of the world's people speak English as their first or second language.

4. Rodney Koeneke, *Empires of the Mind: I. A. Richards and Basic English in China, 1929-1979* (Palo Alto, CA: Stanford University Press, 2004), 213.

5. Bradley A. Thayer, "The Case for the American Empire" in Christopher Layne and Bradley A. Thayer, eds., *American Empire: A Debate* (New York: Routledge Press, 2007), 7.

6. Francis Bacon, *The New Atlantis* (Whitefish, MT: Kessinger Publishing, 2004), 309.

7. Francis Bacon, 321.

8. Bronwen Price, *Francis Bacon's New Atlantis: New Interdisciplinary Essays* (Manchester, UKL Manchester University Press, 2002), 131-134. See also a critical analysis in Marina Leslie, *Renaissance Utopias and the Problem of History* (Ithaca, NY: Cornell University Press 1998), 81-119.

9. Paul A. Rahe, *Republics Ancient and Modern: The Ancien Régime in Classical Greece* (Chapel Hill, NC: The University of North Carolina Press, 1994), 87.

10. James Madison, *Notes of Debates in the Federal Convention of 1787* (New York: W. W. Norton Company, 1987), xiv.

11. James Madison, E. H. Scott, ed., *Journal of the Federal Convention Kept by James Madison* (Chicago, IL: Scott, Foresman and Company, 1898), 257.

12. James Madison, Gaillard Hunt, ed., *The Writings of James Madison: 1803-1807* (New York: G. P. Putnam's Sons, 1908), 92.

13. Thomas Jefferson, George Tucker, ed., *The Life of Thomas Jefferson: Third President of the United States* (Philadelphia, PA: Carey, Lea and Blanchard Company, 1837), 85-87.

14. Thomas Jefferson, Henry Stephens Randall, ed., *The Life of Thomas Jefferson* (New York: Derby and Jackson, 1868), p. 316.

15. Irving Brant, *James Madison: The President, 1809-1812* (Indianapolis, IN: Bobbs-Merrill Company, 1956), 68-69.

16. Gordon S. Wood, *Empire of Liberty: A History of the Early Republic, 1789-1815* (New York: Oxford University Press, 2009), 632.

17. James Madison, Gaillard Hunt, *The Writings of James Madison* (New York: G. P. Putnam's Sons, 1906), 88.

18. Gordon Wood, 632.

19. James Madison, Gaillard Hunt, ed., 88.

20. Gordon Wood, 632.

21. James Madison, Gaillard Hunt, ed., 88.

22. Gordon S. Wood, 633.

23. James G. Wilson, *The Imperial Republic: A Structural History of American Constitutionalism from the Colonial Era to the Beginning of the Twentieth Century* (Aldershot, U.K.: Ashgate Publishing, 2002).

24. Melvin M. Johnson, *The Beginnings of Freemasonry in America* (New York: George H. Doran Company), 367.

25. Charles. M. Andrews, *Colonial self-Government* (New York: History of Colonial America Press, 1904).

26. Francis G. Wilson, *The American Political Mind: A Textbook in Political Theory* (New York: McGraw-Hill, 1949).

27. Evarts B. Greene, *The Foundations of American Nationality* (New York: American Book Company, 1922), 376.

28. Evarts Green, 173.

29. Benjamin Franklin, "Join, or Die," *The Pennsylvania Gazette*, May 9, 1754.

30. Willard G. Bleyer, *Main Currents in the History of American Journalism* (New York: Boston & Houghton Mifflin, 1927), 76.

31. Evarts Greene, 377.

32. Benjamin Franklin, Walter Isaacson, ed., *A Benjamin Franklin Reader* (New York: Simon and Schuster, 2003), 160.

33. For a bibliographical account, see Kent Logan Walgren, *Freemasonry, Anti-Masonry and Illuminism in the United States, 1734-1850: A Bibliography* (Worcester, MA: American Antiquarian Society, 2003).

34. The list is prepared through a careful analysis of various sources, including the Article of Confederation for The United Colonies of North America proposed on July 21, 1775 in Benjamin Franklin, Walter Isaacson, ed., *A Benjamin Franklin Reader* (New York: Simon and Schuster, 2003), 260-264 and *The Constitutions of the Free-Masons* in James Anderson (1723), which was reprinted by Benjamin Franklin (1734). A rare copy is available in the Library of the Supreme Council in Washington, D.C.

35. Benjamin Franklin, Walter Isaacson, ed., 259-261.

36. Thomas E. Burke, "The Albany Plan of Union, 1754" in Stephen L. Schechter, ed., *Roots of the Republic: American Founding Documents Interpreted* (Lanham, MD: Rowman and Littlefield Publishers, 1990), 112.

37. Ibid.

38. Thomas E. Burke, 113.

39. Benjamin Franklin, Walter Isaacson, ed., 161.

40. Benjamin Franklin, Frank Woodworth Pine, ed., *The Autobiography of Benjamin Franklin* (Garden City, NY: Garden City Publishing Company, 1916), 244.

41. Christopher Sowrs, a German printer, wrote to Conrad Weiser on September 6, 1755, bitterly complaining of the activities of Benjamin Franklin and his fellow Freemasons. See Sidney Hayden, *Washington and His Masonic Compeers* (New York: Masonic Publishing and Manufacturing Company, 1869), 296. This correspondence was first published in the *Historical Magazine of New York* in 1755, according to the *Masonic Review*, 1860, Vol. 23, 152.

42. William H. Seward, George E. Baker, ed., *The Works of William H. Seward* (Boston, MA: Houghton, Mifflin and Company, 1884), Vol. 1, 51.

43. The phrase "Manifest Destiny" was introduced by John O'Sullivan when his editorial "Annexation" first appeared in 1845 to promote the annexation of Texas and the Oregon Country to the United States. See John O'Sullivan, "Annexation," *United States Magazine and Democratic Review Vol. 17,* No.1, July-August 1845, 5-10.

44. William Seward, 58.

45. John Quincy Adams, Josiah Quincy, ed., *Memoir of the Life of John Quincy Adams* (Boston, MA: Crosby, Nichols, Lee and Company, 1860), 96.

46. Ibid.

47. John Gallagher and Ronald Robinson, "The Imperialism of Free Trade," *The Economic History Review*, Vol. VI, No. 1, 1953,13.

48. Thomas Paine, Isaac Kramnick, ed., *Common Sense* (New York: Penguin Books, 1982), 86.

49. Thomas Paine, Hypatia B. Bonner, ed., *Rights of Man* (London, UK: Watts and Company, 1906), 112.

50. Remarks by President George W. Bush at the California Business Association's breakfast meeting in the Sacramento Memorial Auditorium on October 17, 2001. See the entire speech outlining the war efforts in response to the 9/11 attack on the White House webpage: http://www.whitehouse.gov/news/releases/2001/10/20011017-15.html

51. George W. Bush, *The National Security Strategy of the United States of America* (Washington, D.C.: The White House, 2002).

52. See the National Security Council's strategy released on September 17, 2002 on the White House webpage: http://www.whitehouse.gov/nsc/nssintro.html

53. See the second Inaugural Address of President George W. Bush on January 20, 2005 on the White House webpage:
http://www.whitehouse.gov/news/releases/2005/01/20050120-1.html

54. George W. Bush, 17-20.

55. See *the National Security Strategy of the United States of America*, "Ignite a New Era of Global Economic Growth through Free Markets and Free Trade" (Chapter VI), 18.

56. Letter by Thomas Jefferson to Thomas Pinckney in Philadelphia on May 29, 1797. See Thomas Jefferson, Paul Leicester Ford, ed., *The Writings of Thomas Jefferson: 1795-1801* (New York: G. P. Putnam's Sons, 1896), 129.

57. William Cabell Rives, *History of the Life and Times of James Madison* (Boston, MA: Little, Brown and Company, 1881) 394.

58. Harold James, *The Roman Predicament: How the Rules of International Order Create the Politics of Empire* (Princeton, NJ: Princeton University Press, 2006).

59. Harold James, 1.

60. See Hermon Atkins McNeil's statement in the United States Supreme Court webpage at http://www.supremecourtus.gov/about/eastpediment.pdf

61. Joseph E. Stiglitz, *Freefall: America, Free Markets, and the Sinking of the World Economy* (New York: W. W. Norton and Company, 2010).

62. Joseph E. Stiglitz, 296.

63. Joseph E. Stiglitz, 278.

64. Thomas Paine, Isaac Kramnick, ed., *Common Sense* (New York: Penguin Books, 1982), 31.

65. David Shambaugh, ed., *Deng Xiaoping: Portrait of a Chinese Statesman* (New York: Oxford University Press, 1995), 88.

66. See a historical account in Suzanne Ogden, *Inklings of Democracy in China* (Boston, MA: Harvard University Press, 2002), 66.

67. Alexander Hamilton, Harold Coffin Syret, ed., *The Papers of Alexander Hamilton* (New York: Columbia University Press, 1979), 13.

68. Richard Bradley, *Harvard Rules: The Struggle for the Soul of the World's Most Powerful University* (New York: HaperCollins Publisher, 2005), xiv.

Epilogue: God's Crucible Nation: Predestiny or Free Will?

1. Following in his father's footsteps, President George W. Bush reiterated the founding vision in his second Inaugural Address on January 20, 2005. See the White House webpage at: http://www.whitehouse.gov/about/presidents/georgewbush.

2. Manly P. Hall, *The Secret Destiny of America* (Los Angeles, CA: Philosophical Research Society, 1944), 77.

3. President Ronald Reagan frequently used this popular phrase, borrowed from former Harvard president and Massachusetts Governor John Winthrop (1587-1649), to describe America in his speeches. The governor delivered this famous "City upon a Hill" sermon, also known as *A Model of Christian Charity,* which is often seen as a forerunner to the notion of American "exceptionalism." See John Winthrop, *The Journal of John Winthrop* (Boston, MA: Belknap Press of Harvard University Press, 1996), xi and 10.

4. Oliver Cromwell's quote was proposed by the 1776 congressional committee consisting of John Adams, Benjamin Franklin and Thomas Jefferson for the seal and motto of the newly independent United States of America. See Charles Adiel Lewis Totten, *The Seal of History: Our Inheritance in the Great Seal of Manasseh* (New Haven, CT: The Our Race Publishing Company, 1897), 3-24.

5. George W. Bush.

6. Richard N. Haass, *War of Necessity, War of Choice: A Memoir of Two Iraq Wars* (New York: Simon and Schuster, 2009), 14-16. See also Ivo H. Daalder and I. M. Destler, *In the Shadow of the Oval Office: Profiles of the National Security Advisers and the Presidents They Served—From JFK to George W. Bush* (New York: Simon and Schuster, 2009), 278-280.

7. George W. Bush.

8. Ibid.

9. Ibid.

10. Ibid.

11. Sun Tzu, Samuel B. Griffith, ed., *The Art of War* (New York: Oxford University Press, 1963), 84.

12. See a historical analysis in Patrick Mendis, *Trade for Peace: How the DNA of America, Freemasonry, and Providence Created a New World Order with Nobody in Charge* (Bloomington, IN: iUniverse Press, 2009).

13. George W. Bush, *The National Security Strategy of the United States of America* (Washington, D.C.: The White House, 2002), 17–20.

14. President Harry S. Truman made these remarks upon receiving an honorary law degree from the University of Kansas City on June 28, 1945. See the American Presidency Project at the University of California at Santa Barbara website at http://www.presidency.ucsb.edu/ws/index.php?pid=12190.

15. Jeremiah 1:5.

16. William Jay, *The Life of John Jay: Miscellaneous and Official Correspondence* (New York: J and J Harper, 1833), 376.

17. Read John Jay's letter to Samuel Miller on February 18, 1822: "It appeared to me that the Trinity was a Fact fully revealed and substantiated, but that the *quo modo* [in that manner] was incomprehensible and consequently inexplicable by human Ingenuity. According to sundry Creeds, the divine Being whom we denominate the *second* Person in the Trinity had before all worlds been so generated or begotten by the *first* Person in the Trinity, as to be his coeval, coequal and coeternal Son. For proof of this I searched the Scriptures diligently—but without Success. I therefore consider the Position of being at least of questionable Orthodox." See James H. Hutson, *The Founders on Religion: A Book of Quotations* (Princeton, NJ: Princeton University Press, 2007), 217.

18. Deuteronomy 30:19.

19. Charles Francis Adams, *The Works of John Adams: Second President of the United States* (Boston, MA: Little, Brown, and Company, 1865), 423.

20. John Adams and Thomas Jefferson, Paul Wilstach, ed., *Correspondence of John Adams and Thomas Jefferson 1812-1826* (Boston, MA: The Bobbs-Merrill Company, 1925), 142.

21. Since Dutch theologian Arminius (1560-1609) attempted to reform Calvinism, the Arminian (or Arian) movement became the basis of the Dutch Remonstrants in the Netherlands. See Jacobus Arminius, *The Works of James Arminius* (Auburn, AL: Berby and Miller, 1853).

22. Swedish scientist and Christian mystic Swedenborg (1688-1772) rejected the doctrine of salvation through Christian faith alone and considered that the both faith and charity are needed for salvation, not one without the other. See Michael Stanley, ed., *Emanuel Swedenborg: Essential Readings* (Berkeley, CA: North Atlantic Books, 2003).

23. James Madison, *A Memorial and Remonstrance: The Religious Rights of Man, Written in 1784-5* (Washington City: S. C. Ustick, 1828), 7.

24. Nathan Schachner, *Thomas Jefferson: A Biography* (New York: Appleton-Century Crofts, 1951), 971.

25. Benjamin Franklin, Henry Stueber, ed., *Works of the Late Dr. Benjamin Franklin* (New York: Samuel Campbell Bookseller, 1794), 86.

26. The U.S. Declaration of Independence in the U.S. Government Archive states: "Drafted by Thomas Jefferson between June 11 and June 28, 1776, the Declaration of Independence is at once the nation's most cherished symbol of liberty and Jefferson's most enduring monument. Here, in exalted and unforgettable phrases, Jefferson expressed the convictions in the minds and hearts of the American people. The political philosophy of the Declaration was not new; its ideals of individual liberty had already been expressed by John Locke and the Continental philosophers. What Jefferson did was to summarize this philosophy in 'self-evident truths' and set forth a list of grievances against the King in order to justify before the world the breaking of ties between the colonies and the mother country." See the founding document at http://www.archives.gov/exhibits/charters/declaration.html.

27. Thomas Jefferson, Henry Augustine Washington, ed., *The Writings of Thomas Jefferson: Autobiography, Correspondence, Reports, Messages, Addresses, and Other Writings* (New York: H. W. Berby, 1861), 152.

28. James Madison, "The Federalist Paper No. 51," in *The Federalist* (New York: Modern Library, 1788), 337.

29. James D. Richardson, *A Compilation of the Messages and Papers of the Presidents, 1789-1897* (Washington, D.C.: Government Printing Office, 1896), 561.

30. Martin Luther King, Jr., James Melvin Washington, ed., *I Have a Dream: Writings and Speeches that Changed the World* (New York: HarperCollins Publishers, 1992), 104.

SELECTED BIBLIOGRAPHY

Adams, John Quincy, and Josiah Quincy, Eds. *Memoir of the Life of John Quincy Adams.* Boston, MA: Crosby, Nichols, Lee and Company, 1860.

Adams, John, and Charles Francis Adams, Eds. *Letters of John Adams.* Boston: Charles Little and J. Brown, 1841.

Adams, John, and Thomas Jefferson, Paul Wilstach, Eds. *Correspondence of John Adams and Thomas Jefferson 1812-1826.* Boston, MA: The Bobbs-Merrill Company, 1925.

Adams, John. *The Works of John Adams: Second President of the United States.* Boston: Charles C. Little and James Brown, 1851.

Albanese, Catherine L. *A Republic of Mind and Spirit: A Cultural History of American Metaphysical Religion.* New Haven: CT: Yale University Press, 2007.

Allen, Brooke. *Moral Minority: Our Skeptical Founding Fathers.* Chicago, IL: Ivan R. Dee Publisher, 2007.

Alsop, Stewart. *The Center: People and Power in Political Washington.* New York: Harper and Row, 1968.

Amar, Akhil Reed. *America's Constitution: A Biography.* New York: Random House, 2005.

Ambrosini, Maria Luisa, and Mary Willis. *The Secret Archives of the Vatican.* New York: Barnes and Noble, 1996.

Anderson, James. *The Constitutions of the Free-Masons.* London: William Hunter, 1723.

Andrews, Charles. M. *Colonial self-Government.* New York: History of Colonial America Press, 1904.

Arminius, Jacobus. *The Works of James Arminius.* Auburn, AL: Berby and Miller, 1853.

Armstrong, Karen. *A History of God: From Abraham to the Present, the 4000-Year Quest for God.* New York: Random House, 1993.

Armstrong, Karen. *The Case for God.* New York: Random House, 2009.

Aurelius, Marcus. *The Meditations of Marcus Aurelius.* London: Elibron Classics, 1887.

Bacon, Francis, and Clark Sutherland Northup, Eds. *The Essays of Francis Bacon.* New York: Houghton Mifflin Company, 1908.

Bacon, Francis. *Advancement of Learning: And Novum Organum.* New York: The Colonial Press, 1900.

Bacon, Francis. *The New Atlantis*. Whitefish, MT: Kessinger Publishing, 2004).

Baldwin, Neil. *The American Revelation: Ten Ideals That Shaped Our Country from the Puritans to the Cold War*. New York: St. Martin's Press, 2006.

Bedini, Silvio A. *The Life of Benjamin Banneker: The First African-American Man of Science*. Baltimore, MD: Maryland Historical Society, 1999.

Bednar, Michael J. *L'Enfant's Legacy: Public Open Spaces in Washington, D.C.* Baltimore, MD: The Johns Hopkins University Press, 2006.

Berg, Scott W. *Grand Avenues: The Story of the French Visionary Who Designed Washington, D.C.* New York: Pantheon Books, 2007.

Berkin, Carol. *Revolutionary Mothers: Women in the Struggle for America's Independence*. New York: Vintage Books, 2006.

Berlet, Chip, and Matthew N. Lyons. *Right-Wing Populism in America: Too Close for Comfort*. New York, NY: Guilford Press, 2000.

Bernstein, Richard B. *Thomas Jefferson: The Revolution of Ideas*. New York: Oxford University Press, 2004.

Billington, James H. *Fire in the Minds of Men: Origins of the Revolutionary Faith*. Edison, NJ: Transaction Publishers, 1999.

Blanchard, Calvin. *The Life of Thomas Paine: Mover of the Declaration of Independence*. New York: D. M. Bennett, 1877.

Boritt, Gabor. *The Gettysburg Gospel: The Lincoln Speech That Nobody Knows*. New York: Simon and Schuster, 2008.

Bradley, Richard. *Harvard Rules: The Struggle for the Soul of the World's Most Powerful University*. New York: HaperCollins Publisher, 2005.

Brady, Cyrus Townsend. *The True Andrew Jackson*. Philadelphia, PA: J. B. Lippincott Company, 1906.

Brant, Irving. *James Madison: The President, 1809-1812*. Indianapolis, IN: Bobbs-Merrill Company, 1956.

Brighton, Simon. *In Search of the Knights Templar: A Guide to the Sites in Britain*. London: Sterling Publishing Company, 2006.

Browder, Anthony T. *Egypt on The Potomac: A Guide to Decoding Egyptian Architecture and Symbolism*. Washington D.C.: Institute of Karmic Guidance, 2004.

Brown, Dan. *The Lost Symbol: A Novel*. New York: Doubleday, 2009.

Bullock, Steven C. *Revolutionary Brotherhood: Freemasonry and the Transformation of the American Social Order, 1730-1840*. Chapel Hill: The University of North Carolina Press, 1996.

Bush, George W. *The National Security Strategy of the United States of America*. Washington, D.C.: The White House, 2002.

Cable, Mary. *The Avenue of the Presidents*. Boston: Houghton Mifflin, 1969.

Caemmerer, Hans Paul. *The Life of Pierre Charles L'Enfant: Planner of the City Beautiful, the City of Washington*. Washington, D.C.: National Republic, 1950.

Callahan, Charles H. *Washington: The Man and the Mason*. Washington, D.C.: Press of Gibson Brothers, 1913.

Cannadine, David. *Mellon: An American Life*. New York: The Random House, 2008.

Cerami, Charles. *Benjamin Banneker: Surveyor, Astronomer, Publisher, Patriot*. New York: Wiley Press, 2002.

Chan, Michael D. *Hamilton on Commerce and Statesmanship*. Columbia: University of Missouri Press, 2006.

Channing, Edward. *A History of the United States: Federalists and Republicans 1789-1815*. New York: The Macmillan Company, 1917.

Chernow, Ron. *Alexander Hamilton*. New York: Penguin Press, 2004.

Church, Forrest. *So Help Me God: The Founding Fathers and First Great Battle Over Church and State*. Orlando, FL: Houghton Mifflin Harcourt, 2007.

Clark, Ronald W. *Benjamin Franklin: A Biography*. London: Phoenix Press, 1983)

Claudius Ptolemy, Frank E. Robbins, Eds. *Ptolemy: Tetrabiblos*. Cambridge: Harvard University Press, 1980.

Coil, Henry W. *Freemasonry through Six Centuries*. Fulton, MO: Ovid Bell Press, 1967.

Cromwell, Wesley. *The Negro in American History: Men and Women Eminent in the Evolution of the American of African Descent*. Washington, D.C.: The American Negro Academy, 1914.

Daalder, Ivo H. and I. M. Destler. *In the Shadow of the Oval Office: Profiles of the National Security Advisers and the Presidents They Served—From JFK to George W. Bush*. New York: Simon and Schuster, 2009.

Dallek, Robert. *Lyndon B. Johnson: Portrait of a President*. New York: Oxford University Press, 2004.

de Hoyos Arturo, and S. Brent Morris, Eds. *Freemasonry in Context: History, Ritual, Controversy*. Lanham, MD: Lexington Books, 2004.

de Montesquieu, Charles. *The Spirit of Laws*. New York: Cosimo Classic, 2007.

de Tocqueville, Alexis, and Henry Reeve, Eds. *Democracy in America*. Cambridge, MA: Sever and Francis, 1863.

de Tocqueville, Alexis, and Henry Reeve, Eds. *The Republic of the United of States of America*. New York: A. S. Barnes and Company, 1856.

Dershowitz, Alan M. *Blasphemy: How the Religious Right is Hijacking Our Declaration of Independence*. Hoboken, NJ: John Wiley and Sons, 2007.

Dickens, Charles. *American Notes and Pictures from Italy*. Alcester, U.K.: Read Books Press, 2007.

Dickens, Charles. *The Works of Charles Dickens*. London: Chapman and Hall, 1898.

Dirksen, Everett McKinley. *The Education of a Senator*. Urbana, IL: University of Illinois Press, 1998.

Dulles, Allan. *Great True Spy Stories*. New York: Harper and Row, 1968.

Dupuis, Martin, and Keith Boeckelman. *Barack Obama: The New Face of American Politics*. Santa Barbara, CA: Greenwood Publishing, 2008.

Dyer, Joel. *Harvest of Rage: Why Oklahoma City is Only the Beginning*. Boulder, CO: Westview Press, 1998.

Einstein, Albert, and Maurice Solovine. *Albert Einstein, Letters to Maurice Solovine*. Paris: Gauthier-Villars, 1956.

Emerson, Ralph Waldo. *The Conduct of Life and Society and Solitude*. London: McMillan and Company, 1883.

Fay, Bernard. *Franklin: The Apostle of Modern Times*. Boston, MA: Little Brown and Company, 1929.

Fay, Bernard. *Revolution and Freemasonry, 1600-1800.* Boston, MA: Little Brown and Company, 1935.

Feinberg, Barbara. *The Articles of Confederation: The First Constitution of the United States.* Brookfield, CT: The Millbrook Press, 2002.

Ferguson, James. *Astronomy Explained Upon Sir Isaac Newton's Principles.* Philadelphia: Matthew Carey, 1809.

Fischer, David Hackett. *Paul Revere's Ride.* New York: Oxford University Press, 1995.

Foley, John P., Ed. *The Jeffersonian Cyclopedia: A Comprehensive Collection of the Views of Thomas Jefferson.* New York: Funk and Wagnalls Company, 1900.

Forbes, Esther. *Paul Revere and the World He Lived In.* New York: Houghton Mifflin company, 1942.

Franklin, Benjamin, and Albert Henry Smyth, Eds. *The Writings of Benjamin Franklin.* New York: The MacMillan Company, 1906.

Franklin, Benjamin, and Frank Woodworth Pine, Eds. *The Autobiography of Benjamin Franklin.* Garden City, NY: Garden City Publishing Company, 1916.

Franklin, Benjamin, and Henry Stueber, Eds. *Works of the Late Dr. Benjamin Franklin.* New York: Samuel Campbell Bookseller, 1794.

Franklin, Benjamin, and Walter Isaacson, Eds. *A Benjamin Franklin Reader.* New York: Simon and Schuster, 2003.

Franklin, Benjamin, and William Temple Franklin, Eds. *Memoirs of Benjamin Franklin.* New York: Derby and Jackson, 1859.

Franklin, Benjamin. *Poor Richard: The Almanacks for the Years 1733-1758.* New York: Limited Editions Club, 1964.

Frary, Ihna Thayer. *They Built the Capitol.* Freeport: Books for Libraries Press, 1969.

Freidel, Frank. *Franklin D. Roosevelt: A Rendezvous with Destiny.* Newtown, CT: American Political Biography Press, 2005.

Frost, David. *Billy Graham in Conversation with David Frost.* Oxford, England: Lion Publishing, 1998.

Gibbs, Nancy, and Michael Duffy, *The Preacher and the Presidents: Billy Graham in the White House.* New York: Center Street, 2007.

Gilbert, Felix. *To the Farewell Address: Ideas of Early American Foreign Policy.* Princeton, NJ: Princeton University Press, 1970.

Goode, James M. *The Outdoor Sculpture of Washington, D.C.: A Comprehensive Historical Guide.* Washington, D.C.: Smithsonian Institution Press, 1974.

Goodwin, Doris Kearns. *Team of Rivals: The Political Genius of Abraham Lincoln.* New York: Simon and Schuster, 2006.

Goodwin, Jason. *Greenback: The Almighty Dollar and the Invention of America.* New York: Macmillan, 2003.

Gordon-Reed, Annette. *Thomas Jefferson and Sally Hemings: An American Controversy.* Charlottesville, VA: University of Virginia Press, 1998.

Green, Constance McLaughlin. *The Secret City: A History of Race Relations in the Nation's Capital.* Princeton, NJ: Princeton University Press, 1967.

Greene, Evarts B. *The Foundations of American Nationality.* New York: American Book Company, 1922.

Grizzard, Frank E. Jr. *The Ways of Providence: Religion and George Washington*. Buena Vista, VA: Mariner Companies, Inc., 2005.

Grubb, Norman. *Modern Viking: The Story of Abraham Vereide, Pioneer in Christian Leadership,*. Grand Rapids, MI: Zondervan Publishing House, 1961.

Gurney, George. *Sculpture and the Federal Triangle*. Washington, D.C.: Smithsonian Institution Press, 1985.

Gutheim, Frederick Albert and Antoinette J. Lee, Eds. *Worthy of the Nation: Washington, DC, from L'Enfant to the National Capital Planning Commission*. Baltimore, MD: The Johns Hopkins University Press, 2006.

Gutjahr, Paul. *An American Bible: A History of the Good Book in the United States, 1777-1880*. Palo Alto, CA: Stanford University Press, 1999.

Haass, Richard N. *War of Necessity, War of Choice: A Memoir of Two Iraq Wars*. New York: Simon and Schuster, 2009.

Hall, Manly P. *The Secret Destiny of America*. Los Angeles, CA: Philosophical Research Society, 1944.

Hall, Manly P. *The Secret Teachings of All Ages*. Baltimore, MD: Forgotten Books, 1928.

Hamilton, Alexander, and Harold Coffin Syret, Eds. *The Papers of Alexander Hamilton*. New York: Columbia University Press, 1979.

Hamilton, Alexander, and John Hamilton, Eds. *The Works of Alexander Hamilton*. New York: John F. Throw Printer, 1850.

Hamilton, Alexander, James Madison, and John Jay. *The Federalist Papers*. Stilwell, KS: The Digireads.com Publishing, 2004.

Harland-Jacobs, Jessica. *Builders of Empire: Freemasons and British Imperialism, 1717-1927*. Chapel Hill, NC: The University of North Carolina Press, 2007.

Harley, Lewis Reifsneider. *The Life of Charles Thomson: Secretary of the Continental Congress and Translator of the Bible from the Greek*. Philadelphia, MD: George W. Jacobs and Company, 1900.

Harper, John Lamberton. *American Machiavelli: Alexander Hamilton and the Origins of U.S. Foreign Policy*. New York: Cambridge University Press, 2004.

Harris, William Conley. *E Pluribus Unum: Nineteenth-Century American Literature and the Constitutional Paradox*. Iowa City, IO: University of Iowa Press, 2005.

Hieronimus, Robert, and Laura Cortner. *The United Symbolism of America: Deciphering Hidden Meanings in America's Most Familiar Art, Architecture, and Logos*. Franklin Lake, NJ: Career Press, 2008.

Hietala, Thomas R. *Manifest Design: American Exceptionalism and Empire*. Ithaca, NY: Cornell University Press, 2003.

Higginbotham, Don. *George Washington: Uniting a Nation*. Lanham, MD: Rowman and Littlefield Publishers, 2002.

Higginson, Thomas Wentworth. *Makers of America: Life of Francis Higginson, First Minister on the Massachusetts Bay Colony, and Author of New England's Plantation, 1630*. New York: Dodd, Mead and Company, 1891.

Hobbes, Thomas. *Leviathan: Or, The Matter, Forme and Power or a Commonwealth, Ecclesiastical and Civill*. London: C. J. Clay and Sons, 1904.

Hogan, Michael J. *The Marshall Plan: America, Britain, and the Reconstruction of Western Europe, 1947-1952*. New York: Cambridge University Press, 1989.

Holmes, David Lynn. *The Faiths of the Founding Fathers*. New York: Oxford University Press, 2006.

Hoover, Herbert, *The State Papers and Other Public Writings of Herbert Hoover*. New York: Doubleday, Doran and Company, 1934.

Horowitz, Mitch. *Occult America: The Secret History of How Mysticism Shaped Our Nation*. New York: Random House, 2009.

Hume, David. *An Enquiry Concerning Human Understanding*. Oxford, England: Clarendon Press, 1902.

Hume, David. *Essays: Moral, Political, and Literary*. London: Longmans, Green and Company, 1898.

Hutson, James H. *The Founders on Religion: A Book of Quotations*. Princeton, NJ: Princeton University Press, 2007.

Isaacson, Walter. *American Sketches: Good Leaders, Creative Thinkers, and Heroes of a Hurricane*. New York: Simon and Schuster, 2009.

Isaacson, Walter. *Benjamin Franklin: An American Life*. New York: Simon and Schuster, 2003.

Jacob, Kathryn Allamong. *Testament to Union: Civil War Monuments in Washington, D.C.* Baltimore, MD: The Johns Hopkins University Press, 1998.

James, Harold. *The Roman Predicament: How the Rules of International Order Create the Politics of Empire*. Princeton, NJ: Princeton University Press, 2006.

Jay, William. *The Life of John Jay: Miscellaneous and Official Correspondence*. New York: J and J Harper, 1833.

Jeffers, Harry Paul. *Dark Mysteries of the Vatican*. New York: Citadel Press, 2010.

Jeffers, Harry Paul. *Freemasons: A History and Exploration of the World's Oldest Secret Society*. New York: Citadel Press, 2005.

Jeffers, Harry Paul. *The Freemasons in America: Inside the Secret Society*. New York: Citadel Press, 2006.

Jefferson, Thomas, and Andrew A. Lipscomb, Eds. *The Writings of Thomas Jefferson*. Washington, D.C.: The Thomas Jefferson Memorial Foundation, 1904.

Jefferson, Thomas, and George Tucker, Eds. *The Life of Thomas Jefferson: Third President of the United States*. Philadelphia, PA: Carey, Lea and Blanchard Company, 1837.

Jefferson, Thomas, and Henry Augustine Washington, Eds. *The Writings of Thomas Jefferson: Autobiography, Correspondence, Reports, Messages, Addresses, and Other Writings*. New York: H. W. Berby, 1861.

Jefferson, Thomas, and Julian P. Boyd, Eds. *The Papers of Thomas Jefferson, March 1789 to November 1789*. Princeton, NJ: Princeton University Press, 1958.

Jefferson, Thomas, and Paul Leicester Ford, Eds. *The Works of Thomas Jefferson*. New York: G. P. Putnam's Sons, 1905.

Johnson, Melvin M. *The Beginnings of Freemasonry in America*. New York: George H. Doran Company.

Joost-Gaugier, Christiane. *Measuring Heaven: Pythagoras and His Influence on Thought and Art in Antiquity and the Middle Ages*. Ithaca, NY: Cornell University Press, 2006.

Jusserand, Jean Jules. *With Americans of Past and Present Days*. New York: Charles Scribner's Sons, 1916.

Kagan, Robert. *Of Paradise and Power: America and Europe in the New World Order*. New York: Knopf, 2003.

Kant, Immanuel, and Carl J. Friedrich, Eds. *The Philosophy of Kant: Immanuel Kant's Moral and Political Writings*. New York: Modern Library, 1949.

Kant, Immanuel. *Project for a Perpetual Peace: A Philosophical Essay*. London: S. Couchman for Vernor and Hood, 1796.

Key, Francis Scott. *Poems of the Late Francis S. Key*. New York: Robert Carter and Brothers, 1857.

King, Jr., Martin Luther. James Melvin Washington, Ed. *I Have a Dream: Writings and Speeches that Changed the World*. New York: HarperCollins Publishers, 1992.

Kirkland, Caroline Matilda. *Memoirs of Washington*. New York: D. Appleton and Company, 1857.

Kite, Elizabeth Sarah. *L'Enfant and Washington 1791-1792: Published and Unpublished Documents Now Brought Together for the First Time*. Baltimore, MD: The Johns Hopkins Press, 1929.

Kitman, Marvin. *The Making of the President 1789: The Unauthorized Campaign Biography*. New York: Grove Press, 2000.

Knight, Christopher, and Robert Lomas, *The Book of Hiram: Freemasonry, Venus, and the Secret Key to the Life of Jesus*. New York: Sterling Publishing Company, 2005.

Koch, Adrienne. *Jefferson and Madison: The Great Collaboration*. New York: Alfred Knopf, 1950.

Kocis, Robert. *Machiavelli Redeemed: Retrieving His Humanist Perspectives on Equality, Power, and Glory*. Bethlehem, PA: Lehigh University Press, 1998.

Koeneke, Rodney. *Empires of the Mind: I. A. Richards and Basic English in China, 1929-1979*. Palo Alto, CA: Stanford University Press, 2004.

Kuo, J. David. *Tempting Faith: An Inside Story of Political Seduction*. New York: Simon and Schuster, 2006.

Lambert, Frank. *The Founding Fathers and the Place of Religion in America*. Princeton, NJ: Princeton University Press, 2003.

Leigh, Richard, Henry Lincoln, and Michael Baigent, *The Holy Blood And The Holy Grail*. New York: Random House, 2004.

Leslie, Marina. *Renaissance Utopias and the Problem of History*. Ithaca, NY: Cornell University Press 1998.

Lewis Jan Ellen, and Peter S. Onuf, Eds. *Sally Hemings and Thomas Jefferson: History, Memory, and Civic Culture*. Charlottesville, VA: University of Virginia Press, 1999.

Lichtman, Allan J. *White Protestant Nation: The Rise of the Conservative Movement*. New York: Atlantic Monthly Press, 2008.

Liebling, Alvin, Ed. *Adlai Stevenson's Lasting Legacy*. New York: Palgrave Macmillan, 2007.

Lincoln, Abraham. *The Gettysburg Address*. New York: Houghton Mifflin Company, 1998.

Lind, Michael. *Up from Conservatism: Why the Right is Wrong for America*. New York: Simon and Schuster, 1997.

Lodge, Henry Cabot. *George Washington*. Boston, MA: Houghton Mifflin, 1917.

Lomas, Robert. *Turning the Solomon Key: George Washington, the Bright Morning Star, and the Secrets of Masonic Astrology.* Beverly, MA: Fair Winds Press, 2007.

Luria, Sarah. *Capital Speculations: Writing and Building Washington, D.C.* Hanover, NH: University of New Hampshire Press, 2006.

Lynn, Barry W. *Piety and Politics: The Right-Wing Assault on Religious Freedom.* New York: Random House, 2007.

Machiavelli, Niccolo. Quentin Skinner and Russell Price, Eds. *Machiavelli: The Prince.* New York: Cambridge University Press, 1998.

Mackey, Albert Gallatin. *An Encyclopedia of Freemasonry and Its Kindred Sciences.* Philadelphia: Moss and Company, 1879.

Mackey, Albert Gallatin. *The History of Freemasonry: Its Legendary Origins.* Minneola, NY: Dover Publications, 2008.

Madison, James, and E. H. Scott, Eds. *Journal of the Federal Convention Kept by James Madison.* Chicago, IL: Scott, Foresman and Company, 1898.

Madison, James, and Gaillard Hunt, Eds. *The Writings of James Madison: 1803-1807.* New York: G. P. Putnam's Sons, 1908.

Madison, James. *A Memorial and Remonstrance: The Religious Rights of Man, Written in 1784-5.* Washington City: S. C. Ustick, 1828.

Madison, James. *Notes of Debates in the Federal Convention of 1787.* New York: W. W. Norton Company, 1987.

Madsen, Deborah L. *American Exceptionalism.* Edinburgh, U.K.: Edinburgh University Press, 1998.

McGraw, Barbara. *Rediscovering America's Sacred Ground: Public Religion and Pursuit of the Good in a Pluralistic America.* Albany, NY: SUNY Press, 2003.

Meacham, Jon. *American Gospel: God, the Founding Fathers, and the Making of a Nation.* New York: Random House, 2007.

Meacham, Jon. *American Lion: Andrew Jackson in the White House.* New York: Random House, 2008.

Mead, Walter Russell. *Special Providence: American Foreign Policy and How It Changed the World.* New York: Alfred A. Knopf, 2004.

Melling, Philip H. *Fundamentalism in America: Millennialism, Identity and Militant Religion.* Edinburgh, U.K.: Edinburgh University Press, 1999.

Mendis, Patrick. *Human Side of Globalization: The Political Economy of Glocalization as if the Washington Consensus Mattered in Asia, Africa, and the Americas.* Deer Park, NY: Linus Publications, Third edition, 2009.

Mendis, Patrick. *Trade for Peace: How the DNA of America, Freemasonry, and Providence Created a New World Order with Nobody in Charge.* Bloomington, IN: iUniverse Press, 2009.

Meyer, Jeffrey F. *Myths in Stone: Religious Dimensions in Washington, D.C.* Berkeley, CA: University of California Press. 2001.

Micklethwait John, and Adrian Wooldridge. *The Right Nation: Conservative Power in America.* New York: Penguin Press, 2004.

Miller, Nathan. *Spying for America: The Hidden History of U.S. Intelligence.* New York: Dell Press, 1989.

Moore, Jerry D. *Architecture and Power in the Ancient Andes: The Archaeology of Public Buildings.* New York: Cambridge University Press, 1996.

Morris, S. Brent, and John W. Boettjer. *Cornerstones of Freedom: A Masonic Tradition.* Washington, D.C.: Scottish Rite Supreme Council, 1993.

Morse, Sidney. *Freemasonry in the American Revolution.* Whitefish, MT: Kessinger Publishing, 1992.

Newton, Isaac. *Four letters from Sir Isaac Newton to Doctor Bentley Containing Some Arguments in Proof of a Deity.* London: R., and J. Dodsley, 1756.

Nolan, James Bennett. *Benjamin Franklin in Scotland and Ireland.* Philadelphia: University of Pennsylvania Press, 1956.

Obama, Barack. *Dreams from My Father: A Story of Race and Inheritance.* New York: Three Rivers Press, 2004.

Obama, Barack. *Words on a Journey: The Great Speeches of Barack Obama.* Rockville, MD: Arc Manor Classics, 2008.

Ovason, David. *The Secret Architecture of Our Nation's Capital: The Masons and the Building of Washington, D.C.* New York: HarperCollins Publishers, 1999.

Ovason, David. *The Secret Symbols of the Dollar Bill: A Closer Look at the Hidden Magic and Meaning of the Money You Use Every Day.* New York: HarperCollins Publishers, 2004.

Paine, Thomas, and Hypatia B. Bonner, Eds. *Rights of Man.* London, UK: Watts and Company, 1906.

Paine, Thomas, and Isaac Kramnick, Eds. *Common Sense.* New York: Penguin Books, 1982.

Paracelsus, Nicholas Goodrick-Clarke, Eds. *Paracelsus: Essential Readings.* Berkeley, CA: North Atlantic Books, 1999.

Pearce, Alfred John. *The Science of the Stars.* London: Simpkin, Marshall and Company, 1881.

Perry, William Stevens. *Episcopate in America: Sketches Biographical and Bibliographical of the Bishops of the American Church.* New York: The Christian Literature Company, 1895.

Pike, Albert. *Morals and Dogma of the Ancient and Accepted Scottish Rite of Freemasonry.* New York: Masonic Publishing Company, 1874.

Pippenger, Wesley. *District of Columbia Original Land Owners, 1791-1800.* Westminster, MD: Heritage Books, 2007.

Pomeroy, Sarah, Stanley Burstein, Walter Donlan, and Jennifer Roberts. *Ancient Greece: A Political, Social, and Cultural History.* New York: Oxford University Press, 1999.

Prentice, Ezra, and John Egan. *The Commerce Clause of the Federal Constitution.* Chicago: Callaghan and Company, 1898.

Price, Bronwen. *Francis Bacon's New Atlantis: New Interdisciplinary Essays.* Manchester, UKL Manchester University Press, 2002.

Rahe, Paul A. *Republics Ancient and Modern: The Ancien Régime in Classical Greece.* Chapel Hill, NC: The University of North Carolina Press, 1994.

Reed, Henry Hope. *The United States Capitol: Its Architecture and Decoration.* New York: W. S. Norton and Company, 2005.

Richardson, James D. *A Compilation of the Messages and Papers of the Presidents, 1789-1897.* Washington, D.C.: Government Printing Office, 1896.

Rives, William Cabell. *History of the Life and Times of James Madison.* Boston, MA: Little, Brown and Company, 1881.

Roberts, Cokie. *Founding Mothers: The Women Who Raised Our Nation.* New York: William Morrow, 2004.

Robertson, Pat. *The New World Order.* Dallas, TX: Word Publishing, 1991.

Robinson, John J. *Born in Blood: The Lost Secrets of Freemasonry.* New York: Dorset Press, 1989.

Rockefeller, David. *Memoirs.* New York: Random House, 2002.

Roosevelt, Theodore, and Joseph Bucklin Bishop, Eds. *Theodore Roosevelt and His Time Shown in His Own Letters.* New York: Charles Scribner's Sons, 1920.

Rothschild, Emma. *Economic Sentiments: Adam Smith, Condorcet, and the Enlightenment.* Cambridge, MA: Harvard University Press, 2001.

Rudhyar, Dane. *The Astrology of America's Destiny.* New York: Random House, 1974.

Rush, Benjamin, and Dagobert Runes, Eds. *The Selected Writings of Benjamin Rush.* New York: Philosophical Library, 2008.

Schachner, Nathan. *Thomas Jefferson: A Biography.* New York: Appleton-Century Crofts, 1951.

Schechter, Stephen L. Ed. *Roots of the Republic: American Founding Documents Interpreted.* Lanham, MD: Rowman and Littlefield Publishers, 1990.

Schlenther, Boyd Stanley. *Charles Thomson: A Patriot's Pursuit.* Newark, DE: University of Delaware Press, 1990.

Schwerin, David. *Conscious Capitalism: Principles for Prosperity.* Woburn, MA: Butterworth-Heinemann, 1998.

Scott, Pamela, and Antoinette Lee. *Buildings of the District of Columbia.* New York: Oxford University Press, 1995.

Selengut, Charles. *Sacred Fury: Understanding Religious Violence.* Lanham, MD: Rowman and Littlefield Publishers, 2008.

Seward, William H., and George E. Baker, Eds. *The Works of William H. Seward.* Boston, MA: Houghton, Mifflin and Company, 1884.

Shackelford, George Green. *Jefferson's Adoptive Son: The Life of William Short, 1759-1848.* Lexington, KY: University Press of Kentucky, 1993.

Sharlet, Jeff. *The Family: The Secret Fundamentalism at the Heart of American Power.* New York, Harper's, 2008.

Sizemore, William G. *Dynamic Freedoms: Our Freedom Documents.* Washington, D.C.: The Supreme Council, 1988.

Smith, Adam. *An Inquiry into the Nature and Causes of the Wealth of Nations.* London: T. Nelson and Sons, 1852.

Smith, Adam. *The Theory of Moral Sentiments.* London: A. Millar, 1759.

Smith, Gary Scott. *Faith and the Presidency: From George Washington to George W. Bush.* New York: Oxford University Press, 2006.

Smith, Roy C. *Adam Smith and the Origins of American Enterprise: How America's Industrial Success was Forged by the Timely Ideas of a Brilliant Scots Economist.* New York: St. Martin's Press, 2004.

Soltan, Karol Edward, and Stephen L. Elkin. *The Constitution of Good Societies.* University Park, PA: Penn State University Press.

Staloff, Darren. *Hamilton, Adams, Jefferson: The Politics of Enlightenment and the American Founding.* New York: Hill and Wang, 2005.

Stanley, Michael. Ed. *Emanuel Swedenborg: Essential Readings*. Berkeley, CA: North Atlantic Books, 2003.

Stassen, Harold Edward, and Marshall Houts, Eds. *Eisenhower: Turning the World Toward Peace*. St. Paul, MN: Merrill Publishing Corporation, 1990.

Steblecki, Edith J. *Paul Revere and Freemasonry*. Boston, MA: Paul Revere Memorial Association, 1985.

Stevenson, David. *The Origins of Freemasonry: Scotland's Century, 1590-1710*. Cambridge, UK: Cambridge University Press, 1990.

Stiglitz, Joseph E. *Freefall: America, Free Markets, and the Sinking of the World Economy*. New York: W. W. Norton and Company, 2010.

Stillson, Henry Leonard. Ed. *History of the Ancient and Honorable Fraternity of Free and Accepted Masons and Concordant Orders*. Boston, MA: The Fraternity publishing Company, 1890.

Stimson, Frederic Jesup. *The Law of the Federal and State Constitutions of the United States*. Clark, NJ: The Lawbook Exchange, 2004.

Symth, Albert Henry, Ed. *The Writings of Benjamin Franklin*. New York: The McMillan Company, 1906.

Tabbert, Mark. *American Freemasons: Three Centuries of Building Communities*. New York: New York University Press, 2005.

Tatsch, J. Hugo. *Facts about George Washington as a Freemason*. Whitefish, MT: Kessinger Publishing, 1998.

Totten, Charles Adiel Lewis. *The Seal of History: Our Inheritance in the Great Seal of Manasseh*. New Haven, CT: The Our Race Publishing Company, 1897.

Tucker, Robert, and David Hendrickson. *Empire of Liberty: The Statecraft of Thomas Jefferson*. New York: Oxford University Press, 1990.

Tyler, Lyon Gardiner. *The Cradle of the Republic: Jamestown and James River*. Richmond, VA: Whittet and Shepperson Printers, 1900.

Versluis, Arthur. *The Esoteric Origins of the American Renaissance*. New York: Oxford University Press, 2001.

Walch, Timothy. *Guardian of Heritage: Essays on the History of the National Archives*. Washington, D.C.: National Archives and Records Administration, 1985.

Waldman, Steven. *Founding Faith: Providence, Politics, and the Birth of Religious Freedom in America*. New York: Random House, 2008.

Walgren, Kent Logan. *Freemasonry, Anti-Masonry and Illuminism in the United States, 1734-1850: A Bibliography*. Worcester, MA: American Antiquarian Society, 2003.

Washington, George, and Jared Sparks, Eds. *The Writings of George Washington*. Boston: MA: Ferdinand Andrews Publisher, 1839.

Washington, George, and John C. Fitzpatrick, Eds. *The Writings of George Washington from the Original Manuscript Sources, 1745-1799*. Washington, D.C.: U.S. Government Printing Office, 1939.

Washington, George, and Julius Friedrich Sachse, Eds. *Washington's Masonic Correspondence as Found among the Washington Papers in the Library of Congress*. Lancaster, PA: Press of the New Era Printing Company, 1915.

Washington, George. *The Diaries of George Washington*, Volume 6. Charlottesville, VA: University Press of Virginia, 1979.

Washington, George. *The Writings of George Washington: Being His Correspondence, Addresses, Messages, and Other Papers, Official and Private.* Boston, MA: Little, Brown, and Company, 1855.

Washington, George. *Washington's Farewell Address to the People of the United States.* Baltimore, MD: John L. Cook, 1810.

Washington, George. Worthington Chauncey Ford, Eds. *The Writings of George Washington.* New York: G. P. Putnam's Sons, 1891.

Wasserman, James. *The Secrets of Masonic Washington.* Rochester, VT: Destiny Books, 2008.

Weinberger, Caspar, and Gretchen Roberts, *In the Arena: A Memoir of the 20th Century.* Washington, D.C.: Regnery Publishing, 2001.

Whalen, William Joseph. *Christianity and American Freemasonry.* San Francisco, CA: Ignatius Press, 1998.

Wilson, Francis G. *The American Political Mind: A Textbook in Political Theory.* New York: McGraw-Hill, 1949.

Wilson, James G. *The Imperial Republic: A Structural History of American Constitutionalism from the Colonial Era to the Beginning of the Twentieth Century.* Aldershot, U.K.: Ashgate Publishing, 2002.

Wilson, Woodrow, and Donald Day, Eds. *Woodrow Wilson's Own Story.* Boston, MA: Little, Brown and Company 1952.

Winthrop, John. *The Journal of John Winthrop.* Boston, MA: Belknap Press of Harvard University Press, 1996.

Withey, Lynne. *Dearest Friend: A Life of Abigail Adams.* New York: Simon and Schuster, 2002.

Wolanin, Barbara A. *Constantino Brumidi: Artist of the Capitol.* Washington, D.C.: U.S. Government Printing Office, 1998.

Wood, Gordon S. *Empire of Liberty: A History of the Early Republic, 1789-1815.* New York: Oxford University Press, 2009.

Wood, Gordon S. *The Americanization of Benjamin Franklin.* New York: Penguin Press, 2004.

Woodford, Adolophus Frederick. *A Defense of Freemasonry.* London: George Kenning, 1874.

Wright, Dudley. *Roman Catholicism and Freemasonry.* Whitefish, MT: Kessinger Publishing, 2003.

Zagorin, Perez. *Francis Bacon.* Princeton, NJ: Princeton University Press, 1999.

INDEX

ACKNOWLEDGEMENTS

Though this book has but one father, it has many godparents. Even before the publication of my previous book *TRADE for PEACE* in February 2009, I engaged in extensive conversations with friends, colleagues, and other experts on America's role in the world. In the midst of the 2008 historic political campaign and the presidential election, they convinced me to postulate a theory focusing on trade (in goods, services, and most importantly, American ideas) and Providence as the nation seemed destined to have Barack Obama as president. Although I would like to thank each and every person of various political persuasions for their insightful comments and suggestions, I do not claim either the infallibility or the originality of any statements to advance such a grand theory. Adhering to my previous book's research on trade and further study of Freemasonry literature, I strove to organize fragmented materials in a coherent and integral manner in order to present a convincing "theory of commercial providence" and to advance these conversations beyond scholastic and traditional confinements.

In this respect, I am intrigued by 33° Freemasonry grand master for Missouri and 33rd U.S. President Harry S. Truman's profound observation: "The only thing new in the world is the history you don't know." This transformative world leader, who fully integrated African Americans into the military, had a unique, "brotherly" worldview much like his founding Masonic brethren George Washington did. While I have incorporated Masonic influence into the foundation and ethos of American exceptionalism, my theory also offers perspectives to address concerns raised by those perennial critics and cynics of America along with a pantheon of conspiracy theorists and religious fundamentalists. To that end, President Truman viewed America as "built by all nations." The illustrious Freemason may have been elated to learn about Obama's brisk ascendancy to the White House.

There is nothing unusually new in this book compared to the previous one. Nonetheless, the mood of the nation has changed and it is inevitable that I should begin to see things differently than I did before. With President Obama, we are living through one of the most fundamental shifts in American history—almost as if undergoing a rebirth of the nation. During his first State of the Union address on January 27, 2010, the subtle image of his podium captured the very essence of America's founding vision and national identity outlined in this book. On the president's left side stood Speaker Nancy Pelosi from the state of California, that bastion of liberal and western diversity, who is also the highest-ranking women ever to serve in Congress. On the president's right side was Vice President Joe Biden, a Catholic elected to the U.S. Senate from the "Eastern Establishment" state of Delaware. Closing the virtuous circle and taking center stage was a president of Hawaiian and mid-western heritage, more precisely from the state of Abraham Lincoln, Illinois. The new nation proudly presented a remarkable portrait of American trinity and unity. Alongside the smaller-and-bigger states from each coast, Obama himself symbolizes the "global nation" (a hybrid of his Kenyan scholar-father and white Kansan author-mother) that resembles Hawaiian diversity and mixed human stock. The occult (unseen) national conviction, *E Pluribus Unum,* "Out of many, one," portrays the Founding Fathers' idea of unity and equilibrium in gender, religion, and race. The image also illustrates America's operative principle of autonomy and interdependence for human progress. The theory of commercial providence subtly but ubiquitously undergirds this founding vision and celebrates its eventual destiny.

Over the past eighteen months, I have been working on this manuscript while at the Johns Hopkins University's School of Advanced International Studies (SAIS), and during my book and lecture tours in Asia and America. Having benefited from the contributions of many people, I might fail in the difficult task of thanking them all as they really deserve. Among them, I am very grateful to Professor David "Mike" Lampton (dean of the faculty) and Dr. John Harrington (associate dean) for their support and assistance, as well as Dr. Carla Freeman and Ms. Zhaojin Ji at SAIS China Center. I would also like to extend my gratitude to Professor Dingli Shen (Fudan University), Professor Jan Kiely (Nanjing University), Dr. Wenquan Otto (Chinese Foreign Affairs University),

Professor Ting Wai (Hong Kong Baptist University), Professor Tang Xiaosong (Guangdong University of Foreign Studies), and their staff members. I am very appreciative of the early support extended by Professor Shelton Williams (president of the Osgood Center for International Studies). I also benefited from discussions with Professor Brian Atwood (dean of the Humphrey Institute), Professor Robert Kurdrle, and Dr. Margaret Carlson at the University of Minnesota. I extend my deepest thanks to all of them.

It was a tremendous honor to get book endorsements from a panoply of distinguished statesmen, diplomats, scholars, and entrepreneurs. I would like to sincerely thank the Honorable Thomas Daschle, former U.S. Senate majority leader and distinguished senior fellow at the Center for American Progress for his thoughtful book endorsement and enduring support. I also wish to convey my gratitude to his able staff, especially Jody Bennett and Lindsey Wagner. It was a privilege to receive praise from the Honorable Robert "Bob" Livingston, who was chosen to succeed Newt Gringrich as Speaker of the U.S. House of Representatives. Founder of the Livingston Group, the congressman is also a descendent of Chancellor Robert Livingston of New York, who gave the inaugural oath of office to President George Washington on a *Masonic Bible* from the St. John's Masonic Lodge in New York City (both the president and the chancellor were Freemasons).

I also extend my heartfelt appreciation to Admiral William Sizemore (a 33° Freemason, the Grand Cross, and the grand executive director of the Supreme Council of the Scottish Rite Freemasonry) and distinguished journalist James Fallows (the national correspondent for the *Atlantic Monthly* and the founding chairman of the New America Foundation) for their book endorsements and support. It was a great delight to receive a note of high recommendation from former Grand Master Akram Elias of the Grand Lodge of Free and Accepted Freemasons in Washington, D.C. He helped me to better understand the hidden meaning and Masonic symbolism of the nation's capital.

For her commendation, I am very grateful to Ambassador Paula Dobriansky, former undersecretary of state for democracy and global affairs under President George W. Bush and senior fellow at Harvard University's John F. Kennedy School of Government. It was a great honor to work with Dr. Dobriansky at the State Department, and to count on her unfailing support and goodwill. I am equally grateful to Ambassador Frank Loy, former undersecretary of state for global affairs under President Bill Clinton, who commissioned me to chair an interagency policy working group that subsequently produced a handbook on intellectual property rights and the C-175 process.

Above all, I am most grateful to President Stephen Joel Trachtenberg of the George Washington University for his thoughtful foreword. As a revered academic and global leader (as well as a 33° Freemason and the Grand Cross), I am privileged to have his undying support, wise guidance, and constant inspiration. I also extend my sincere thanks to Helene Interlandi (executive assistant to President Trachtenberg) for her assistance.

A trio of superb editors made significant contributions to the success of this book project. In the first place, Leah Green, my good friend and academic partner, helped me research and edit the book. Naturally gifted, her gentle critique, advice, and restructuring of my arguments were extremely valuable. She clearly understands American history, foreign policy, and world affairs as we both have worked together while at Norwich University, and subsequently co-authored articles and papers related to national security and international affairs. I am enormously grateful to Leah for her dedication, sense of humor, and indefatigable support. Miryam Lindberg, an author and translator who is engaged in various projects around the world, is not only a critical reviewer of my work but also a talented researcher, editor, and advisor. She always provided me with alternative viewpoints to better develop my arguments. Andy Lei, my friend and colleague, is an intellectually versatile and linguistically gifted world traveler, and a highly cultured man. I benefited from his experience in the Middle East and Asia. Their collective insights and meticulous editing have been definitive for the end product. I am honored to have had their support and assistance, especially the thought provoking questions and remarks that often led me to rewrite and restructure my arguments.

A group of anonymous reviewers offered valuable feedback to improve my manuscript. In addition, a great number of colleagues and friends provided their specific subject matter expertise, knowledge, and support. I would like to express my appreciation to Professor John Bessler, Thomas Bork, Gene Calonge, Kenneth Gibala, Timothy Giblet, Jeff Hayes, Donnie Hachey, Arturo de Hoyos, Kenneth Insley, Mark Levine, Dr. Neil Marple, Hon. Al Mathiowetz, Don McAndrews, Dr. Brent Morris, Alden Mulabdic, Christopher Mullaney, Joan Sansbury, Marion Smith, Marcus Trelaine, Larissa Watkins, Robert Watkins, and Carl